John Sandford

The Mission and Extension of the Church at Home

John Sandford

The Mission and Extension of the Church at Home

ISBN/EAN: 9783337813277

Printed in Europe, USA, Canada, Australia, Japan

Cover: Foto ©Lupo / pixelio.de

More available books at **www.hansebooks.com**

THE
BAMPTON LECTURES FOR MDCCCLXI.

Luke iv. 18, 19.

Πνεῦμα κυρίου ἐπ' ἐμέ, οὗ εἵνεκεν ἔχρισέ με εὐαγγελίσασθαι πτωχοῖς, ἀπέσταλκέ με [ἰάσασθαι τοὺς συντετριμμένους τὴν καρδίαν,]

Κηρῦξαι αἰχμαλώτοις ἄφεσιν καὶ τυφλοῖς ἀνάβλεψιν, ἀποστεῖλαι τεθραυσμένους ἐν ἀφέσει, κηρῦξαι ἐνιαυτὸν κυρίου δεκτόν.

THE

MISSION AND EXTENSION

OF

THE CHURCH AT HOME,

CONSIDERED

IN EIGHT LECTURES,

PREACHED BEFORE

THE UNIVERSITY OF OXFORD,

IN THE YEAR MDCCCLXI.

AT THE LECTURE FOUNDED BY

THE LATE REV. JOHN BAMPTON, M.A.

CANON OF SALISBURY.

BY

JOHN SANDFORD, B.D.

ARCHDEACON OF COVENTRY.

LONDON:
LONGMAN, GREEN, LONGMAN, AND ROBERTS.
M.DCCC.LXII.

TO

THE MEMORY OF

ERSKINE DOUGLAS SANDFORD,

LATE SHERIFF OF GALLOWAY, N.B.

AND OF

DANIEL KEYTE SANDFORD, D.C.L., KNIGHT,

FORMERLY PROFESSOR OF GREEK IN THE

UNIVERSITY OF GLASGOW,

THESE LECTURES ARE INSCRIBED

IN FAITH, HOPE, AND LOVE,

BY THEIR SURVIVING BROTHER.

EXTRACT

FROM

THE LAST WILL AND TESTAMENT

OF THE

REV. JOHN BAMPTON,

CANON OF SALISBURY.

—— " I give and bequeath my Lands and Estates to
" the Chancellor, Masters, and Scholars of the University
" of Oxford for ever, to have and to hold all and sin-
" gular the said Lands or Estates upon trust, and to the
" intents and purposes hereinafter mentioned; that is to
" say, I will and appoint that the Vice-Chancellor of the
" University of Oxford for the time being shall take and
" receive all the rents, issues, and profits thereof, and
" (after all taxes, reparations, and necessary deductions
" made) that he pay all the remainder to the endowment
" of eight Divinity Lecture Sermons, to be established
" for ever in the said University, and to be performed in
" the manner following:

" I direct and appoint, that, upon the first Tuesday in
" Easter Term, a Lecturer be yearly chosen by the Heads
" of Colleges only, and by no others, in the room ad-
" joining to the Printing-House, between the hours of ten
" in the morning and two in the afternoon, to preach
" eight Divinity Lecture Sermons, the year following, at
" St. Mary's in Oxford, between the commencement of

"the last month in Lent Term, and the end of the third week in Act Term.

"Also I direct and appoint, that the eight Divinity Lecture Sermons shall be preached upon either of the following Subjects—to confirm and establish the Christian Faith, and to confute all heretics and schismatics — upon the divine authority of the holy Scriptures — upon the authority of the writings of the primitive Fathers, as to the faith and practice of the primitive Church — upon the Divinity of our Lord and Saviour Jesus Christ — upon the Divinity of the Holy Ghost — upon the Articles of the Christian Faith, as comprehended in the Apostles' and Nicene Creeds.

"Also I direct, that thirty copies of the eight Divinity Lecture Sermons shall be always printed, within two months after they are preached, and one copy shall be given to the Chancellor of the University, and one copy to the Head of every College, and one copy to the Mayor of the city of Oxford, and one copy to be put into the Bodleian Library; and the expense of printing them shall be paid out of the revenue of the Land or Estates given for establishing the Divinity Lecture Sermons; and the Preacher shall not be paid, nor be entitled to the revenue, before they are printed.

"Also I direct and appoint, that no person shall be qualified to preach the Divinity Lecture Sermons, unless he hath taken the degree of Master of Arts at least, in one of the two Universities of Oxford or Cambridge; and that the same person shall never preach the Divinity Lecture Sermons twice."

PREFACE.

The printing of these Lectures has been delayed by illness, which for some months after they were delivered, prevented their being prepared for the press. Meanwhile popular interest in the questions of which they treat is manifestly on the increase; and the writer believes that the views which they advocate are daily gaining ground.

In his own case they are the result of many years' reflection and experience. But they express the convictions of multitudes in our day, who, uninfluenced by prejudice, and untrammelled by party, exercise an unbiassed judgment on matters in which they are personally concerned, and on which they claim an individual opinion.

No man can have watched the progress of the Church in England — still less have been himself actively engaged in its service, for nearly half a century — without appreciating the mighty changes that during that time have taken place in its condition and its prospects.

Views, which fifty years ago were regarded with distrust, are now accepted as established truths; reforms which were then denounced as Utopian, have since been effected. Every year has seen prejudices which were viewed as insurmountable, give way; and partitions that for long had separated brethren, taken down. Men have learned to look one another in the face, and have discovered that they are children of the same God, and belong to the same household of faith.

Above all, the Christian laity are awakening at once to their privileges and responsibilities, and beginning to take that share in the deliberations and work of the Church, which more than anything else indicates recovered life and is the earnest of progressive improvement.

Who, then, that reads aright the signs of our times can distrust God's presence at this moment with His Church in this land? Or who can doubt that if it obeys His voice it shall prevail and prosper? May He imprint on our hearts that word, "he that is not with me, is against me; and he that gathereth not with me, scattereth abroad!"

To Him be glory in all the churches, both now and for ever! Amen.

SUMMARY.

LECTURE I.

(*Delivered February 24th, 1861.*)

NATURE AND OFFICE OF THE CHURCH.

Acts ii. 47.

" *And the Lord added to the Church daily such as should be saved.*"

Ὁ δὲ κύριος προσετίθει τοὺς σωζομένους καθ' ἡμέραν τῇ ἐκκλησίᾳ.

Statement of the subject, page 1.
Its importance and appropriateness, 2.—Spirit in which it ought to be treated, 3.—Moral and religious aspect of the country, 6.—Indications of recovered life in the Church, 7.—Doctrine of toleration better understood, 9.—Desirableness of correct views on the nature of the Church itself, 11.—General design of these Lectures, 12.—Nature of the Church, 13.—Its mission, 18.—Its credentials, 24.

LECTURE II.

(*Delivered March 10th, 1861.*)

DISTINCTIVE FEATURES OF THE ENGLISH CHURCH.

1 Timothy iii. 15.

" *That thou mayest know how thou oughtest to behave thyself in the House of God, which is the Church of the living God, the pillar and ground of the Truth.*"

Ἵνα εἰδῇς πῶς δεῖ ἐν οἴκῳ θεοῦ ἀναστρέφεσθαι, ἥτις ἐστὶν ἐκκλησία θεοῦ ζῶντος, στῦλος καὶ ἑδραίωμα τῆς ἀληθείας.

Position of our Church, 37.—Its Antiquity, 40.—Its Catholicity, 41.—Its love of Scripture, 45.—Its use of tradition, 48.—Its comprehensive spirit, 52.—Its Diocesan and Parochial System, 55.—Its connection with the State, 57.

LECTURE III.

(*Delivered April 14th*, 1861.)

HINDRANCES OF THE CHURCH.

JEREMIAH XIII. 20, 21.

"*Where is the flock that was given thee, thy beautiful flock? What wilt thou say when He shall punish thee?*"

Tests to which the Church is exposed, 65.—Religious condition of our people, 67.—Commercial standard of morality, 69.—Prevalence of dissent, 70.—Its political antagonism, 71.—Differences amongst Churchmen, 72.—Spiritual destitution, 74.—Causes of; 1. the Parochial System in abeyance, 75.—2. Want of church accommodation, 76.— 3. Densest populations the poorest, 80.—4. Poverty of endowments, 81.—5. Lower type of Clergy, 82.

LECTURE IV.

Delivered April 28th, 1861.

WANTS OF THE CHURCH.

LUKE X. 2.

"*Therefore said he unto them, The harvest truly is great, but the labourers are few: pray ye therefore the Lord of the harvest, that he would send forth labourers into his harvest.*"

Ἔλεγεν οὖν πρὸς αὐτούς· ὁ μὲν θερισμὸς πολύς, οἱ δὲ ἐργάται ὀλίγοι· δεήθητε οὖν τοῦ κυρίου τοῦ θερισμοῦ, ὅπως ἐκβάλῃ ἐργάτας εἰς τὸν θερισμὸν αὐτοῦ.

The work of the Church in a great measure of a missionary character, 86.—Need of increased spiritual agency, 92.—Subdivision of parishes, 94.—Poverty of many of our populous cures, 96.—Remedies for this; 1. Relief afforded by Ecclesiastical Commissioners, 98.— 2. Diocesan efforts, 98.—3. Recognised responsibilities of property, 99.—4. Use of the offertory, 101.— 5. More equitable assessment of benefices, 103.— 6. Increase of the Episcopate, 105.— 7. Lay agency, 112.

LECTURE V.

(*Delivered May 5th*, 1861.)

CLERICAL AGENCY.

2 Timothy ii. 15.

" *Study to show thyself approved unto God, a workman that needeth not to be ashamed, rightly dividing the word of truth.*"

Σπούδασον σεαυτὸν δόκιμον παραστῆσαι τῷ θεῷ, ἐργάτην ἀνεπαίσχυντον, ὀρθοτομοῦντα τὸν λόγον τῆς ἀληθείας.

Clerical office and standard, 116.—Precautions taken by the Church to exclude unfit persons, 117.—Need of clergy discipline, 120.—Of clerical training, 123.—Deficiencies complained of, 124.—Diversity of gifts, 125.—Distinctive training required. How far afforded by the Universities, 128.—Theological colleges; 1. as a substitute, 130.—2. As auxiliary, 131.—Objections to these, 131.—What we ask of the Universities, 135.—More of practical training required, 137.—Address to candidates, 139.

LECTURE VI.

(*Delivered May 12th*, 1861.)

NATIONAL EDUCATION AS SUBSIDIARY TO THE CHURCH.

Proverbs ii. 10, 11.

" *When wisdom entereth into thine heart, and knowledge is pleasant unto thy soul; discretion shall preserve thee, understanding shall keep thee.*"

The Church in favour of education, 143.—Church view of education, 143.—Must be religious, 144.—Secular education in America, 145.—Must be in the principles of the Church, 147.—National interest in the cause of education, 148.—

Main obstructions in its way, 149.—What is chiefly wanted, 150.—Moral and religious training, 151.—Importance of clerical supervision, 152.—Necessity of retaining hold on the young, 152.—Sunday schools, 153.—Evening schools, 154.—Middle schools, 155.—Injury to the Church from neglect of these, 156.—Old educational Foundations, 157.—Importance of Middle class education, 159.—Public schools, 160.—Work effected by Dr. Arnold, 161.—Lessons of corporate life to be imparted, 162.—Special office of the Universities, 164.—Importance of this, 165.—Undervalued by certain classes, 166.—Faults of student life, 167.—Special dangers of student life, 169.—More of intercommunion between the governing and undergraduate body required, 170.—Sermons in college chapels, 171.

LECTURE VII.

(*Delivered June 2nd*, 1861.)

FABRICS AND SERVICES OF THE CHURCH.

1 CHRONICLES XXIX. 1.

"*For the Palace is not for man, but for the Lord God.*"

Neglected condition of our churches in a former age, 172.—Source of this, 173.—Revival of church architecture, 174.—Design of Christian worship, 175.—Common rights of worshippers, 177.—Evils of appropriation, 179.—Need of temporary fabrics, 180.—Example afforded by Jewish Church, 181.—Such fabrics supplemental and exceptional, 182.—True principles of religious worship, 182.—Contrast with foreign churches, 183.—How to attract the poor and win the operative classes, 184.—Liturgical revision, 186.—How far admissible, 187.—Principles on which it ought to be conducted, 188.—Are Dissenters to be won? 190.—True means of attracting to our services, 193.

LECTURE VIII.

(*Delivered June 9th, 1861.*)

THE CHURCH, AS IT WAS, AS IT IS, AS IT MIGHT BE.

Acts ix. 6.

"*Lord, what wilt Thou have me to do?*"

Κύριε, τί με θέλεις ποιῆσαι;

Recapitulation and concluding argument. Aim of these Lectures, 195.—State of the Church at the beginning of the present century, 198.—Admitted defects, 199.—Real cause of these, 200.—True hope of the Church, 201.—The Church contrasted with other religious systems, 202.—The Church expresses the mind of our people, 205.—What is required of its teachers, 206.—Importance of lay co-operation, 207.—Office of warden, 208.—Lay co-operation in counsel required, 209.—Individual responsibility, 210.—This often overlooked, 211.—Influence of example, 214.—Woman's mission, 216.—Conclusion, 219.

LECTURE I.

Acts ii. 47.

"*And the Lord added to the Church daily such as should be saved.*"

"*'Ο δὲ κύριος προσετίθει τοὺς σωζομένους καθ' ἡμέραν τῇ ἐκκλησίᾳ.*"

THE Mission and Extension of the Church in England, with special reference to its present exigencies and resources, is the subject selected for these Lectures. Various considerations render this one of grave and critical importance. It embraces topics and involves interests that more or less concern every man amongst us, that affect almost every relation of life, and underlie our whole social and religious condition as a people.

And in our day it may be said more than any other to force itself on the public attention, to engage thoughtful and earnest minds, and to furnish occupation for the statesman and the philanthropist. No theme would appear to excite more general and lively interest, or to be more frequently in the mouths of men in the day in which we live.

It therefore specially demands the consideration of our Universities, to which are committed such weighty trusts, and which possess such manifold means of stimulating and directing national thought. And in bringing it before you on this occasion, I not only claim your indulgence, but ask your prayers that God would give to me the " spirit of power, and of love, and of a sound mind;"[a] and enable me to discharge the duty I have undertaken, in a manner befitting the importance of my Subject and worthy of the Office which I hold.

In my treatment of the various topics which will come before us, I may have to depart somewhat from the course pursued by previous lecturers on this Foundation. But this, I trust, will be justified by the nature of the inquiries on which we are about to enter. These will not be of the speculative and recondite character of some which have instructed and delighted an auditory in this place. On the contrary, I shall have to deal with matters of a strictly practical nature, which have come more immediately under my own observation, and on which I may be able to address you from familiar acquaintance and personal experience.

But here it may be necessary to notice an objection that meets me at the threshold.

It may be said that my subject, however interesting in itself, hardly falls within the scope of a Lec-

---

[a] 2 Timothy i. 7.

tureship designed for the elucidation and confirmation of religious evidence.

It may be urged that there are reasons in the circumstances and temper of our day why, more especially on this occasion, the usual course should be rigidly adhered to. Opinions, it may be said, have been recently expressed, and are now unhappily current, involving assaults on the very foundations of revealed truth; and that these it is the special province of this Lectureship to meet. It may even be viewed as a providential provision against them.

Admitting this,— and the more readily, because, as it appears to me, it is in the pulpits of our Universities, and before learned audiences, rather than when addressing a mixed congregation,— with the pen rather than in oral debate — that questions, requiring calm investigation and the precision of the practised theologian, should be handled (1) — it may be inferred, that had any course of lectures addressed to what may be deemed by some the more immediate necessities of academic thought been before the electors, it would not have been my privilege to address you to-day.

I am myself of opinion that what we most want in times of religious perplexity are themes practical, rather than polemic. To me it appears that, under such circumstances, the clergy ought to address themselves more than ever to the consciences and the hearts of men ; and that the way for us all to solve controversy and to stifle doubt, is to face the realities of the Christian life and the difficulties and necessities of the world around us, and each to engage manfully and heartily in the duties which devolve on himself.

Both Scripture and experience seem to teach that the road even to transcendental truth, lies not in theory, but in action,—not in speculation, but in obedience,—that the way to "grow in the knowledge of God and of our Lord Jesus Christ,"[a] is not so much the exercise of the intellectual powers,—still less the indulgence of the imagination,—but an humble acquiescence in what is revealed, and a simple compliance with what is commanded. The path of personal holiness is the highway, of which we read that the "wayfaring men, though fools, shall not err therein;"[b] and it is the declaration of Christ Himself, "He that doeth the will of my Father which is in Heaven, shall know of the doctrine whether it be of God."[c]

I therefore trust that you will bear with me, if I direct your attention, on the present occasion, to topics of a more homely and practical character than those which have recently engaged the academic mind; if I suggest questions like these— Why am I here? What am I living for? What does God require me to do? But if censured for not speaking enough to the times, let the reply of Archbishop Leighton suffice, "Suffer one poor brother to preach for Eternity."

2 Peter iii. 18.   [b] Isaiah xxxv. 8.   [c] John vii. 17.

My subject then, as I have stated, is the mission and extension of Christ's Church in this land. I desire to treat this in the following lectures, not controversially, or so as to expose and widen differences which, wherever they exist amongst Christian men, obstruct and mar the work of God, — but with that breadth of view and in that spirit of charity, which we believe to be the characteristics of our own communion, and which are assuredly required of a national Church.

To idolize our own Ecclesiastical system—to see nothing but good in ourselves as churchmen, and evil in those who differ from us — what can this serve, but to confirm both them and us in error? How inconsistent with a creed which professes to "prove all things, and to hold fast that which is good?"[a] How futile in an age, which takes nothing on trust ; but tests all things, both secular and sacred, by their obvious utility and practical results ? How irreconcileable with the warnings of history, the lessons of experience, the yearnings after what is real and true — which we boast in as the special signs of our times — if our simple desire be not to learn the will of God, in order that we may do it ! And if the more we know of God's ways, the more we learn to distrust our own, — if we see every day how His cause is injured, and His designs are retarded by the unfaithfulness and incompetence of human agents, — does it not become us as a Church,

[a] 1 Thessalonians v. 21.

to renounce now, and for ever, the language of self-gratulation—to cease " to measure ourselves by ourselves, or to compare ourselves among ourselves," [a] — and to desire that " every high thought that exalteth itself against the knowledge of God be cast down, and every thought be brought into captivity to the obedience of Christ?" [b]

That any right-minded man can contemplate the moral and religious state of this country without serious misgivings, is next to impossible. The national standard and practice so often at variance with Scripture — the multiform shapes of misbelief and infidelity, which among us no longer seek the shade, but court observation—the discontent and socialism of large and banded masses of our operatives —the flagrant and unblushing vice and intemperance of our streets (2) —the inadequate influence exercised by the Church over the bulk of the people — the numerous separatists from its fold — added to which, the attitude of hostility which many of these have recently assumed; above all, the feuds and divisions within the Church itself — what Christian man can view these things without great heaviness and continual sorrow of heart!

When to this we add the terrible amount of heathenism in our great cities and populous districts,— for which the Church and Nation are clearly responsible, inasmuch as multitudes are still unpre-

[a] 2 Corinthians x. 12.   [b] 2 Ibid. x. 5

vided with the means of grace — how monstrous does anything like self-complacence appear! To whose lips ought not the confession to rise, "O Lord, righteousness belongeth unto Thee; but unto us belongeth confusion of face ... to our kings, to our princes, and to our fathers, because we have sinned against Thee"?[a] What becomes us but humble penitence for the past, and hearty endeavours at future amendment?

In saying this, I am, of course, not unmindful of the efforts to roll away our reproach, which signalize the Christianity of our age and country; nor of the signs and pulsations of quickened life within our own communion. Nor do I for a moment distrust the vitality of our Church, nor its power, in the cause and strength of God, to cope with and overcome every conceivable amount and form of evil. To do this would be to doubt God Himself; to disbelieve His tokens; to regard neither the operation of His hands, nor the times of refreshing that have come to us from His presence.[b] It were impossible for any religious mind to contrast the present aspect of the Church with what it bore some years ago — and this within the memory of many of ourselves — without both gratitude and encouragement (3).

Of the indications of recovered life which characterise our age, perhaps the most hopeful is the deepened and diffused interest on the subject of the Church itself, in relation to its nature, its mission

[a] Daniel ix. 7, 8.   [b] Psalm xviii. 8.

and its wants. And if the questions, to which this has given birth, have not always tended to godly edifying in the faith, but when pursued in an irreverent or captious spirit have gendered strife; if even in the case of some sincere and devout, but, as we must believe, ill balanced minds, they have resulted in defection, deplorable alike for the seceders and the Church which, in the case of a distinguished few, has been deprived of a light in which it had rejoiced — what else was to be expected in a time of extraordinary religious resuscitation and reaction, like our own? It is our wisdom, while we lament these things, to learn from them; to profit by the rebuke they are meant to convey; solemnly to ponder in our hearts how far we may have been ourselves responsible for them — how far greater zeal, greater faithfulness, more of Christ's Spirit, closer conformity to His example, would have prevented or would have healed them: — in short, not to blame others, that we may exculpate ourselves ; but freely and heartily to acknowledge our own sins and shortcomings, and to ask grace to pardon and help to amend.

I can conceive no other spirit in which a Christian man ought to meet either the complaints of friends or the taunts of enemies. Had it been uniformly exhibited, what crimes and calamities by which the cause of religion has been stained and obstructed,— what strife and divisions — what tears and blood would it have averted !

And this in no part of Christendom more than in our own, where — whatever form of faith has been in the ascendant—whether Roman Catholic, or Protestant, Anglican, or Nonconformist — pleas for intolerance and persecution have never been wanting.

Witness even by-gone attempts at pacification between the Church and the Sects,—in which it is difficult to say whether the domineering spirit of the one or the narrow-mindedness and contumacy of the other was most to be deplored. And though possibly no allowable concessions might have satisfied litigious demands, yet who can now doubt that a healing and remedial course might have averted many of the evils which have flowed from our subsequent divisions?

Is it sanguine to predict that both churchmen and dissenters would manifest a better spirit in the times in which we live, were a like occasion to be given; that the doctrine of toleration is now better understood (4); that we have learned at least thus much from our religious disruptions and the manifold and infinite griefs they cause?

For instance, is it credible that churchmen would at this day treat remonstrants as the Prolocutor Weston did, when, in the time of Mary, he said to his opponents, "You have the Word, but we have the sword?" Or as Bishop Sheldon, in the reign of the second Charles, when he expressed his fear lest Nonconformists might be satisfied with the scant measure of concession then dealt out to them. Or as, in a later age, a legal dignitary of this country, who was regarded as a bulwark of the Church, — though he supported it only as an establishment, — when addressing a deputation of Dissenters, he allowed himself, and with an oath, such words as these: "If your own religion were established I would support it; but when you were up, you kept us down, — and now we are up, we will pay you back" (5).

And though compromise on either side is neither to be advocated nor desired — and comprehension, however we may long for it, in punishment of our sins may still be unattainable — yet a recent correspondence between a Colonial Bishop, — once a lecturer on this Foundation, — and an eminent Nonconformist divine, is not without promise for the future. It cannot be read without exciting admiration for both. It breathes throughout a manly, healthy, genial tone. It indicates that the spirit in which churchmen and separatists strove together in the Hampton Court and Savoy Conferences, has undergone a change (6).

So with the wider rent and sorer loss in the time of Wesley. Admitting that all has not been lost to the cause of a common Christianity, of which our Church was then deprived; yet who that reads the history of those days, and knows what Wesleyan Methodism has since effected for the quickening of souls, and the revival and spread of religion in many a benighted district of this country, but must mourn that the followers of John Wesley had not adhered to the example and admonition he bequeathed to them, and raised no separate and rival altars? Who but must long for the return to our Church's bosom of the zeal, and the piety, and the power, of which it has been so long deprived (7)?

Never by a rigid adherence to non-essentials, when these are found to separate Christian men, can the cause of Christ be served. Never by an imperious and rough refusal, when concessions are admissible, can any Church retain waverers, or recover alienated children, or promote the cause of truth, and peace, and godliness, in the world.

And this renders it so important that we of the present day should have clear and definite views, and afford a true reflection of the Church itself — that we should understand what, as a Divine institution, it really is — that we should rightly appreciate the work it has to effect in the world. Above all, that we should exhibit its influence on our own hearts and lives, and present it to others, in its true and attractive features, as the Spouse of Christ and the Shepherd of the souls for which He died.

I therefore propose to consider in detail, in the course of these Lectures, the office and qualifications of the English Church as a National establishment, and to state some of the main difficulties and obstructions it has at present to contend with.

I shall point out what appear to be the chief causes of its weakness and its failures; and shall suggest some of the remedial measures and agencies required.

I shall be thus led to dwell upon the training of our Clergy, and the functions of our Elementary, and Middle, and Public Schools; and also upon the special work of our Universities.

I shall have to notice questions affecting the Fabrics and religious Services of our Church, and their better adaptation to the existing necessities and future prospects of our people.

And I shall conclude with some practical remarks on what seems to be more especially required of us, as Citizens and Churchmen, in this momentous and critical period of our history.

In the present Lecture I shall endeavour, within the compass allowed me, to treat of the Nature, Office, and Credentials of the Church, and its means for effecting the mission in which it is engaged.

And first, as to the true nature of the Institution designated in Holy Scripture as the Church.

That on this preliminary point—which to those who take Scripture for their guide, might have been presumed to be so plain—perplexities and controversies have existed, and now divide Christian men, is notorious. And that anything advanced by myself should meet with universal acceptance, is not to be expected. Some, as has been remarked by a great writer, will so narrow their definition, as if

LECTURE I.

their object was not to comprehend, but to exclude. "They define, not by that which the Church essentially is, but by that wherein they imagine their own more perfect than the rest are." Others, as we see in every age, and never more than in our own, in their desire to embrace, confound all differences, and eliminate all lines of demarcation. In their hope of comprehending those that are without, they are apt to forget the terms under which they are themselves concluded, and to pay too little regard to the conscientious difficulties of their brethren. It may be even said of them, that in many things they allow a latitude to separatists, and display a sympathy towards them, which they refuse to churchmen.

Happily, however, on this preliminary, but cardinal point, there is nothing in Scripture, that can be truly represented as incompatible with the language of the Anglican formularies and accredited standard of doctrine. Both of these recognise the Church as the Kingdom of God on earth; the general Assembly of the first-born, whose names are written in Heaven[a]; the whole Company of Christian people dispersed throughout the world; the mystical Body of the Son of God, which is the blessed company of all faithful people[b]: or to quote words to which most of us have subscribed as an article of faith, "A Congregation of faithful men in which the word of God is preached, and the Sacraments be duly ministered,

---

[a] Hebrews xii. 23. [b] Communion Service.

according to Christ's ordinance in all those things that of necessity are requisite to the same."[a]

Such, happily, are the terms, sufficiently comprehensive, and yet sufficiently defined, employed in the Formularies and Confession of the Church of England.

We believe them to be sanctioned by the word of God, and at the same time concurrent with the dictates of charity and the demands of human nature. They do not challenge controversy, but they meet practical requirements. They imply a society, founded by God Himself, to constitute His visible Kingdom upon earth, involving a corporate life, with relations and affections, and sympathies and duties, springing out of this. They describe that living body of men, called by God out of this world to exhibit what humanity was, is, and will be, to the end. They denote a brotherhood, into which we are born by Baptism, and in which we are made, through the Incarnation and Spirit of the Lord Jesus, as children of God and heirs of Christ, partakers of the Divine nature.

And inasmuch, as God's blessing on the members of this body collectively and individually, and the growth and prevalence thereof in the world, depend on the degree in which its various relations and mutual interdependencies, and the correlative functions and obligations which emanate from these are

[a] Article XIX.

felt and carried out; the points, which I have enumerated, seem to be those which it most concerns us to insist on. In them we may find the solution of inquiries which, to bring peace and contentment, must be practically dealt with. They supply the antidote to theories which perplex, even when they do not lead to serious aberration. They suggest the spirit, in which, as members of a body—of which our blessed Lord is the Head, and the end is the salvation of mankind—we are, one and all of us, to co-operate in the work for which He gave Himself. And he who considers them, not in a curious and litigious spirit—not for the indulgence of his imagination, or from vain and vague inquisitiveness — but with a simple desire to learn, in order that he may do God's will, will find them full of instruction in the practical and every-day duties of life. He will be brought to see his own individual share in this holy and blessed fraternity, and the solemn and stringent obligations it imposes. And haply, he may be led to inquire, as The Apostle did, when his eyes were opened to see our Lord Himself, and he learned His identity with His members,— " Lord what wilt thou have me to do?"[a]

When thus considered, it seems full of promise that the Nature of Christ's Church, as a corporate body, is attracting such general attention; and that the privileges and correlative duties of its members are

[a] Acts ix. 6.

becoming daily better understood. We may rejoice that among intelligent persons the form of expression which used to limit the Church to the Clergy is nearly exploded. We may hope that few churchmen would, in the present day, object to the definition of Dr. Arnold — when, in allusion to the memorable aphorism of the Abbé Sièyes, he described the Laity as "the Church minus the clergy" (8). We may hope that still fewer will deny, that the aim and end of such a corporation, as the Church, is to unite and fraternise all ranks and conditions of men; to make them of one mind in the Lord; to promote among them unity of sentiment and action; to make them all, male and female, clerical and lay, "Kings and Priests unto God."[a]

To what, but the prevalence of correct views on this cardinal and vital point, can we look for the spread and eventual triumph of Christ's kingdom upon earth? To these our divisions, and the jealousies and feuds which spring from them, are confessedly the greatest hindrance. When men shall have mastered the truth, that as in Christ we are all members one of another, we may hope that they will forego what has so long kept them asunder. We shall no longer "bite and devour one another, and be consumed one of another."[b] "The envy of Ephraim shall depart, and the adversaries of Judah shall be cut off; Ephraim shall not envy Judah, and Judah shall not

[a] Revelations i. 6; xx. 6; Peter ii. 5, 9.
[b] Galatians v. 15.

vex Ephraim."[a] We shall cease to hear of the power of the Church, as if it were something sacerdotal and political, as separate from and adverse to the people,— as if the people were not in fact the Church, and the clergy but the servants of the people for Jesus' sake.

Let us, therefore, learn more and more to regard the Church in its collective character; to view it as an aggregate of many members; to remember that "by one Spirit we are all called into one Body, and have been all made to drink into one Spirit."[b] For then we shall put on charity, which is the bond of perfectness[c]; and the grace of God shall reign in our hearts; and Christ shall be all in all; and it may be said again, as of old, "Look, how these Christians love one another." And though the care of the individual soul must be the primary consideration of each, let us bear in mind that it is not as isolated units, but as members of a family, and as such as incorporated with Christ Himself, that we approach God, and address Him as our Father which is in Heaven.

The whole of the Christian Economy proclaims this. The human nature of our Lord, the common work He has achieved for us, the prayer which bears His name, the new commandment which is the badge of His discipleship, the sacraments by Himself appointed, His promised presence with those who meet together in His name and with His Church

[a] Isaiah xi. 13.   [b] 1 Corinthians xii. 13.   [c] Colossians iii. 11.

unto the end of the world — all teach this great truth,—that our union with Christ incorporates us with His members, identifies us with all whom He is not ashamed to call His brethren.

And just in proportion as we enter into the import and fulness of this our common church life, shall we realise the blessings it implies. Then, and then only, shall we be built together for an habitation of God through the Spirit[a], and have nourishment ministered to us through our Head[b], and grow up to Him in all things, and make increase of the body, unto the edifying of itself in love.[c] Then shall we understand what has hitherto withered the graces, and paralysed the efforts, and dwarfed the growth of that Church which was meant to bring us all, in the unity of the faith, and of the knowledge of the Son of God, unto a perfect man, unto the measure of the stature of the fulness of Christ.[d]

It will further elucidate the nature of the Church, if we consider for what it was called out of the world, and endowed with the gifts and graces of the Holy Spirit.

It was to open men's eyes, and to turn them from darkness to light, and from the power of Satan unto God, that they might receive forgiveness of sins, and inheritance amongst them that are sanctified by faith which is in Christ Jesus.[e] It was to incorporate

[a] Ephesians ii. 22.
[b] Colossians ii. 19
[c] Ephesians iv. 15, 16.
[d] Ephesians iv. 13.
[e] Acts xxvi. 18.

them in one united and harmonious brotherhood, in and under Christ. It was to make them, collectively and individually, partakers of the Divine nature.

To effect this, it was to impersonate the mind and life of God, and thus to manifest that it comes from God, and represents His nature and His will. The standard and the pattern of the Church is humanity, in union with the Godhead, as revealed and exhibited in Jesus Christ.

Now we know what our Lord's own mission was. He Himself proclaimed it in the pregnant and thrilling words with which He commenced His ministry at Nazareth :—" The Spirit of the Lord is upon me, because He hath anointed me to preach the Gospel to the poor. He hath sent me to heal the brokenhearted, to preach deliverance to the captives, and recovery of sight to the blind, to set at liberty them that are bruised."[a]

And this Christ did, in virtue of His humanity. His ministry was founded upon homely and familiar intercourse, and an intense personal sympathy with man. It behoved Him, as we are told, to be made like unto His brethren. And thus He became amenable to the conditions of human nature. He took part with flesh and blood; He submitted to privation and suffering ; He was touched with the feeling of our infirmities; He bare our sicknesses; He was in

[a] Luke iv. 18.

all points tempted like as we are; He was made sin for us.^a

Christ's ministry was also founded on sacrifice and self-surrender. Though He were a son, yet learned He obedience by what He suffered. He abdicated what was His own. He became capable of loss and detriment, for the good of others. Though rich, for our sakes He became poor, that we through his poverty might be made rich. He emptied Himself, and took on Him the form of a servant. He said, "Not My will, but Thine be done." He became obedient unto death.^b

And when He instituted His Church, it was upon the principles He had Himself exemplified, and which are, in fact, essential to its success. The Church must needs be conformed to its Divine exemplar: its essence must be sympathy: its life consists in self-surrender. "For as the body is one and hath many members, and all the members of that one body being many are one body, so also is Christ." "The members are to have the same care one of another. And whether one member suffer, all the members are to suffer with it, or one member be honoured, all the members are to rejoice with it."^c

This, therefore, is what the Church is to enforce and to exhibit. It grew and multiplied at the first

---

^a Hebrews ii. 14,17; iv. 15; Matthew viii. 17; 2 Cor. vi. 21.
^b Hebrews v. 8; Philippians ii. 7, 8; 2 Corinthians viii. 9; Luke xxii. 42.   ^c 1 Corinthians xii. 12, 26.

because it did so. It enunciated and it illustrated the law of brotherhood. It fraternized the members of the human family, on the broad ground of common necessities and the common provision made for all these in the Gospel.

Hence, as has been finely observed, at once the opposition Christianity encountered, and its triumphs. It was to the Greeks foolishness, and to the Jews a stumbling block.[a] But it was light for the blind, help for the helpless, hope for the despairing, succour for the lost.

"It is written, Eye hath not seen, nor ear heard, neither have entered into the heart of man, the things which God hath prepared for them that love Him."[b] To tell those who gloried in social and religious exclusiveness, that God is no respecter of persons — that access to His favour was as open to the Samaritan and the Gentile, as to the Jew,—to the publican and the adulteress and the thief, as to the Pharisee,— to the illiterate, as to the philosopher, — must have been offensive to those who rested on the very distinctions which the Gospel thus summarily and for ever abolished. The natural man received it not — it was foolishness unto him — he could not know it, because it is spiritually discerned.[c] But it coincided with the universal and irrepressible instincts of the human soul; it enfranchised with the liberty which makes men free; it neutralised

---

[a] 1 Corinthians i. 23.   [b] Ibid. ii. 9.   [c] Ibid. ii. 14.

distinctions of race, and creed, and clime, and speech, and outward condition, which served under a different economy to dissocialise, and embitter, and enslave. It proclaimed that there is " neither Greek nor Jew, circumcision nor uncircumcision, Barbarian, Scythian, bond, nor free, but Christ is all, and in all,"[a] and on the ground of this, it required men to put on " charity which is the bond of perfectness." [b]

And what man was in the first century, he is now; his instincts, his needs, his cravings are still the same. The edicts of men, the disparities of fortune, the usages of society may stifle and repress,—but they cannot extinguish these. And as man, when most embruted, is still conscious of the image in which he was created,— and when most enslaved, of his equality with those who coerce him,— so even when in a state of savage and soured isolation, he still feels the yearnings and the aspirations which are common to all men, and inherent in the nature he inherits.

These it is the office of the Church to satisfy. And to do so, it has but to teach and to impersonate the lessons of the Gospel. For this is to impart the freedom and the fellowship for which men pine; this, to restore what was lost in Adam, but has been recovered in Jesus Christ. Our Lord's incarnation embodied, and His personal mission taught this.

---

[a] Colossians iii. 11; Galatians iii 28.   [b] Colossians iii. 14.

His lowly birth, His humble station, His participation in the ills He came to relieve — in a word the life-long sacrifice, of which His humanity was the vehicle, may teach the Church the nature of the work to which it is called, and the only manner in which that work can be accomplished (9).

A like lesson is conveyed in Christ's Commission to His Church, "As the Father hath sent me, so send I you; He that receiveth you, receiveth Me."[a]

For what do these words imply? That His Apostles were to teach as He had taught, to walk as He had walked, to minister as He had ministered. He enjoined this literally, when He said "Heal the sick, cleanse the lepers, raise the dead, cast out devils: freely ye have received, freely give."[b] He promised that the works He did, they should do, and greater, because He went unto the Father.[c] And to enable them to do so, after His ascension He endued them with power from on high, He baptized them with the Holy Ghost and with fire, He wrought with them, and confirmed their word with signs following.[d]

And thus we read in the verses preceding my text, "and many wonders and signs were done by the apostles. And all that believed were together, and had all things common; and sold their possessions, and goods, and parted them to all men, as every man had

[a] John xx. 21; Matthew x. 40; John xiii. 20; xvii. 18.
[b] Matthew x. 8.   [c] John xiv. 12.
[d] Acts i. 8; xiv. 3.

need. And they continuing daily with one accord in the temple, and breaking bread from house to house, did eat their meat with gladness and singleness of heart, praising God and having favour with all the people. And the Lord added to the Church daily such as should be saved."[a]

Eighteen centuries have elapsed since these scenes were enacted; and the picture they present is painfully contrasted with what we see around us now. When we contemplate the schisms and the deadness of the Church in times succeeding,—with its divided state and comparatively inoperative character in the present day,—we are even tempted to distrust its mission and Christ's continued presence with it,—though this falling away is predicted in the very record that narrates those early triumphs.

And yet we know that the Church's Credentials are the same now, as in the day of primitive believers,—that its commission is identical with that conferred on the apostles,—that the presence of our Lord is as much assured to us as it was to them,—and that our safeguard against both despondency and presumption must be found in believing this, and acting on this persuasion.

For how, it may be asked, was the Church originally equipped for its mission; and what are its present organization and instruments, as a divine institution?

They may be specified as the Christian ministry,

[a] Acts ii. 43—47.

the Sacraments, the Holy Scriptures, the Church's Forms of Devotion embodying its Creeds, and its Corporate Fellowship and Action.

These all emanate from our Lord Himself, or have the sanction of His Holy Spirit. They were given the Church to profit withal. They are the channels through which the Holy Ghost ordinarily works. We have them now. They owe their efficacy, not to any counsel or work of man, but to the presence, and the power, and the blessing of our Lord Himself.

To attempt to expound these various means of grace, is not my province now. I shall not, for instance, be required to enforce the divine institution of Holy Orders. It is admitted by all who take Scripture for their guide, that "God gave apostles for the perfecting of the saints, for the work of the ministry, for the edifying of the body of Christ:"[a] and that, as our Lord ordained twelve to be with Him, invested them with a plenary commission, and breathed on them the ordaining spirit, so He assured them of His presence with their Office unto the end of the world.[b]

It is unquestionably the doctrine of our Church, that our Bishops are the successors of the Apostles; that our Priests are the representatives of those on whom any of the Twelve laid holy hands; that our Deacons exercise an office equivalent to that possessed by the earliest Seven. Our Church proclaims

[a] Ephesians iv. 11.
[b] Mark iii. 13; John xx. 21, 22, 23; Matthew xxviii. 20.

that the unworthiness of the agent does not invalidate the truth of God or annul His commission; that the message may be true, though he who delivers it may not himself believe it; that the blessings he dispenses are real, though he may not himself partake them.[a] It teaches, in a word, that the treasure imparted is of God, though conveyed in earthen vessels; and its announcement is now, as of old, "Believe on the Lord your God, so shall ye be established; believe His prophets, so shall ye prosper."[b]

In like manner, with the Holy Sacraments. The Church maintains that they are the means of manifesting to us the mind and life of God, and making us, through the incarnation, partakers of the divine nature: that "they be certain sure witnesses, and effectual signs of grace and God's good will towards us, by the which He doth work invisibly in us, and doth not only quicken, but also strengthen and confirm our faith in Him"[c]: that they are rounds of the ladder reaching up to heaven, upon which the angels ascend and descend, while the Lord stands above it.[d]

Baptism, we are taught, is the bath and grave of sin, in which the soul is both cleansed and vivified, and through the Holy Ghost participates in Christ's atoning blood and resurrection power; "whereby, as by an instrument, they that receive it rightly are grafted into the Church; and the promises of the

[a] Article XVI.   [b] 2 Chronicles xx. 20.   [c] Article XXV.
[d] Genesis xxviii. 12, 13.

forgiveness of sins, and of our adoption to be the sons of God by the Holy Ghost, are visibly signed and sealed"ᵃ (10).

The Supper of the Lord, we are taught, is "a sacrament of our redemption by Christ's death: insomuch that to such as rightly, worthily, and with faith, receive the same, the Bread which we break is a partaking of the Body of Christ; and likewise the Cup of Blessing is a partaking of the Blood of Christ."ᵇ In it "we eat the flesh and drink the blood of Christ, we dwell in Christ, and Christ in us."ᶜ As churchmen we embrace without controversy this great mystery of godliness; we believe that it conveys God to us, and incorporates us with Himself; that in it "our fellowship is with the Father and with His Son Jesus Christ." We neither say with Nicodemus, "How shall these things be?"ᵈ nor with them of Capernaum, "Can this man give us His flesh to eat?"ᵉ We do not question, when we should rejoice,—or cavil, when we should adore.

Controversies there have been, and probably ever will be, in the present state, on mysteries so high above the compass of our finite faculties. But the significance with which the Sacraments symbolise the leading truths of the Gospel, can hardly be disputed. They proclaim our fall in Adam, our recovery in Christ, our need of atonement and renovation, and the altered relations towards both

---

ᵃ Article XXVII. ᵇ Article XXVIII. ᶜ Communion service.
ᵈ John iii. 9. ᵉ Ibid. vi. 52.

God and man into which we are introduced in virtue of the incarnation; how we are transferred from a state of nature to a state of grace, are born into God's family, and incorporated with His Church, have living union with our Lord and with all His members. Thus far the teaching of Holy Scripture is express. It tells us that "as many of us as have been baptized into Christ, have put on Christ;" that "by one Spirit are we all baptized into one body;" that "we are saved by baptism," and "by the washing of regeneration and renewing of the Holy Ghost."[a] It enables us to ask with the Apostle, and in words which, with those who admit the authority of Scripture, ought to settle this question for ever,—"the cup of blessing which we bless, is it not the communion of the blood of Christ? the bread which we break, is it not the communion of the body of Christ?"[b] And on the ground of our sacramental communion with our Lord, it establishes our fellowship with one another. "For we being many, are one bread, and one body: for we are all partakers of that one bread."[c]

And although the very means by Christ ordained to unite us with Himself and with one another, have proved a source of multiplied divisions; and the Sacraments themselves, and the Scriptures which describe them as the badge and bond of our union,

[a] Galatians iii. 27; 1 Corinthians xii. 13; 2 Peter iii. 21; Titus iii. 5.
[b] 1 Corinthians x. 16. [c] Ibid. 17.

have been tortured into subjects of contention—yet to humble and docile spirits, conscious of their needs, thirsting for acceptance and communion with God, opening their mouths wide that they may be filled with His fulness, how simple and how suitable, how significant and how healing, are the mysteries which are "hid from the wise and prudent, but revealed unto babes!"

Enough, assuredly, for us that the Sacraments impart and maintain union with Christ and with His people; that the one is the consummation of the work of which the other is the beginning; that they both secure the indwelling of the Holy Spirit; that they cause the faithful recipient to grow and increase with the increase of God;—and by the grace which they convey qualify us at once for the duties of this life and for the scenes of a better. What have we to do as believers in Revelation, but to accept what God bestows,—to wash that we may be clean, to eat that we may be satisfied!

Thus also, with Holy Scripture, of which the Church is the keeper and expounder,—we believe that it is the incorruptible seed of which we are born again,—that it is given us by inspiration of God, —that it is able to make us wise unto salvation, through faith which is in Christ Jesus.[a]

The very existence of the sacred Volume is a proof of the fidelity with which the Church has

---

[a] 1 Peter i. 23; 2 Timothy iii. 16.

discharged her trust. But History also attests the reverence with which its canon was fixed, the care with which its integrity has been preserved, the submission with which its dictates have ever been received by her. Whatever heresies have disturbed the Church, whatever catastrophes have befallen the world, the Word of God remains intact. The controversies and contentions of men, and their mutual jealousies have but served to vindicate its inspiration, and maintain its authority. We know it was the standard universally acknowledged, and to which every disputant appealed. And as long as it is held whole and undefiled, and deferred to with unhesitating reverence, the Church will be true to its mission, and have the means of discharging it. The Oracles of God will unlock to her the secrets of all hearts, and furnish the weapons none can resist and the arguments none can gainsay. Nor can we doubt that the questions which present controversies have stirred, will only render this armoury more available and more serviceable.

Another means with which the Church is supplied for preserving and propagating truth, and promoting Christian fellowship, are her Formularies of devotion. In them, she believes are deposited and perpetuated truths which are the only sure and sound interpreters of Scripture. She regards them not merely as forms of prayer, but also as confessions of faith. She knows that they emembody and embalm her creed; that they show what has been taught and believed by her in every age from the beginning. And therefore apart from their intrinsic value,—as the forms in which from apostolic ages saints have worshipped God, and their confessions, prayers, and praises, have come down to us,—the Church esteems these formularies, as witnessing to the doctrines and usages of days contemporaneous with the Apostles, or immediately succeeding them.

Thus the liturgies which bear the names of St. John, St. James, St. Mark, whether or not the veritable productions of those holy men, at least attest the religious practices and the sacred truths associated with their persons, and stamped with their authority. They also establish by their variations in form, though not in substance, the separate independence of the Churches in which they severally prevailed. In all we find a substantial uniformity, a common order, an identity of ideas and expressions. In this way they may be viewed as constituting an important part of Christian evidence — as a sacred repository of the truth. They are the breathings of the Church's soul,— the utterances of its innermost shrine. They convey to us, in the fulness of confidence and love, and in forms concealed from others, her secret communings with Him to whom all hearts are open, all desires known, and from whom no secrets are hid.

I would notice briefly, in conclusion, the corporate Fellowship and Action which all these means are intended to further, and on which the true life and strength of the Church depend.

For how is the Church described in Scripture? As "a body fitly joined together, and compacted by that which every joint supplieth, according to the effectual working in the measure of every part, making increase unto the edifying of itself in love."[a] As "a body into which all are baptized by the same Spirit and made to drink into the same Spirit,—in which all the members should have the same care one of another, and should suffer and rejoice together,— in which there should be no schism." As "a building fitly framed together and growing unto an holy temple in the Lord, in whom all are builded together for an habitation of God through the Spirit."[b] As a society in which there should be "no divisions, but all should be perfectly joined together in the same mind and in the same judgment." While in the healthy and harmonious action of this corporate life, each member has to witness and to work for God.

As, then, in our social and civil relations,— just as families thrive and states prosper in proportion as their mutual ties and interdependencies are maintained,— so with the Household of faith. When the multitude of them that believed were of one heart and of one soul, great grace was upon them. When they were all together, and of one accord, nothing could withstand them. The ad-

[a] Ephesians iv. 16.
[b] 1 Corinthians i. 10 ; xii. 13, 25, 26 ; Ephesians ii. 21, 22.

versaries were confounded, the churches were multiplied, the Lord added to the Church daily such as should be saved.

When therefore men talk of Christianity as an effete system; when they taunt us with its dwarfed stature and its feeble growth, and the slight influence it exercises in the world; and we are ourselves all too conscious of differences and divisions within the Church,—can we doubt that the corrective of this must be sought in the law of sympathy, which is the law of life and the end and essence of the religion of Christ?

We have learned the use of combination in all that affects the interests of this world. We ground on it our schemes of profit and philanthropy. We trust in it for the diffusion of knowledge, for the promotion of liberty, for the spread of civilisation. We feel that to promote union and joint action amongst men, is the surest way to further their welfare and happiness. We commend whatever tends to draw closer the ties of human brotherhood. Distinctions which for centuries have kept those apart whom God meant to be united, are now rejected as ignoble and irrational. To reclaim free action, to abolish caste, to remove civil and religious disabilities, are the foremost objects of our day. It is only when the unity of the Church, and the fellowship of the Gospel, and the communion of Saints are contended for, that the principle of brotherhood is forgotten.

And thus with multitudes in our day the Church is a mere abstraction. With others the tie to it is but traditional, or conventional, or political. They succeed to its membership as a matter of inheritance; they value it only as an Establishment; they adopt its usages and formularies merely as in accordance with their tastes, and suited to their social position, and agreeable to their sense of propriety. On such grounds as these they are classified in its census, designated as its members, to be seen in its solemn assemblies, and, perhaps, periodically partake of its most sacred rite. But of the real nature of the Church as a Divine institution, and a corporate fellowship, and a living body,— or of the duties which its membership imposes — they entertain no distinct or adequate conception. They have no loyal, earnest, clinging attachment to its altars. They never think of it as a centre of unity and a source of blessedness; they never turn to it amid the cares and distractions of this world as a refuge and a home for their hearts. It has no hold on their imaginations and no place in their affections.

What wonder that to labour for the Church, or to make sacrifices for its sake constitutes no part of the religion of these men! that its cause excites no enthusiasm, and its wrongs arouse no resistance; that the Church thus offers no compact front to assailants, — while the apathy and supineness of its members are often painfully contrasted with the opposite qualities in Separatists! It is not that such men are incapable of attachment, or of self-surrender, or of heroic efforts for what they value. But they have been wont to view the Church as a thing external to themselves — in which the clergy are chiefly interested, and for which the clergy are mainly responsible — and religion as a matter that concerns only a man's own soul, and for which he is accountable to God alone.

So with many in our day of far more promise, and of far higher stamp of character, but who are impatient of dogmatism in religion, weary of forms unaccompanied by the power of godliness, suspicious of pretentious profession, and to whom polemics are distasteful.

To win such persons by theories, or sway them by authority, is clearly impracticable. We can only influence them by the force of example.

They ask for what may commend itself to every man's conscience in the sight of God; for living and practical exemplifications of truth; for something which they may taste, and touch, and handle; — in a word, for the spirit which quickened the world in the first century of Christianity, and revived the Church at the time of the Reformation. To rouse the apathetic, to satisfy the inquirer, to convince gainsayers, to evangelise those amongst us who are without God and without hope in the world, to make sound and living members of the Church, this is what is wanted.

Therefore, if we would have our Church survive the shock of these latter days, and "walk the waters as a thing of life and beauty," winning to its bosom those that are without, and sheltering all that are within, we must realise our corporate life as churchmen, and be ourselves an epistle of Christ, to be seen and read of all men. In no other way can we hope to recommend and endear the Church. To gain acceptance for its ministry, we must evince the blessings of which it is the channel. To have its sacraments esteemed, we must display their quickening and sanctifying power. To maintain its standard of Scripture, we must make this the rule of our own lives. To vindicate our beautiful forms of devotion, we must heartily and habitually join in them ourselves.

Otherwise, men will say of us that we have a name to live while we are dead; that, like those of old, we cry, "the Temple of the Lord, the Temple of the Lord, the Temple of the Lord are we,"[a] while we deny the Lord of the Temple; that like theirs, our profession is a pretence and our hope a delusion.

[a] Jeremiah vii. 4.

LECTURE II.

1 TIMOTHY III. 15.

"*That thou mayest know how thou oughtest to behave thyself in the House of God, which is the Church of the living God, the pillar and ground of the Truth.*"

ἵνα εἰδῇς πῶς δεῖ ἐν οἴκῳ θεοῦ ἀναστρέφεσθαι, ἥτις ἐστὶν ἐκκλησία θεοῦ ζῶντος, στῦλος καὶ ἑδραίωμα τῆς ἀληθείας.

IT is impossible to contemplate the English Church, whether in reference to our own age and people, or to the world at large, without admitting the greatness and importance of its position. And every one who has the true interests of religion at heart, must desire to see it duly qualified for its mission, and heartily engaged in discharging this.

Called out of Christendom to witness to the truth of God, placed by Him as a city upon a hill, representing the religious mind of a great nation, its influence for good, if duly exercised, must be incalculably great. By a strict adherence to the canon of Scripture, by an exemplary standard of devotion, by impersonating in word and act the mind and life of God, it may shine as a light in the world, and vindicate its divine original by arguments that none can gainsay.

And in days of doubt and debate like these, when so many on every side of us are asking who shall show us any good,—when all things seem in a transition state,—when on the flow and reflux of popular opinion men's minds are drifting hither and thither, —we have reason to bless God for the landmarks and safeguards which such an institution affords.

It is the glory of the English Church, though with some a plea to disparage it, that it maintains the mean between extremes. For what does this imply? That it "tries the spirits whether they be of God,"— discriminates between the divine oracles and the traditions and opinions of men, — "proves all things, and holds fast that which is good."

It is this, in the words of an eloquent statesman, that makes our national Church "a shelter and a home, a signal of rallying to the combatant and a refuge for the fallen." With no unseemly precipitation, in no compromising spirit,—but after full deliberation, and with a clear apprehension of consequences, were its standard and formularies framed. And with no faltering tongue does it pronounce at the present time on subjects on which men's minds were divided centuries ago, and are divided now.

Our Anglican reformers were men not only valiant for the truth, but also of great practical experience, of ripe scholarship, of vast and varied erudition. They were mighty in the Scriptures: they were also versed in primitive records, and profound in patristic theology. Above all, they were men who, after they were illuminated, had endured a great fight of afflictions; had been proved by imprisonment, and exile, and the spoiling of their goods, and the edge of the sword, and the violence of fire. Theirs were not days for captious doubts, or reckless innovation; but when the senses were exercised to discern both good and evil, and men wrote and spoke with their lives in their hands, and all they valued on earth and in heaven at stake.

Our Reformers were no mere adventurers in theology, neither were they actuated by a blind animosity to Rome. They were only bent on vindicating the independence of their national Church, on purging it from base accretions, on rescuing from corruption or decay truths which had been obscured, distorted, or denied. They but sought to precipitate error, and leave pure and limpid the Gospel stream. Surely it becomes us to speak of such men with tenderness, to make allowance for their difficulties and consequent short-comings, and to receive with thankfulness and self-distrust the inheritance they have transmitted.

The Church of England is a fact of history. It stands before us to-day as the religious institution of a great, and free, and understanding people. It is in an important sense a type of our national character, and like our civil constitution, has been the growth of ages. It has stood the test of adversity; for it has seen evil days, and suffered sore reverses. But it has survived the storms that swept over it, and has struck its roots wide and deep into our social and political system, and it may be hoped into the hearts of our people.

No one can dispute its antiquity. And whether or not planted by St. Paul himself in his mission to the utmost bounds of the West, we know, from the coincidence of native records with foreign testimony, that a society similarly organised, with like creed and like polity, existed in these realms at a date coeval with the age of the Apostles.

The vestiges of the early British Church are indeed few and scanty. But we have evidence of its threefold ministry, its monastic institutions, its version of the Bible, and its ritual (10). While history records that when afterwards incorporated with the Church founded by Augustine, and indebted to that great man for its revival, extension, and permanent establishment, it maintained its struggles from time to time, against the inordinate demands and gross corruptions of the Romish Church. And when restored to its independence at the Reformation, it purified its doctrine and discipline according to the Word of God and the primitive and apostolic practice.

We have already seen that the Church was designed for the restoration of men to the image and favour of God ; that its mission is to gather and incorporate them in one spiritual body,—of which Christ Himself is the pattern and the head,— and to make them partakers of the divine nature. It may be reasonably inferred that the necessary conditions of such an institution are Divine appointment, grace in the Sacraments, succession in the Ministry, visibility and permanence in the Body.

Such are, consequently, the credentials of the English Church,—which it maintains to have belonged to it from the beginning, and to have been reasserted and fully recognised at the Reformation. It claims to be primitive in its type, scriptural in its teaching, and catholic in its spirit.

To discuss the validity of English Orders, the efficacy of the sacraments administered amongst us, the presence of our Lord in our ordinances and assemblies, would carry me far beyond the space allowed for these Lectures, and into ground which has been previously and ably occupied by others. I must therefore be content to assume that the commission and inheritance of the early Church have been transmitted to ourselves, and to refer you to the testimony of those who followed close on the footsteps of the Apostles, and who enumerate and classify the three orders retained in our communion as of divine or apostolic institution and continuous succession.

And if I dwell for a moment upon the principles avowed by the leaders of the Reformation in this and other lands, and accredited in our own recognised rule of faith, it is only in passing, and with a view to my younger brethren present.

We find, then, Cranmer maintaining the divine authority of priests and bishops, the superiority of bishops, and their succession from the Apostles. We notice in documents, put forth by authority, the gift or grace of ministration in Christ's Church asserted to be given of God to Christian men by the consecration and imposition of the bishop's hands, and to be intended to continue to the end of the world.

We further find it declared in the Ordinal drawn up in 1549, that from the Apostles' times there have been three orders of ministers in Christ's Church — bishops, priests, and deacons; and that none were admitted to them but by public prayer with imposition of hands.

Lastly, in the Ordinal now is use,—and which is expressly sanctioned and authorised, not only as part of the Book of Common Prayer, but by the thirty-sixth article,—we have episcopal ordination enjoined; with a declaration that none shall be hereafter accounted or taken to be a lawful bishop, priest, or deacon in our Church, who has not had episcopal consecration or ordination.

On the general question of the need of a call and separation to the ministry, other reformed Communions are not at issue with ourselves. Luther condemns the denial of this as an error invented by the devil. The Confession of Augsburg speaks of the ministry of the word and sacraments as divinely instituted. The Helvetic Confession of the Zuinglians declares the office of the ministry to be ancient, and ordained of God, not of recent or of human ordination. Calvin says that no one must be accounted a minister of Christ except he be regularly called.

And even on the subject of Episcopacy, on which these communions unhappily differ from us, it was not willingly that they renounced it. On the contrary, the Lutherans earnestly protested their desire to retain episcopacy, and adhere to the canonical government, if only the bishops would cease to exercise cruelty upon the Churches.

The Calvinists, though in like manner rejecting their bishops, who would have bound them to Rome, declared that they were ready to submit to a lawful hierarchy. Even John Knox may be instanced as a witness for the distinction of bishops and presbyters; and Beza pronounced it insane to reject all episcopacy, and prayed that the Church of England might continue to enjoy for ever that singular bounty of God (11).

I desire, however, not to be misunderstood on this matter. It is one thing to unchurch those who differ from us, and another to uphold our own position. For myself I subscribe to the language of our great divine, uttered in reference to foreign reformed Churches:—" This their defect and imperfection I had rather lament than exagitate,—considering that men oftentimes, without any fault of their own, may be driven to want that kind of polity which is best, and to content themselves with that which either the irremediable error of former days or the necessity of the present has forced upon them."

For ourselves, it behoves us to take heed lest we be surpassed by those less endowed, in labours, and eloquence, and personal holiness. We are witnesses to the works of faith and the labours of love, and the patience of hope in our Lord Jesus Christ and in the sight of God our Father, which distinguish many among them, and prove their election of God. We recognise their talents and their virtues, their powerful advocacy of the great truths of Christianity, and the success with which their efforts are often crowned. May we be able to surpass them in these respects, and to say with truth, in the words of the Apostle, "Are they ministers of Christ? I am more!"

We, indeed, believe our own doctrine and practice to be more in accordance with Scripture and Apostolic usage; and that their tendency is to humble the soul, to exorcise self, to promote an absolute and habitual dependance upon God, and thus to subordinate the man to the system and diminish his personal importance. We believe that the language of a heart duly penetrated by the sense of a divine commission and of delegated trusts, is " Woe is me, that I am a man of unclean lips:"[a] "Not that we are sufficient of ourselves to think anything as of ourselves, our sufficiency is of God:"[b] "We have this treasure in

[a] Isaiah vi. 5.   [b] 2 Corinthians iii. 5.

earthen vessels, that the excellency of the power may be of God, and not of us:"[a] "Unto me, who am less than the least of all saints, is this grace given, that I should preach the unsearchable riches of Christ."[b] We feel, that the denial of self, the renunciation of self, the going out of self, are the conditions of clerical acceptance with both God and man. We admit, in the fullest sense, that we ought not to boast of our titles, but only to be what they imply; and that to rest in credentials which a man degrades, and a ministry which he does not discharge, is of all infatuations the most deplorable, or of all impostures the most contemptible.

Less liable to controversy or mistake is the feature of the English Church, to which I now proceed — I mean her reverential love of Scripture, and her implicit submission to it as a rule of faith and practice. That she is a faithful witness and keeper of Holy Writ is her strongest claim to the national allegiance, and her firmest hold on the national mind. And no one can be acquainted with the principles of our Church, or have regularly worshipped in her courts, or been conversant with her pious poor, without admitting that she possesses this. Her constant and copious use of Scripture in her public services, her invariable appeals to it from the pulpit, her desire to have her own pretensions tried and her doctrines tested by this alone, the encouragement which she gives to all

[a] 2 Corinthians iv. 7.   [b] Ephesians iii. 8.

her members to search the Scriptures for themselves, sufficiently evince the implicit submission of the Church of England to the written word of God. An open Bible in their mother tongue is the inheritance of all her people. Her public assemblies, her judicial courts, her private dwellings, her village schools all attest this.

But we owe it to our Anglican reformers that it is so. Time was, as we well know, when the Bible was a sealed book in our land; when its blessed truths were wrung out like drops of blood from those who had the custody of it; when it was death to read its sacred pages without their permission; when fragments of it were hung by them in derision round the necks of their victims at the scaffold. Our reformed Church has sown the Bible broadcast amongst her people. She can say to one and all, "that from childhood they have known the Scriptures, which are able to make them wise unto salvation through faith that is in Christ Jesus." She can echo the memorable words of one of her noblest confessors at the stake: "Good people, I have taught you nothing but God's holy word, and those lessons which I have taken out of God's blessed book; and am prepared this day to seal it with my blood" (12).

Never, we may hope, will the candle these men lighted be extinguished in our land, nor the reverence and the affection of our people for the Book for whose sake they gave their bodies to be burnt, abate or languish.

And in the supreme regard entertained in our communion for the Word of God, we but follow in the steps of the early Church.

We hold with Irenæus, "that the Scriptures are perfect, being spoken by the Word of God and His Spirit."

With Tertullian, we "reverence the fulness, and adore the perfection of Scripture," and with him "fear the woe which is destined for him who adds or takes away."

With Origen we maintain "that in the two Testaments every word that appertains to God may be sought out and discussed, and from them all knowledge of things may be understood."

With Athanasius we believe "that the holy and divinely inspired Scriptures are of themselves sufficient to the enunciation of truth, in them alone is the doctrine of salvation contained, and no man must add or take therefrom."

With Basil "we receive those things which are written; the things which are not written we seek not."

With Ambrose we ask, "How can we use those things which we find not in the Scriptures?"

With Augustine we hold "that in those things which are plainly laid down in Scripture, all things are found, which embrace faith and morals" (13).

But then, as our Church maintains that Scripture is perfect, and abundantly of itself sufficient for all things, she also believes that, for the avoiding of heresy, the line of interpretation must be directed according to the rule of ecclesiastical and catholic sense. And this mainly constitutes the difference between our Church and the Sects.

The English Church claims for itself authority in controversies of faith [a] (14). In deciding these it takes as its rule of truth the confession of the early and undivided Church: it avails itself of the light of primitive testimony and of general practice. And I put it to men of understanding,—whether without this it were possible to curb the wantonness of private interpretation, or prevent the unstable wresting the Scriptures to their own destruction. "It is the lust of solitary pride,"—I quote an illustrious statesman, an alumnus and representative of this University,— "which engenders speculations injurious to the faith, and claims for its own fancies the deference which it refuses to the collective voice."

But primitive tradition testifies to facts, and carries us to the fountain head. It records what was believed and practised in the earliest age of Christianity, expounding primitive doctrine by primitive practice. It settles the canon of Scripture, and furnishes the proof that the sacred books were written by those whose names they bear.

And, therefore, while our Church rejects tradition as a distinct and independent authority, it welcomes it as a help and guide to the true understanding of

---

[a] XXth Article of Religion.

the Bible. It rests on no human sanction; it admits no testimony to be superior or equal to the Scripture. But it avails itself of the confession of the early Church, as evidence of what was early believed and early taught, and demonstrating that its own doctrine and usages are primitive and apostolical.

That such was the course sanctioned and approved by our Reformers is notorious. Their controversy with Rome was that that Church had departed from primitive doctrine and usage, to which they desired to submit themselves. Their own wish was to approach, as near as they could, to the Church of the Apostles, and of the ancient Catholic bishops and fathers. They declared that they had ordered, not their doctrines alone, but also the sacraments and forms of public prayer by the pattern of primitive rites and institutes.

"I protest," said Cranmer, "that it was never in my mind to write, speak, or understand anything, but what I have learned of the sacred Scriptures, and of the Holy Catholic Church of Christ from the beginning; and also according to the exposition of the most holy and learned fathers and martyrs of the Church."

"I repair," said Ridley, "to the usages of the primitive Church."

"We have approached," said Jewel, "as nearly as we could, to the Church of the Apostles, and of the ancient Catholic bishops and fathers."

The appeal was, in every case, from the corruptions of the Latin Church in the sixteenth century, to the consent and practice of the Church Catholic in its primitive purity (15).

In fine, the principle of interpretation adopted by the English Church, is well laid down by Dr. Waterland. "We allow," he says, "no doctrine as necessary, which stands only on the fathers or on tradition, oral or written. We admit none for such, but what is contained in Scripture, and proved by Scripture, rightly interpreted. And we know no way more safe in necessaries, to preserve the right interpretation, than to take the ancients along with us. We think it a good method to secure our rule of faith against impostures of all kinds; whether of enthusiasm, or false criticism, or conceited reason, or oral tradition, or the assuming dictates of an infallible chair. If we thus preserve the true sense of Scripture, and upon that sense build our faith, we then build upon Scripture only,—for the sense of Scripture is Scripture."

And then, if it be asked where the hermeneutical tradition of the English Church may be found? the question was recently proposed to myself in a tone of triumph within the walls of the Vatican — we answer in the Book of Common Prayer. You must seek our Church's exposition of Scripture in its Liturgy, by which its Articles are interpreted. You will find its standard of doctrine, as well as its forms of devotion, *there* (16).

And, therefore, over and above its value as a vehicle of worship, we prize our Book of Common Prayer, as an exponent of apostolical teaching and practice. We send inquirers to its pages for the confession of our faith. We present it as a solemn and deliberate adoption of the doctrine and the rule of the early Church. We say here you have the sense and the judgment of our reformers on the faith which was once for all delivered to the saints. Here is transmitted the form of sound words, which our fathers had heard in faith and love which are in Christ Jesus,—and which is now committed to our keeping.

"Public forms of liturgy,"—I quote Bishop Jeremy Taylor,—"are the great securities and basis to the religion and piety of the people. This is all that most men know of their religion,—and they cannot in any way know it better than by those forms of prayer which publish their faith and their devotion to God and all the world." And "thus it is not," observes Professor Blunt, "to any impracticable principle that our Church appeals, when she refers her members to primitive tradition. She does not bid them range for themselves over the wide field of patristic theology, however advantageous it may be to do so, for those who have leisure for the work. But she bids them abide by the Prayer Book, a small volume, a volume within the reach of all, within the comprehension of all, with which she furnishes all; a standard of faith and practice, which has hitherto kept the Church constantly true to itself, counteracting from time to time its obliquity, whichever way it might bear."

Allow me to continue for a moment in the words of this great divine. "How reasonable it is, and yet how impassioned! How catholic, and yet how true to the wants of every man's own heart! How hearty are its accents of self-abasement! How touching its cries for mercy! How earnest its petitions! How high and animating its notes of thanksgiving and praise! How elastic it is! How affecting in its simplicity, when it cheers our humble village church! How sublime in its majesty, when it puts forth the fulness of its strength in our cathedrals! How suited to all ranks and conditions of men! How grateful to the scholar! How acceptable to the peasant! What multitudes of hearts has it lifted up to God! What multitudes of souls has it led to Paradise. *Esto perpetuum!*"

That the Church should have a distinct and definite creed and rule, is, of course, essential. "Hers is not," says an eloquent writer, "that sceptical neutrality, which, amidst the multiplicity of opinions, considers all as equally acceptable to God." On the contrary, she knows that the foundations of Christian unity must be laid in Christian truth.

Yet we believe that the spirit of our Church is neither narrow nor sectarian: that it does not desire to limit the terms of its communion, or fetter men's consciences by restrictions sanctioned neither by Scripture nor expediency. It would be irreconcilable with its duty as a national institution to do so. Of such the necessary conditions are, Truth, Comprehension, Charity. Its tests and formulas of doctrine ought, therefore, to be few and simple, laying traps for none, excluding none who do not perversely exclude themselves. Otherwise, the Church becomes a sect. It separates itself from the sympathies of good, and true, and thoughtful men. It precludes the return of those who are without, and thwarts the aspirations and endeavours of those within. And at a time when so many are yearning to see our Church, in practice as well as theory, the spiritual mother of our people, displaying a large and all-embracing charity, dealing its blessings on every side, carrying its ministrations to every door, enlisting under a common banner all that love the Lord Jesus Christ in sincerity, exclusiveness on her part were not only unchristian, but suicidal (17).

Men of other communions, even the most largehearted and generous amongst them, are unconscious or incredulous of this state of feeling. They give the Church credit for neither the efficacy of its system nor for the spirit by which it is pervaded. They look rather to the bubbles on its surface than to the strong deep current underneath. They know comparatively little of the clerical mind.

" The Clergy," says an eminent Nonconformist, " meet in Convocation to talk and do nothing; they protest against the slightest symptom of progress; they proclaim that no steps can be taken for fifty years to come; they will not recognise the propriety of altering in the least old forms; they profess their utter inability to make a new prayer." In contrasting them with certain of their lay brethren, he designates them as "muttering shadows, the ghosts of the past, rather than living men of flesh and blood, with arms and hands to do something" (18).

Churchmen — least of all those who are conversant with our clergy, and know what is stirring in the bosom of the Church itself — will not be greatly moved by such allegations. They have full confidence in their cause — they record with gratitude the blessing which attends it — they believe that it will wax stronger and stronger, while rival systems will fail and collapse — and of its eventual triumph they entertain no manner of doubt.

But what justifies their hope,—but the strength of the foundation on which our Church reposes, and her full and articulate admission that there is nothing necessary for salvation but may be found in the Scriptures? For this is the revelation of what all hearts are in want, and all feeling after,—the real, the infinite, the true. It is no mere enunciation of dogmas, no congeries of spiritual abstractions, no dry scheme of theology, — but the revelation of a living Being in His boundless capacity to bless, and His personal relation to ourselves. This it is, for which all souls are thirsting, and all minds are groping after.

And this we hold that the teaching of our Church embodies and imparts. Its Creeds we maintain are confessions of God's name; its Sacraments symbols and channels of communion with Him; its formularies of devotion means and helps to approach Him. In this way they are suited to simple minds and earnest hearts, to children and peasants as well as to scholars and philosophers. They are the food of hungry souls, and the solace of wearied spirits. And though theologians may dispute about them, and captious spirits carp at them, yet artless minds and humble hearts in every age have found in them the confession of their mouths unto salvation, and the belief of their hearts unto righteousness.

That an institution, such as has been described, is fitted for the work assigned it, will be generally admitted; nor can it be denied that there are special advantages in the organization and machinery of the English Church for the discharge of its all-important duties.

Of these, its Parochial and Diocesan system — the theory of which, indeed, is nearly perfect — may be considered the foremost.

It professes to subdivide the country into plots of manageable area and population; to locate in each of these a man separated by his calling to offices of love and mercy, fitted by education and previous habits for intercourse with all ranks of society, and bound by solemn obligations to whatever can adorn and sanctify human nature; to afford him access to every man's door, and avenues to every man's heart; to supply him with the motives and the materials for a work, the holiest, most blessed, and most beneficent that can be assigned to man (19). Moreover, to provide in all our parishes an adequate supply of lay officers for such purposes, connected with the social order, fiscal arrangements, and general well-being of their respective localities, as can be suitably discharged by laymen.

Over these parochial subdivisions our Church further professes to have placed chief pastors — with an area proportionately adjusted — to whom both sacred and secular agents shall be accountable; who may exercise over them a wise, fatherly, and careful supervision, pervading their several districts, visiting each parish in succession, coming into contact with all ranks and classes, familiarised and endeared to all, lay and clerical, rich and poor, young and old, by personal presence and apostolic ministrations.

The duties attached by our Church to the Episcopal office, are set forth in the Form of consecration. A bishop is to feed the flock, to preach the word, to administer godly discipline, to be vigilant, sober, given to hospitality, apt to teach, as a wise and faithful servant to give to God's family their portion in due season. He is to hold up the weak, to heal the sick, to bind up the broken, to bring again the outcasts, to seek the lost; to be to such as believe a wholesome example, in word, in conversation, in charity, in spirit, in faith, in purity.

Such is the parochial and diocesan theory of our Church. And were the functions it implies duly and adequately discharged — were our Pastorate and our Episcopate commensurate with the requirements of the Church and the nation, it would be impossible to exaggerate the blessings we might look for. Even as a picture it is pleasant to contemplate, and it is one which some amongst us may even live to see accomplished.

The last feature of the English Church, to which I shall allude in this Lecture, is her connection with the State.

This alliance, as is well known, has been long objected to by separatists, and their scruples have been shared, in recent days, even by some members of our own communion. But by the majority of churchmen the interdependence between Church and State has been ever viewed as indispensable. They regard it as the result of mutual obligations, as implying trusts and duties inseparable from the constitution of each, as not to be neglected by either with impunity.

The Church, it is urged, is bound to "pray for all in authority,"[a] "to uphold the powers that be,"[b] "to be subject for conscience' sake,"[c] to show an example of reverence for law, to further all the ends for which government is established.

The Church is to diffuse knowledge, to foster liberty, to advocate legality, to cultivate social charity, to promote in every way the moral and material interests of man.

The Church educates men to understand their

[a] 1 Timothy ii. 2.   [b] 1 Titus iii. 1.
[c] Romans xiii. 1—7.

position as subjects and as citizens. It teaches man that civil and social duties spring from religion. It witnesses in its formularies that God has appointed powers—that law is from Him. The recognition of its duty in this respect may be traced in its Liturgies from the first; and it has ever been the aim of the Church to promote the temporal prosperity of States.

In like manner, it is maintained to be both the duty and the interest of the State to foster and uphold the Church. It is held that no commonwealth can throw off its responsibility to do so. "That kings should be the nursing fathers of the Church, and queens its nursing mothers",[a] is contended to be both a law of God and an instinct of religion.

The origin and nature of this alliance between Church and State are, however, often misunderstood. By not a few in our day it is viewed as a thing of modern date, and a political contrivance — as a mere conventional contract — as the offspring of state-craft and priest-craft. Whereas it is, in fact, as has been already said, a necessity of our secular and religious institutions, and even of the very nature we inherit. It springs up wherever men learn their own weaknesses and wants, and begin to feel after God; and is not a sudden and arbitrary compact, but a gradual and spontaneous growth. It was embodied in the Jewish

[a] Isaiah xlix. 23.

Theocracy. It existed in the time of the Patriarchs. It is implied when it is said of Abraham, who was in his own person both priest and king,—"I know him, that he will command his children, and his household after him; and they shall keep the way of the Lord, and do justice and judgment."[a]

When Constantine established Christianity in the fourth century, and his example was followed throughout Christendom, it was because by religion, "kings reign and princes decree justice;" because religion is the fountain of authority and the guardian of property, and the foundation of law; because right is the offspring of religion, and right is might.

The Church has been opprobriously designated as the creature of the State. Nor can it be denied that occasionally it has furnished pleas for such a taunt. But this has been when it has forgotten its commission and betrayed its trusts, and sought in the favour of princes and in legal enactments the help that cometh only of the Lord; and then found to its confusion, when the reed on which it leaned has broken and pierced it, that "Cursed is he that trusteth in man, and maketh flesh his arm, and departeth from the Lord."[b]

But the Church is the pillar and the ground of the truth[c], and therefore the strength of states, and the prop of thrones, and the cheap defence of nations, and the stability of the times. Of it, as of

[a] Genesis xviii. 19.   [b] Jeremiah xvii. 5.
[c] 1 Timothy iii. 15.

ancient Israel, it may be said, "Blessed is he that blesseth Thee, and cursed is he that curseth Thee."[a] Without it institutions collapse and dynasties melt away. It is the security of the very sects that disclaim it, though they find their shelter beneath its bulwarks,—and would assuredly discover, were it overthrown, that its ruin involved their own.

Our fathers sought to associate religion with everything; to hallow with it domestic tie, and civil contract, and secular arrangement, and national custom, —and thus to preserve the essential relation between spiritual and civil life, and to render, as far as might be, law and religion identical (20).

The tendency of modern legislation has been too often to reverse this. Our legislature has rightly abolished tests which, to create civil disabilities, profaned a sacrament, and were practically an outrage to religion. But unhappily it has proceeded to supplant Baptism by an act of registration, to degrade Matrimony into a civil contract, to divorce ties which the Church still proclaims to be indissoluble. It even threatens to allow affinities which Scripture seems to interdict and nature shrinks from. The danger is, lest such attempts to denationalise the Church should eventually desecrate the nation, should introduce distrust and pollution into families, and poison the sources of public and domestic purity and happiness.

[a] Numbers xxiv. 9.

That churchmen should provoke or precipitate such a catastrophe by a single hour — that they should not rather do all in their power to check, if they cannot avert what would ensue, were the alliance under which states have thriven and waxed great, which has secured them the favour of God and the allegiance of true hearts, to be dissevered,—seems almost incredible. And yet even some such in our day chafe at a connection, which they consider to damage the interests and cripple the action of religion. They represent the Church as in fetters to the State,—and urge instances of mal-administration in patronage, and apathy in the correction of abuses and the suppression of disorders, as justifying their assertion. And they long for the freedom and the elasticity from which they conceive the Church to be at present debarred, and which would in their eyes more than compensate for what would be sacrificed by the severance of Church and State.

But theory is not unfrequently at variance with actual experience. And while we may hope that, as religion spreads and deepens, and the resources of our Church are more fully developed, causes of complaint may cease, yet an acquaintance with countries where our ecclesiastical system is not established and no alliance with the State interferes with the operation of the Church, may show us that the remedy proposed might be worse than the disease. The history of episcopacy in Scotland and America conveys such warning. And the domination of vestries, and the contention of synods, and the feuds between bishops and presbyters,— where there is no interposition on the part of Government—may render us both grateful for what we enjoy and tolerant of what we cannot amend.

Better the ills we know than those we might encounter! The words of an American professor whom, many years ago, when I was an undergraduate, I conducted over this University,—and to whom, when full of admiration at what he saw and heard of our institutions, I suggested possible imperfections, often recur to my mind. "A man," he said, "must have lived half his life without the blessings you seem to undervalue, to know how to appreciate them. You in England bask in the sunshine, till you learn to spy motes in the sun."

It may be true that the benefits of the alliance between the civil and the ecclesiastical power are greatly in favour of the State. Yet who can deny the advantages conferred by it on the Church? Such are its secure possession of endowments, its sole and undisturbed occupancy of our parish churches, the influential social position of its clergy, its chief direction of the national education, access for its ministrations to rich and poor, opportunities and facilities of every kind for the discharge of its sacred mission. To deny or undervalue these advantages would be irrational, while to sacrifice them would be both criminal and suicidal. Nor can any one fairly dispute that a state, which sanctions and protects such interests as these, has both a claim on the loyalty of churchmen, and a right to demand an account of their stewardship, and to see that the trusts committed to them be faithfully and efficiently discharged.

Admitting that there are flaws in our present ecclesiastical system, — grievances which call for redress, deficiencies to be supplied, occasional incompetence and unfaithfulness in administration, contradictions between ecclesiastical and civil law, — yet these are all capable of remedy. And for this it is the duty of churchmen to contend.

Only let the spirit in which we do so be one of reverence for the structure which the piety and wisdom of former generations has established. The interests at stake are sacred and precious beyond all others. They ought to be approached, not with sectarian and selfish aims, not for the indulgence of party strife, not to carp or cavil; but with humility and self-distrust, and a fear of touching with unhallowed hands the ark of God.

Let us be humble; let us be reverent. Let us bear in mind that the conditions of progressive improvement, in Church as in State, are, a value for what we already possess, a recognition of God's hand in bestowing it, gratitude for what we owe to those who have bequeathed to us such a goodly inheritance, and a determination—as far as in us lies—to transmit it unimpaired to our children's children.

LECTURE III.

JEREMIAH XIII. 20, 21.

"*Where is the Flock that was given thee, thy beautiful Flock? What wilt thou say when He shall punish thee?*"

IN my last Lecture I spoke of certain prominent and distinctive features of the English Church, which denote its fitness for its mission, and entitle it to the national adherence and support.

I showed that it was primitive in its model, scriptural in its teaching, and by its principles and organization qualified to be the religious teacher of an intelligent and practical people.

It will, probably, besides be admitted that our Church was never more alive than at present to its trusts, or more efficient in the discharge of these; that there has been of late a great and general revival of religious light and life within its borders; that its clergy as a body are zealous and exemplary, and its lay members increasingly awake to their privileges and their duties; and that in consequence the services of the Church are better performed and better attended, and its ordinances more generally valued than in a previous generation.

Still it is not, as has been already observed, by measuring ourselves by ourselves, that we can be justified—least of all in a day when privileges of every kind are understood to imply duties, and all systems are canvassed and tested. Nor can any one, who has at heart the true interests and real welfare of the Church, object to its being submitted to the ordeal to which all other institutions are exposed.

Granting, it will be said, that the Church as by law established is all you describe it,—granting its divine commission, its continuous succession, its scriptural standard, the excellency of its parochial and diocesan system, and its preponderating influence from its alliance with the State:—granting, moreover, its present resuscitation in inward life and practical efficiency,—the question is as to the results?

The Church professes to be the religious institution of the nation, the teacher and shepherd of the people, the guardian of public morality and religion, the authorised exponent of doctrine. Both its pretensions and its means are great. It has exclusive privileges, and large endowments, and a well adjusted and extensive organization. And its trusts and responsibilities are commensurate. What is the result? Has it accomplished its mission and done its work? Is it faithful? Is it efficient? Can it show seals of its apostleship? Has it a hold on the affections of the nation? Do men avail themselves of its ministrations and rejoice in them? Do we see its fruits in a moral, a religious, and a united people? That diocesan and parochial system with which you have girdled the country, has it proved a zone of life, and light, and blessing?

Now to deny failures or defects that may be justly urged against the Church can answer no purpose whatever, and is unworthy of honest and godly men. A churchman's only solicitude should be to ascertain in what these blemishes originate, how they may be removed, whether they are incidental or inherent, whether our system itself is faulty, or is only not carried out.

In the present and succeeding Lecture I shall endeavour to answer this inquiry.

That, as a people, we have been largely endowed and eminently blessed in our civil and religious condition, we, as Englishmen, are ever ready to avow. Our sense of national superiority is notorious. And our assumption on account of it has proved not less offensive to others than injurious to ourselves. It has subjected us to charges of insular pride; and has exasperated foreigners to charge us with all possible and impossible enormities — with an utter want of religion, with a neglect of social and domestic obligations, with an indifference to the welfare of our humbler classes at home, and of our Colonial dependencies. It has done us more serious disservice; for it has blinded us to our national deficiencies and national delinquencies, and has thus retarded our national improvement. In the contemplation of our material and political advantages, we ask what nation is so great? in the sense of our spiritual inheritance, who has God so nigh? Our intelligence, our industry, our prowess, our progress in physical science and temporal prosperity, our religious independence and scriptural purity are engraven on the heart of the nation, and too often flaunted in the face of the world.

And yet it must be admitted that there exists amongst us at this moment an amount of practical heathenism, perhaps unexampled in any other nation of Christendom; and that masses of our population are sunk in the grossest ignorance and sensualism, and live and die without God, and without hope. Six millions in England are calculated never to enter a place of worship or make any profession of religion (21). The National Church has little hold on the operative classes. Of the middle order of the community in our large cities many are disaffected to the Establishment. And as to the bulk of the humbler classes of our people, it would be easy to furnish instances from amongst them of as profound an ignornace of God, and of a moral degradation as gross and intensified, as ever existed in Pagan Rome, or could be found to-day in Central Africa (22).

Neither can it be denied that, as a necessary consequence, monstrous forms of misbelief and fanaticism are rife amongst us; that infidel and anarchical principles prevail extensively; that licentious publications freely circulate amongst our people; that disaffection to our institutions spreads and deepens; that political privileges are coveted and clamoured for by many with a view to revolution. And all who have investigated our social condition know that, however it may strike superficial observers, there smoulders beneath the surface a mass of lawlessness and irreligion which may explode at any moment and rend society in pieces (23).

Even in what is patent, as disclosed in our parliamentary discussions, and in the current literature of the day,—and for which we need not search, with our parochial clergy, and City missionaries, and Bible women, in the purlieus and slums of the metropolis, or in our prisons and convict establishments,—but in what meets every eye, and is of almost daily occurrence, — we have abundant cause for humiliation, as a people to whom God has given much, and from whom He requires the more.

Again, it must be admitted, that in many of the qualities which used to reflect honour upon Englishmen, and were esteemed national characteristics, there has been a lamentable and flagrant deterioration. The high conscientiousness, the sterling integrity, the candour in commercial transactions,—"how is the gold become dim! how is the most fine gold changed!"[a] The word of the British tradesman was once like the Bible; his bond was as good as gold; a false

---

[a] Lamentations of Jeremiah iv. 1.

weight and an unjust balance were his abomination. The adulterations, the artifices, the impostures, by which mercantile wealth is now sometimes attained, the forgeries and betrayals of trust which impair credit and destroy confidence, were never heard of, —or if they did occur, excited wonder and consternation. And the meretricious glitter and inflated but unreal pretensions so prevalent in our day, are a miserable substitute for the moderate but just gains, and the unsullied conscience, and the simple habits, and the rugged independence of a by-gone generation (24).

That to counterbalance all this there is much of religious life and practical godliness amongst us, has been freely admitted. There is also in the present day a far greater regard to conventional propriety than in a former age; and the intemperance, profaneness, and indelicacy which then prevailed, are out of date. Religion, also, is more countenanced by the upper classes; while a high standard of principle and practice no longer causes surprise and ridicule, or bars a man's entrance into the highest circles of society, or imperils his professional prospects (25).

And did the Christianity of our land present a compact front—were we at peace amongst ourselves, —we might appeal to our mutual love and united action as a proof that God is with us.

But, unhappily, in religion we are in this country, as a house divided against itself. Our rival sects are innumerable. We count our denominations by hundreds. And of all the hindrances which the Church encounters in its mission, our religious divisions are the sorest. They disorganise its forces; they impede and neutralise its efforts. They cause the inquirer to stumble, and the enemy to blaspheme. And though it has been alleged by some that Separation is no evil, that it even fosters a wholesome emulation — and a spurious charity goes so far as to demand that we should not pray against it, that the word " schism" should be expunged from our Liturgy (26),—are not "variances," and " emulations," enumerated in the Bible among the works of the flesh? And the unity which so many in our day deem both unattainable and undesirable, is it not the subject of the apostle's exhortation, and even of the prayers of the Son of God?

Still it is asserted, that Dissent has become rooted in our land. It is designated by a recent writer as a national institution (27). We are even told that numerically it rivals the Establishment; while recent events have disclosed both its political power, and its sectarian animosity. Its demand is not now for toleration, but for ascendance. It has its political league, and its parliamentary tactics, and its confederation of sects, and its agency active, unscrupulous, and ubiquitous. Its language may be somewhat ambiguous, but its objects are no longer disguised. In its present vocabulary, right of private judgment means resistance to authority; freedom of conscience, dictation to the consciences of others; liberation of religion, the subversion of the National Church and the confiscation of ecclesiastical property.

The question at issue is avowed to be one of supremacy, and the sacred mission of dissenting ministers to be to shatter the National Church, and to give the dust of it to the four winds of heaven. The English Church is declared to be a great national evil, an obstacle to the progress of truth and godliness in the land; to destroy more souls than it saves; and its end, we are told, is most devoutly to be wished by every lover of God and man (28). And unless we are content to see our property alienated, our educational endowments secularised, and our consecrated buildings and enclosures shared with teachers whose doctrines differ from our own, we must be prepared for the struggle that is surely impending.

It is in no spirit of unkindness that these words are spoken, or with the slightest desire to disparage the efforts of others. There are names of dissenting teachers and philanthropists that will be had in honour while the world lasts. And the services rendered by Nonconformists to the cause of science, liberty, and practical godliness cannot be disputed for a moment. Neither is it at present a question how far dissent may have been in some instances justified, or even unavoidable. It is no more my intention to impugn the excellence of individual Separatists than to defend short-comings and inconsistencies in Churchmen.

The question is simply as to the character and tendency of dissent as a system, or rather as to the obstructions which the Church of the nation in our day encounters in its mission. And this preparatory to the consideration of plans for their removal or abatement.

Of these obstructions Dissent is amongst the foremost. It impedes the conscientious and earnest-minded pastor. It undermines his influence and counteracts his ministrations every day. It furnishes a rallying point for the disaffected and the self-willed in all our parishes. It is a snare to both pastor and people,—tempting the one to conceal or compromise his Church's creed, to lower its standard and ignore its rule,—exposing him to charges of unfaithfulness if conciliatory, and of bigotry if rigid;—while it tends to beget in parishioners an indifference to truth. And though it must be met, like all other hindrances, in the spirit of the Gospel, it is not less to be deplored. It has wrought, and is working vast and extensive evil, and imperilling to a fearful extent the faith, the loyalty, and the moral and religious life of our people. Multitudes amongst us feel and deplore this, though they may be unwilling openly to avow it.

Another, though it may be hoped a decreasing hindrance in the way of the Church, is the want of unity amongst its members. Now, amongst brethren disunion is an evil, just in proportion as unity is a blessing. And though to a certain extent there must be discrepancies of opinion, when men's minds are so differently constituted, — and the spirit and platform of our Church recognise and admit these,— yet amongst men bound by the same confessions and the same formularies, and amenable to the same rule, and serving at the same altars, variance is both unreasonable and scandalous. It was to preclude this that our standard was framed — to exclude controversy, to prevent strife, to insure compliance with the apostolic precept, that "all should speak the same thing," and "walk by the same rule," and "be perfectly joined together in the same mind and the same judgment."[a] And therefore nothing can justify the jealousies, the party names, the separate interests, which embroil and divide churchmen. Those particoloured banners under which silly men and women range themselves,— those criminations which they bandy to and fro—their jubilations at the preference and preponderance of their own clique,—the readiness with which they receive and propagate reports injurious to those who differ from them,—impede religion, and degrade the Church. They foster hatred, variance, emulations, wrath, strife, envyings, and such like, which exclude from the kingdom of Heaven[b]; and the temporary ascendance and the party triumphs thus obtained are at the price of what true hearts

[a] Philippians iii. 16; 1 Corinthians i. 10.
[b] Galatians v. 10.

chiefly prize—truth, unity, and concord. Need I add that while the worst tempers of the world are cherished in the bosom of the Church, and "the spirit that is in us lusteth unto envy,"[a]— and the aim is not so much to hush, and to hide divisions, as to inflame, and to intensify, and to expose them,— the blessing of God cannot rest upon us, or the cause of religion prosper in our land?

But I come now to hindrances of a different kind, which impair and imperil our Church and preclude its action and extension. And since for these we are all more or less responsible,—inasmuch as they clearly admit of correction,—with these in an age of enterprise and action we are specially called to grapple. It is, of course, easy to account for miscarriages; as it is to suggest correctives that do not depend upon ourselves. And thus the doctrines of the Church, and the polity of the Church, and its connection with the State are blamed; and men seek in the reform of our Liturgy, and the abolition of religious restrictions, and the disruption of our existing institutions, for remedies that are really to be found in the healthy action and full development of our system as it is.

In respect, then, of the Spiritual Destitution which prevails so extensively amongst us, which we all admit to be a calamity and a scandal, and which has reached in our day to such an appalling extent, as to concentrate public attention, and to constrain the

[a] James iv. 5.

notice of the legislature, and to stir to their depths all earnest and benevolent minds — the question is not so much, Is the Church responsible for this? but rather, Is this the consequence of its system, chargeable on its system? Is it not notoriously and inevitably the result of setting that system at nought?

The theory of our parochial scheme is a church and a clergyman for every thousand of our people. In town parishes two or three thousands may be fairly intrusted to a single pastor. But the testimony of our most experienced and painstaking clergy is, that no man, whatever be his physical energy and pastoral gifts, can effectively minister to a greater number. A population of three thousand is considered to justify a grant from our Clergy aid Societies.

When, therefore, in not one, but in multiplied instances,—and this too in scenes of commercial enterprise, where the population increases annually by thousands,—we find not two or three, nor even ten or twenty, but even thirty and forty thousand assigned to a single incumbent,—in one instance seventy-eight thousand so apportioned, with church accommodation for about fourteen hundred, and of this only two hundred sittings free;—to suppose that under such circumstances the Church can do its work,—or to charge the failure on its system,— is irrational.

It is an accredited fact that in our Metropolis we have a parish with a population of forty thousand, with only one church in a corner of the district, and on one side of it ten thousand souls without church, chapel, or school of the Church of England, and not a single room capable of holding twenty persons: — that in the very centre of the civilisation, the enterprise, the wealth and power, as well as of the government of this great empire, there is less spiritual provision than in any other county in England: — that allowing to each clergyman the care of two thousand persons, there is required for that part of the metropolis which is within the Diocese of London, an increase of at least five hundred and twenty-seven clergymen (29).

Nor if we extend our inquiry to the Provinces, is the aspect of things much improved.

Thus, in Liverpool, we find a parish containing sixteen thousand persons, with only one clergyman in charge, with no church accommodation whatever for the poor, and an average attendance at public worship of only two hundred persons of any kind. Another parish of twenty-five thousand souls, with but one church, not a farthing of endowment, and the seats for the poor so situated that their occupiers can neither see nor hear. A third with a population of twenty thousand souls, with accommodation in church for only one hundred and thirty-three of the poor. We are told, that in the midst of a dense population, there are in that city, churches originally built exclusively for the rich, of which the proprietors have migrated to other parts, and carried away the keys of their pews with them.

In another of the hives of teeming life and thriving commercial speculation,—where hecatombs of souls are yearly sacrificed on the altar of Mammon,—we have one parish, containing thirty-four thousand persons, with only two clergymen, and church accommodation for from two hundred to four hundred of the poor; and another, containing nearly thirteen thousand souls, with no free seats at all.

While at Bradford in Yorkshire, where the spiritual destitution of our land seems to have reached its culminating point, we had, till very recently, a population connected with the parish church, amounting to seventy-eight thousand, with only fourteen hundred sittings for all classes, and of these, at the very outside, only two hundred free, and of course in the worst parts of the church (30).

But even such statements as these furnish a very inadequate picture of the spiritual destitution of this country. Nor does a mere recital of numbers ever produce any commensurate effect upon the mind. You can only realise the state of things by a contrast, such as was once put before myself by a preacher in the town of Birmingham. " The city of Worcester," he said, " has a population of about thirty-two thousand, with a supply of twelve churches besides the cathedral, and at least twenty parochial clergy. I have an equal population to this, increasing annually at a ratio of two thousand, committed to myself and two curates."

Now picture to yourselves this city of Oxford.—with

its present spiritual provision of seventeen parishes and a suitable staff of clergy — reduced to one church and one clergyman; and even then you will have a very faint idea of what prevails elsewhere in many a district of the same extent; for there are spiritual resources here, extra-parochial, of which those who ply the looms and forges which minister to our national wealth and comfort, when without the ordinary means of grace, are devoid.

But there is another feature of the case to be further considered in the course of these Lectures, but which I cannot pass even now without remark. I mean the scanty and miserable accommodation for the poorer classes in many of our churches. To me this has ever seemed one of the greatest blots on our national Christianity. It openly contravenes the law of God; it is in express violation of the law of our land; and it militates against our claim to be a National Church.

Yet it is in evidence, and indeed notorious, that in many of our parish churches no provision is made for the poor: that in others they are thrust into corners, out of sight and hearing, where they feel outraged and degraded, — and are most forcibly reminded of their poverty, just where the distinctions of this earth should cease, and are forbidden by the Word of God. That even in churches built by public grants for the accommodation of the poor, and in which a large proportion of the seats is reserved by express stipulation for them, they are deprived of their right. Seats marked "free" are in some instances as much dealt with as private property, as the pews with doors paying rent. It is in evidence on the testimony of one who held the office of archdeacon, that in a church in which, by act of parliament, one third of the sittings was reserved for the poor, the warden, on being asked to point them out, said at last, "I have *one* free sitting to *one* pew." It was a little bracket in the passage. "But," said he, "the poor never come here ; it serves me to put my hat upon."

In the rectory district of Marylebone in London containing thirty-three thousand persons, there are free sittings for about five hundred in a church built for the accommodation of two thousand five hundred persons; the rest are let for pew-rents: the other few free sittings in this parish are in proprietary chapels, and may be withdrawn at any moment.

Again, in St. George's, Hanover Square, with a population in the season of twenty-five thousand, there are open free seats for three hundred persons, in the passages or against the walls. The other sittings are let for rents amounting to nearly one thousand pounds a year.

In another church in London it was elicited by the Bishop of Exeter, that the free sittings, which are in the roof, out of sight of the minister in both the pulpit and the reading-desk, must be reached by an ascent of nearly one hundred steps. "Are the lame and halt," inquired the Bishop, "expected to climb those three hundred steps to get to their free sittings?" "I have never seen more than one person in those places," replied the rector, "though there may have been others out of sight."

In the face of these facts is it a matter of surprise, if our parish churches are deserted by the humbler classes; if millions frequent no place of worship, least of all those of the Establishment—if in consequence vice, infidelity, and crime abound; and where the name of God is known at all, it is only to be blasphemed?

A circumstance which aggravates the difficulties of the Church is this,—that for the most part the densest populations are the poorest, and the habitations of the wealthy are severed from those of the poor. Operatives are congregated by the necessities of trade in masses; while the wealthy migrate to suburban villas, or to more fashionable quarters; and the seats which were appropriated to them, as I observed before, are shut against the poor. Churches, built for the accommodation of the rich, we find hemmed in by those who are classified by one witness, as "the respectable poor, the struggling poor, the destitute poor, the immoral poor, and the vicious and dangerous poor." The rich employer spends his wealth elsewhere. And thus, where there is most destitution, there is least relief. Every want is best supplied where aid is least required; and every want is worst supplied where necessities are most abundant and most urgent (31).

Another hindrance to the mission of the Church—and that of terrible magnitude—is the poverty of many of our most laborious incumbencies. It may even be stated, as the rule, that the clergy are worst remunerated where their duties are most onerous. The cry, till very recently, has been for *buildings*, when the primary consideration should have been *endowment*. And public and private charity has been lavished upon churches, while the clergymen who serve them have been left to starve.

The evil in every way of such a system is tremendous. You place a man, with onerous and anxious duties, and with crippled means, in the midst of a dense, and impoverished, and disaffected population. You overtask his physical and mental energies. You throw him into hourly contact with distress, which he can by no possibility relieve. You deprive him of the influence which the exercise of a wise benevolence would procure him. You demand from him superhuman exertions, when his spirit is broken and his rest disturbed by his own domestic anxieties. You drive one incumbent to eke out his livelihood by tuition, and another by secular employment. You extort such confessions as these: "My clerical income is so wretched that I am not able to devote my whole time, as I ought to do, to my Church and district:" "My endowment is only 80*l.*, and being a family man, I am obliged to educate my children myself."

As one consequence, we have a lower type of man

and feebler ministrations, where ability and energy are most required. Ordinarily our best and ablest men are not found in the most important and prominent pastoral positions. Our town parishes are often inadequately served. And just where commanding qualities are most called for—in the centres of intelligence and civilisation—our Church is often the worst represented; while generally there are complaints,—and these loud and increasing,—that the homilies of the clergy fall below both the requirements and the literature of our age, and that the press, and not the pulpit, is the instructor of our people.

Noble exceptions there doubtless are;—and men of lofty intellect, and a zeal truly apostolic, may be found labouring on a pittance in the most important, as well as in the poorest and most degraded districts. Yet it is the complaint of one, perhaps the most qualified of any man in England to speak on such a subject,—I mean the present Dean of Chichester,—that the best educated of our clergy are not commonly found in the great manufacturing towns, where their influence is most required: " where we have a commercial aristocracy, full of enterprise and intellect, whose minds, from constant exercise, are vigorous and acute; men of literature and science,—who, if they are to find in the clergy their associates and friends,—must find in them companions, not only their superiors in theological science, but at least their equals in every department of human learning " (32).

And then men talk of the inefficiency of the clergy, of their lack of eloquence and learning, of the failure of the parochial system, of the degeneracy of the Church,— even of Christianity itself as effete, and of the Gospel as having lost its power,— when in fact the action of the Church is suspended, and the agencies of religion are either crippled or withheld. And this in the face of what is now happily established, — that wherever, with a reliance upon God, the suitable agencies are employed, the Church recovers its influence, and the cause of vital Christianity revives.

Meanwhile, in a day in which, perhaps, more than in any other, ability is required in the Christian ministry, there is a danger of our being deprived of this. The ablest of our educated classes who used to feed the ministry of our Church, confessedly, are being drafted into secular professions. My own experience, as an examining chaplain, is, that though the average attainments of candidates for holy orders are improving, there are far fewer instances amongst them, than there used to be, of the highest class of mind. This, of course, may be partially accounted for, by the subsiding of impulses to which the revival of principles, now no longer novel, some years ago gave birth,—by the unsettlement of youthful minds on points of Christian doctrine,—by the not unnatural repugnance of young men of high intellectual calibre and social refinement, to serve under those who are deficient in both these particulars, or to encounter the not unfrequent discourtesies and ignorant intolerance of a vestry, or, it even may be, the violence of a mob (33). But I attribute it mainly to the poverty of so many of our cures, contrasted with the inducements held out by the competitive system in other services; and to the tendency of modern legislation to diminish and impoverish the dignities which used to be the legitimate objects of clerical ambition,—and which, if not always worthily bestowed, acted in the main as a stimulus to learning, and were often the reward of eminent service.

Whatever be the cause, the fact is undeniable; and it justifies the prayer of an eloquent divine, "that the curse may never light upon England, which has been too often evidenced elsewhere, of seeing her clergy sink lower and lower in the scale of education and social position. Against such degradation we ought ever to protest; not, God forbid! from a spirit of pride or self-assertion, but because we know that if that degradation should ever be consummated, the Church will have lost its hold upon the respect and upon the affection of her people" (34).

Another obstacle to the efficient action and extension of our Church,—on which I shall not enter at present,—is the inadequacy of our present Episcopate to the demands of our dioceses; so that an office—which is the very key-stone of our system—is in great measure neutralised,—and with the bulk of our people is neither felt nor appreciated, as it might be.

To do justice to this subject on the present occasion is, however, impossible. And I therefore purpose to consider it in my next Lecture, in which I shall suggest some remedies for the spiritual destitution to which I have now drawn your attention.

Let me only in conclusion remind you, that as the apathy, and lethargy, and supercilious indifference of so-called churchmen are at the root of this destitution —for if the Church were but for one day what she ought to be, it would be remedied before nightfall— so are they the main obstruction to improvement. It will be for each of you to ask himself to-day—How far am I personally implicated in this charge? For it may be, though you are unconscious of it, that the blood of your brother's soul is lying at your door.

LECTURE IV.

LUKE X. 2.

"Therefore said he unto them, The harvest truly is great, but the labourers are few: pray ye therefore the Lord of the harvest, that he would send forth labourers into his harvest."

Ἔλεγεν οὖν πρὸς αὐτούς· ὁ μὲν θερισμὸς πολύς, οἱ δὲ ἐργάται ὀλίγοι· δεήθητε οὖν τοῦ κυρίου τοῦ θερισμοῦ, ὅπως ἐκβάλῃ ἐργάτας εἰς τὸν θερισμὸν αὐτοῦ.

MUCH of the work which devolves upon the Church of England at the present day is of a missionary character. Recent inquiries,—for which we are mainly indebted to a learned and venerable Prelate,—have disclosed, that there are multitudes in the metropolis, and other populous districts of this land, especially in the mining and manufacturing districts, destitute of spiritual instruction and the means of divine worship, and without even the semblance of religion (35).

To talk of such persons, though within the limits of a territorial Christianity, as either churchmen or Christians, would be an abuse of terms. Some of them may have been baptized in their infancy, and are thus, nominally, within the pale of the Church. Many of them have never even assumed the badge of Christianity; for a recent act of the legislature removed the only motive with numbers to seek for their children the initiatory ordinance of the Church. And, practically, both classes are as much without the lessons and influence of religion, as if Christ had never visited the earth. They may live within the sound of the church bells; or they may be even without this audible witness for God. But in either case they never enter a place of worship; the message of the Gospel never falls on their ears; nor have they ever looked into the pages of the Bible. No clergyman is ever seen amongst them. The Sunday brings to them no reminder of a better world, it may be, not even a remission of their week day toil, or only opportunity for sloth and vicious indulgence. With multitudes in this country, it has been thus ever since they were born : it is their normal religious condition : and they pass through the world and out of it, like the beasts that perish.

With others the case in a nominally Christian land is still more pitiable. They have lapsed into practical heathenism through the absence of the moral checks, and the religious lessons, and the pastoral supervision, which they once enjoyed. When the means of grace were within their reach, and religious instruction was afforded,—when the House of God was nigh at hand, and the Pastor knocked at their door,—they may have both employed and valued their religious opportunities. They recall former days with the feeling so exquisitely described by our Lord in the parable of the Prodigal Son. And just as the pent-in alley, and the dingy tenement, and the murky atmosphere, and the noise and the stench of the city are contrasted with the pure air, and the open sky, and the green sward, and the loving and healthy companionship of their village home,—so in their better moments their mis-spent Sundays, and their neglected Bibles, and their estrangement from God and goodness, evoke a sigh for the privileges from which they are debarred, and the duties which they have abandoned.

It is in evidence in the Report on Spiritual Destitution, to which I alluded in my last Lecture, that many who now never enter a church, and have thrown off even the forms of religion, were church-goers and even communicants, when first lured from their provincial homes by the hope of larger gains which a city affords. They came from pious households; they brought with them commendatory letters from their former pastors; for a time they persevered in the religious practices to which they had been used. But they had no place in church, no visit from an appointed pastor, no one to look after them, or drop a word in season, no good example before their eyes. No man cared for their souls. It is the oft-told tale; but the saddest tale of all. A few efforts more or less; a struggle more or less protracted; and then such persons subside into the common way; they go with the multitude; they swim with the stream; they are engulfed in the tide which in our great cities is yearly sweeping souls to destruction.

What the moral and religious condition of a population thus neglected must be, it is easy to conceive. Without schools, without churches, without pastoral visitation, without the ordinances of religion, without the motives or the checks which with ourselves are too often found insufficient to counteract the evil around us and within us,—what can we expect from these untutored and uncared-for multitudes? What but a state,—as we are told,— not merely of vice and irreligion, but of infidelity; not merely a denial of the Christian revelation, but the grossest and darkest heathenism,— an absence of any idea of the existence of a God. Thus it is stated by the chaplain of one of our gaols, that he found thirty-five per cent. of the male, and thirty-nine per cent. of the female prisoners to whom he had to minister, utterly ignorant of our Saviour's name. While it is the testimony of another credible witness, that the whole code of morality, and the only knowledge of right and wrong amongst such persons, is comprised in what the policeman allows or forbids. And this state of things intensifying and propagating itself every day, deepening and spreading in the lower orders of society—the bad habits which are contracted in one part being through the migratory nature of our people carried to another, or again the good habits acquired in one part lost in another; the good ever on the decline, the bad ever on the increase (36).

My brethren, we bewail the ungodliness and inveigh against the vices of our people; we are shocked by the depravity and the crime, the drunkenness and the brutality, which courts of justice bring to light. What should we be, ourselves—the very best amongst us—were we as untaught, as undisciplined, as uncared for, as exposed to the privations and the snares, which the pressure of want and the contagion of example, and the instincts of our lower nature, and the absence of counteracting influences involve? With *us* the violation of the Lord's day is a scandal: our poorer brethren are solicited to it by bribes, and coerced by authority. "They were tempted," depones a witness, speaking of operatives in Government works, "to violate their consciences for money: they have burst into tears in my presence, and said they feared being dismissed if they did not accept the reward of double pay for working on the Sunday" (37).

I confess, when I consider the spiritual disadvantages of such persons, their feeble lights, their slender inducements to a religious profession or a godly life, the positive hindrances in their way, added to their many and fierce temptations, my wonder is that they are no worse. Without religious instruction, or pious example,—without even the restraints which with us society imposes,—with minds beclouded and thoughts engrossed by the necessities of their being, what can we expect from them?

But the question is, how is this destitution to be met? Our population has outgrown the existing machinery of the Church, and is annually on the increase. All the efforts of recent days,—great and truly noble as they have been,—fall short of our requirements. For we have to overtake the over-growth of former years; and to provide for that which the mining, manufacturing, and commercial enterprise of our country calls yearly into being. Granting that much has been effected by recent acts of legislation, by greater elasticity in the Church's ministrations, by the removal of restrictions which have cramped and paralysed religious efforts : granting that a greater number of churches have been erected within the last few years than during the whole previous century : still the evil is on the increase; and the need of the means of grace is every year more and more in excess of the supply.

Take, as an example, the diocese of London, in which during the last four years twenty-nine new churches have been consecrated,— so as to meet the wants of at most ninety thousand persons,—yet the probable increase of the population in that diocese is stated as a hundred and forty thousand (38).

All this is undeniable; and is forced on our attention by debates in Parliament, by visitation charges, by representations from both the pulpit and the press. It is also proved by statistics. The only question is, how are we to arrest an evil, which not only militates against our character as a religious people, and imperils our social security, but also involves the destruction from day to day of multitudes of souls?

What we have to do is to evangelise those who are at once sunk in irreligion, and soured by neglect; to reach them with offers to which they are indifferent, and win them to services to which they are disinclined. We have both to supply the means, and to create the demand.

We want therefore—

First, An increased spiritual agency—men more than buildings.

Secondly, Enlarged facilities for public worship—the synagogue more than the temple.

In the present Lecture I shall treat of the former of these requirements.

By all who have reflected on the subject, the Church's primary want is felt to be an increase of its pastoral staff. Men are wanted of earnest minds and simple habits, with a missionary spirit and missionary gifts, to go amongst the people and labour amongst them, as the first preachers of the Gospel did. We place our trust less than we once did, on the material machinery of religion. We admit the need of a living agency to search out and draw the hitherto reckless and profane; men more than buildings; the missionary first, then the missionary station; the permanent erection, when attention has been excited and interest created, and there is at least the nucleus of a future congregation.

But the crying want is the living agent. We

want evangelists and pastors for the redundant and yearly increasing swarms of our people. We want that house-visiting which begets church-frequenting. We want to bring the English Church in its daily ministrations, into a close, familiar, and pervading contact with all classes of our countrymen. We want the interchange of mind, the intercommunion of spirit, the reciprocation of mutual kindness between the spiritual agent and the people, which constitute the charm of the pastoral relation, and the secret of ministerial success. And without this to claim to be the Church of the country is a pretension, the hollowness of which circumstances are forcing upon us more and more every day.

To plant a large church in the midst of a dense and semi-pagan population, and to locate there one or two clergymen, and to assign them a district of six thousand, ten thousand, twenty thousand, — it may be even forty thousand souls,— and to suppose that in this way we can effect the work of the Church is mere fatuity (39). Under such circumstances, the public services of the sanctuary may be perfunctorily performed — the prayers may be read, and sermons preached — the young may be christened, and couples married, and the dead buried, and the sick and aged cursorily visited; — but even with the most heartfelt devotion in the pastor, how many an aching conscience must there be unprobed — how many a mind diseased never ministered to — how many a scene of squalid misery, and of domestic anguish and bereavement and distress, which the foot of the minister of peace never penetrates, and where his voice is never heard! How many a sufferer on the bed of sickness—how many a dark and troubled spirit, perhaps pining for counsel,—or if not so, only the more to be pitied— must take its flight into eternity, without the teachings, or the consolations, or the ministries of mercy, which the Church was founded, and which it is its bounden duty to afford!

And unless we at least offer these,— to designate ourselves the Church of the nation, and the spiritual mother of its people,—and to resent papal aggression, —and to fret at sectarian intrusion,—and to wonder at the up-growth and spread of Mormonism, and infidelity, and anarchical opinions, or any monstrous outbreak of folly, or of crime, which may be generated by the ignorance or credulity of man,—is a pretension which cannot deceive our own selves, or impose for a moment on an observant, understanding, and reflecting people.

Now the remedy which naturally suggests itself is the subdivision of districts which have become unmanageable. Where a population multiplies annually by thousands, — and many such the manufacturing, mining, and commercial enterprise of our country has created,— such a measure seems essential. We have had our population doubled within the present century: it is increasing at the rate of two hundred thousands a year. We have villages suddenly transformed into populous towns; and districts containing great masses of people, where a few years ago there may have been only green fields, or a few scattered habitations.

The natural suggestion in such cases is, that new parishes should be created. And incumbents for the most part have evinced a laudable willingness to facilitate such arrangement, even when involving sacrifices to themselves. But experience shows the need of caution in such readjustment. To multiply districts, of which the inhabitants are described as "very poor, rapidly increasing, and declining in respectability;" and where there is no adequate provision for a clergyman, is a measure of very questionable expediency. And the matter of Endowment has become in our day one of pressing and primary importance.

I touched upon this point in my last Lecture. It is impossible to contemplate the very slender and disproportionate income of many of our most populous and important cures without emotion. The disclosures on this subject, which recent parliamentary inquiries have led to, are most painful and affecting; and unless a remedy be supplied, and that speedily, the result must be most disastrous to the religious condition of this country. For in directing attention to this subject I have in view not so much the interests of the clergy, as the all-important work to which they have been called.

Of the ten thousand four hundred and thirty-nine

livings in this country, in 1839, there were nearly three hundred stated as under 50*l.*, and nearly two thousand under 100*l.* a year. And thus there are not a few clergymen in this country with cures, either among the poor who need their aid, or the purse-proud who resent poverty as a crime, whose professional income is less than that of the mechanic, or menial servant; and who, in consequence, are often without daily necessaries, and decent clothing. And this in an age distinguished for its wealth, and in which, in every other department, industry and talent command ample remuneration; and whose advance in civilisation demands that its religious instructors should be at once scholars and gentlemen.

I know the specious but fallacious argument with which this statement may be met. We are reminded of the large existing revenues of the Church, of the plethora of wealth under which it labours, of the disproportionate emoluments with which some clerical services are compensated,—and are told that if our resources were more equally distributed, there would be no excessive incomes, to furnish a contrast and create a scandal, but still a sufficiency for all who do the Church's work.

Now it has been shown repeatedly, and recently by the present Bishop of London in his place in Parliament, that were any such redistribution of clerical revenue resorted to,—besides its being at variance with the practice in all other professions, and the general rule by which the tenure of property is regulated,—the result would be both disappointing and pernicious. For it would reduce all our clergy to one dead level, depriving the body of its legitimate incentives, and affording an adequate income to none.

On the general question it seems enough for the ministers of religion to stand on the express warrant of Scripture—"that the labourer is worthy of his hire;"[a] that you should "not muzzle the ox which treadeth out the corn;"[b] "that they which minister about holy things should live of the things of the temple, and they which wait at the altar be partakers of the altar. For even so hath the Lord ordained, that they which preach the Gospel should live of the Gospel."[c]

But I would put it to men of intelligence and generous nature, whether if they expect to have clergy with the education of scholars, and the habits, much more the principles of gentlemen, they must not afford them the means to maintain a respectable position in society — whether if allowed to marry, the clergy should not have provision to bring up and to educate their children — whether if they are to be alert and diligent,—with clear heads, and hearts enlarged in the day-time,—they must not be allowed their night's rest unbroken by the gnawings of care, and the pressure of pecuniary anxiety—whether in a rich and luxurious age like this, when talent finds a ready market, and every

[a] Luke x. 7.　　[b] 1 Corinthians ix. 9.　　[c] Ibid. 13, 14.

profession has its recompense,—the clergy ought to be the dependent ministers of independent congregations.

I urge this more, because the poverty of the pastor and the opulence of his flock are not unfrequently painfully contrasted; and it is in rich and thriving communities that the disproportion between the services and the emoluments of the clergy is at times most observable. While persons of wealth may be found who, instead of emulating the pious munificence of former generations, would be even willing to exonerate themselves of personal charge at the expence of existing Endowments.

It ought, therefore, to be distinctly understood, that to meet the present spiritual destitution of the country in a manner at all commensurate with the exigencies of religion and the requirements of our parochial system, we need an increase of at least two thousand three hundred clergymen; and that to supply even a moderate provision for these, an annual sum of more than half a million is demanded.

A prospective relief is, indeed, now held out by the Ecclesiastical Commissioners. But this is both partial and slow in operation. And the grants proposed depend on equivalent benefactions being made to meet them (40).

On a like principle efforts are being organized at this time in several of our dioceses, in which Lichfield and Oxford are the foremost (41). And in days in which the responsibilities of wealth and the

Christian duty of almsgiving are becoming better understood, it may be hoped that the appeal of religion will not be made in vain.

I speak in the presence of some who, as owners or heirs, have a large stake in the property and wealth of this country. And it is my duty on this occasion to remind them of the very weighty and solemn obligations which worldly possessions of every kind entail. By none, who have the fear of God before their eyes, can these be viewed as otherwise than as a talent, for which they must account. To say, May I not do as I will with my own? is to arrogate the prerogative of God, and in the mouth of a creature is impiety. Man can never be other than a steward of the gifts of God.

Moreover there are instances in which responsibilities are twofold, and to a man's own are superadded those of his ancestors. Such is especially the case with those who have succeeded to lands or other revenues once dedicated to sacred purposes, and charged with religious services—who are, for instance, lay impropriators of tithes, or lay inheritors of church lands — the very designation of whose manors or mansions recalls the act of spoliation, by which these passed from the possession of the Church into secular hands.

It cannot be denied, that of all human possessions such inheritance is most to be regarded as a stewardship for which the owner is accountable to both God and man; and of which one day a strict account will be required. Nor should it be forgotten, among the consequences which the confiscation of ecclesiastical revenue in the sixteenth century—on whatever principles it may be justified—most assuredly entailed,—that it reduced the provision for religion in this country to little more than its amount at the time of the Conquest. It also crippled the resources of the Church to a far greater extent than can be measured by the actual amount of spoliation; for it undermined the security of endowments, and served to check the pious impulses of churchmen, by discouraging the dedication of property henceforth to religious and charitable purposes.

In this way it was the cause of much of the spiritual destitution under which we labour. It serves in a measure to explain how in spite of our accumulated wealth, and national prosperity, and the splendid acts of individual munificence which characterize our age (42), we of the present day have to grapple with arrears of ignorance, and irreligion, and depravity, which have been on the increase for the last three centuries,—and are increasing still.

The responsibilities, however, of which I speak, are of course very far from the only ones to be considered in reference to our existing spiritual necessities. Neither are territorial possessions, or wealth inherited from others, in any wise the only or the main trusts of this nature to be accounted for. An equal, if not weightier responsibility surely rests on those, who if in one sense the producers of our national wealth and material greatness, are proportionably the principal causes of our redundant population. Manufacture and commerce, equally with landed estates and funded wealth, have their grave responsibilities in this respect. And the man who creates a population for purposes of trade, is as much, as the landowner, under an obligation to provide for the spiritual interests of those whom he employs.

It behoves all to whom God has given much to lay these things to heart — if from no higher motives — for the security of their own possessions, and the maintenance of their social position. "For there is that scattereth and yet increaseth,— and there is that withholdeth more than is meet, and it tendeth unto poverty."[a] And not till it is universally felt that privileges imply duties, and that possessions are merely a trust, shall we cease to blush for the spiritual destitution and to tremble for the future of our Fatherland.

It is, of course, the office of the preacher to urge such considerations from the pulpit. But the Church, by means of her Offertory, statedly enforces them. She reminds her worshippers that they are only "stewards of the manifold grace of God,"— that "all things come of Him," and must be rendered to Him again. And while she admonishes them "not to trust in uncertain riches," nor to "withhold more than is meet,"— but to be "rich in good works," "ready to distribute," "willing to communicate,"—

[a] Proverbs xi. 24.

she affords a frequent opportunity for the liberality to which she invites. By her, charity is presented both with motives and occasion of exercise; pious impulses are not allowed to languish or to die for want of an object; and what might otherwise evaporate in mere emotion, is fostered by her care into a habit of benevolence. She thus places Almsgiving on its true foundation as a Scriptural duty, obligatory on every Christian, and essential to our admission into heaven. She urges it, not as a rare and isolated act, but as a constant service of self-denial, in which we are to provide for the wants of others, as methodically as for our own. For such is surely the Christian duty;— not the contribution bestowed a few times a year,— and which must be pleaded for in sermons and on platforms, and canvassed for as a matter of personal favour,—and which is often only a tribute to the popularity or the ability of the advocate ;— but the continuous flow of habitual Almsgiving, which recognizes God as the proprietor of all, and is an item of systematic expenditure (43).

There is, however, another way in which the cause of Church Extension might be materially promoted by the Clergy, and which, while dealing with this topic, I feel constrained to bring forward. It was urged by me thirty years ago when pleading the cause of a clergy charity in a northern diocese; and was powerfully advocated by an influential member of the Lower House at the last meeting of the Convocation of the Province of Canterbury. I mean, by

LECTURE IV.

a more equitable assessment of clerical income than that according to which it is now rated in the king's books.

It cannot be disputed that the present valuation, by which the payments of the clergy to Queen Anne's Bounty are regulated, bears no sort of proportion to actual value. The assessment was originally made in the reign of Henry the Eighth: it has never since been revised: it is not one fourth of the present nett value on average: in the case of some of our larger benefices it is considerably less. Under any circumstances such a valuation is clearly inequitable. But in the present exigencies of the Church,—while we have three hundred of our incumbencies under fifty pounds, and nearly two thousand under one hundred pounds a year,—and while the disproportion between the opulence of some of our benefices to which light duties are attached, and the poverty of many of our populous and laborious cures, is the subject of regret to the Church's friends and of unfriendly comments to its assailants,—it is doubly open to objection. And many feel that, for the credit of the clergy, as well as for the interests of the Church, what is denied by none to be a fictitious valuation ought to be readjusted, and the annual payment to Queen Anne's Bounty to bear a *bonâ fide* proportion to the actual income (44).

Such a measure, as it seems to me, might be pleaded for on many grounds, and would be productive of good in every way. For it would augment the means of benefiting our poorer livings — it would show the disinterestedness of the more wealthy members of the clerical body — it would enlist the sympathies, and stimulate the benefactions of laymen. And however it may have been viewed when suggested thirty years ago, I have no fear that it will now be either misconstrued or resented. On the contrary, I believe that never were the clergy of this country, as a body, more ready for acts of disinterestedness and self-sacrifice than they now are. Every benevolent undertaking, every list of charity, every effort for the spiritual or material welfare of our people proves this. It is admitted that the cause of national education is mainly beholden to the efforts and the contributions of our parochial clergy. It can be shown that their benefactions to purposes of charity are immeasurably greater in proportion, than those of the laity. And were any well-considered plan for the revision and adaptation of the fund of which I speak, to the actual value of our livings and the altered circumstances of our Church, to be recommended by competent authority, the acquiescence of the clergy in such readjustment can hardly be doubted.

Thus far I have been speaking of the exigencies of our Church in respect of the agency and endowment of its parochial Clergy. And yet in the judgment of many — and these amongst the most thoughtful and zealous members of our communion — the most pressing want of our Church, at this time, is an increase of its Episcopate. And this is sought for, not with a view to aggrandize the clerical body,—but to quicken, and invigorate, and increase the Church's agencies, by means of that which contains in itself the nucleus and elements of all other subsidiary efforts.

I believe I am expressing a widely prevalent and deeply rooted conviction amongst churchmen, when I say this. The Church of England is an Episcopal body. It attaches great value to episcopal functions. It receives its orders and confirmation, at the hands of Bishops. It looks to them to take the lead in all Church matters, and to be foremost in whatever affects the honour of God and the welfare of society. And it may be safely asserted that the more their ministrations are multiplied, the more highly are they valued. We have names in our hierarchy of former days which will vie with any in Christendom; and many of our existing prelates are men of apostolic type and exemplary devotion, and are greatly loved and honoured for their works' sake.

But the more that as a Church we value the episcopal office, the more we must desire to have it understood and appreciated, and brought into frequent and homely contact with all ranks and conditions of our people.

To many of these, it may be feared, the episcopal office is a mere abstraction. Nor can it well be otherwise. We have for the nineteenth century, machinery which was deemed wholly inadequate three hundred years ago; since which time the population of the country and the clerical body have been more than quadrupled. Three of our modern dioceses contain a greater number of persons than all of them did at the Reformation. Many of them taken singly are of greater area and population than all the seven dioceses that were committed to the charge of Timothy, and Titus, and Polycarp, and Ignatius, and other apostolic men, by St. Paul and St. John. One of them includes two million souls: in several the episcopal residence is situated at the extremity of a different county from that which contains the cathedral; one prelate has more than a thousand clergy to overlook. And yet the increase of our Episcopate, since the sixteenth century, has been but one (45).

Under such circumstances it is impossible for our existing bishops, whatever be their zeal or their abilities, to meet fully either the demands of the age or the requirements of their office. It cannot be viewed as disrespect, if we say that the thing is too heavy for them, they cannot perform it.

And thus it comes to pass, that there are clergy amongst us who have never spoken to a bishop,— and parishes that have never seen a bishop since Christianity was established,—and thousands of our people whose only conception of a bishop has been taken from the columns of a scurrilous newspaper: while numbers of our middle, and even higher, classes have no acquaintance whatever with the person or with the office of him who is their chief pastor and father in God.

LECTURE IV. 107

I venture on this subject to quote the sentiments of one of more authority than myself.

"I am of opinion," writes the present bishop of Lincoln, "that the erection of new sees, and the subdivision of dioceses, is a measure urgently needed. My own is a district, which it is impossible to superintend with due attention to the circumstances, wants, and condition of each parish and its pastor; and a bishop who should wish to preach in every church in his diocese, and should devote one Sunday to each parish, would require more than fifteen years to make the circuit. The result of this disproportionate size of a diocese to the powers of any one man is, that there cannot be confidential and intimate communication between the bishop and his clergy; that many of the most deserving clergy are unappreciated and unknown; that confirmations are less frequent than they ought to be; and that the bishop, instead of being looked on by the laity as their chief pastor, is known only as a state officer,— rarely seen by any, by many never,— who has to perform certain functions at distant intervals" (46).

Such is the testimony of one—not the least zealous and exemplary of those who now exercise the episcopal office amongst us. And the impression it leaves is surely this,—that were prelates who feel thus to be multiplied,—were they placed where the eyes and hearts of men could rest upon them,—the Church of this land would not be so divided, and so crippled as it now is; the cause of Church Extension would not languish as it does; nor would the evils which disgrace and imperil our common Christianity exist to the fearful extent they now do.

Nay more, the Episcopal office itself would not be so often misunderstood and undervalued. What lately took place in one of our great commercial cities,—when it was asked at a public meeting, " Did you ever see a bishop?" and the answer was a groan,— could not have occurred. Nor could it have been remarked by a great writer on our constitution, with any semblance of truth,—that " all the bishops of England might be swept away to-morrow, without the people ever knowing the change."

I need not dwell upon this subject, because an able and exhaustive writer has recently expressed—what I believe to be a growing and deepening conviction,— that to cope with the evils of the day and meet the existing exigencies of the Church, what we chiefly need is an increase of the episcopal element (47).

The pleas for such a measure may be succinctly stated.

To combat unbelief, to satisfy inquiry, to solve religious doubt, we want a personal application to individuals of the spiritual gifts for which chief pastors ought to be distinguished.

To make an adequate impression on the ungodliness and demoralization of our large towns, we want the agency appointed by Christ and His Apostles for the evangelization of the world.

To administer with the frequency and the unction

demanded, a rite which all pastoral experience attests to be more than any other fraught with spiritual blessings to both pastor and people — and which, under altered circumstances might, by the favour of God, change the entire religious aspect of this country — I mean Confirmation — we want an increase of our Episcopate.

To encourage, stimulate, and direct the clergy; to exercise a salutary and healing influence on the laity, by consulting their wishes, eliciting their sympathies, and exciting their zeal — and both for their own sake and that of the Church at large, securing their hearty cooperation in duties that devolve equally on all the members of Christ's body — we want frequent and familiar intercourse between them and their chief pastors. And to secure this, an augmentation of the Episcopal body is demanded.

Such increase was projected three centuries ago, by leading minds at the Reformation; and was asked for by the nonconformist divines, and promised by Charles II., at the Restoration (48). A measure for effecting it has also been recently recommended by a Royal Commission (49). While the concurrence with which this proposal is regarded by the members of the Church is established by the fact, that petitions in its favour have been signed by six thousand of the clergy, and by many of the most distinguished and influential of our laity (50).

Prelates of an humbler type, less dependent for their station upon outward rank than on the sacredness of their office,—and who would command respect by their learning,—and win affection by their apostolic labours, the innocency of their lives, and their exemplary devotion and self-denial,—is what is asked for. They need not be Peers of Parliament; they could not dispense the same hospitality and extensive charity exacted from our existing Episcopate. But what they lost in worldly pretensions they would gain in actual influence. They would familiarize the people with their office,—would render it with all their ranks a living reality and a household word, —would remove the reproach that the English Church is for the benefit, not of the working or of the middle class, but of the noble and the well-to-do. And the very fact that their office was less an object of worldly ambition and cupidity, would render it less likely to be bestowed from a regard to political and family connection.

Such an Episcopate, it might be confidently expected, would be a source of great and manifold blessings to the national Church; would breathe fresh life into its system, unlock sympathies now dormant in many a heart, develop agencies and resources now withheld. It would do for us at home, what it has already effected for our Church in the Colonies,—where it is matter of experience that wherever a bishopric has been founded, the numbers and efficiency of the clergy have been increased, schools and churches and benevolent institutions have been multiplied, and subsidiary agencies and helps of all kinds have been called into existence (51).

In proof of this we may refer to the diocese of Ripon, in which upwards of half a million sterling has been received for Church purposes within sixteen years from the foundation of that see. The erection of Manchester into a bishopric has led to similar results. And " it may be accepted as an axiom of ecclesiastical economics, that in order to increase the number and efficiency of the parochial clergy, and to relieve their temporal distress, the wisest plan is to provide an adequate number of bishops."

Thus it was urged by the late Dr. Arnold, that " In order to any efficient and comprehensive Church system, the first thing necessary is to divide the actual dioceses. Every large town," he observes, " should necessarily be the seat of a bishop: the addition of such an element into the society of a commercial or manufacturing place would be itself a great advantage." On which Canon Wordsworth remarks : "There is scarcely any large district or populous town in England which does not possess some noble ancient church, distinguished by architectural beauty, which might soon become a cathedral. If the inhabitants of a district or town are desirous of such a result,— and if the desire is right,—let them be enabled to attain it. It would infuse new life into ancient municipalities; it would impart new dignity to the country, and give fresh vigour to those sacred and generous principles and feelings, which unite Christians and Englishmen, in the spiritual and social bonds of piety, loyalty, and peace " (52).

Hitherto I have spoken exclusively of Clerical

agency. But that all should be workers together with God, and witnesses for Him, without distinction of calling or of sex,—and that Lay agency is both recognised in the Christian economy, and has been found of infinite value in the promulgation of the Gospel and the extension of the Church, will be readily admitted. Scripture abounds in testimonies in its favour. Apostles, as we know, both invoked and employed it. By them even women were hailed as "servants of the Church," as "helpers in Christ Jesus;" as "labouring," nay as "labouring much, in the Lord."[a] And the history of Christian effort in every age, and throughout the world, teems with notices of services rendered to the cause of God by those, who have never been separated to the ministry or bound by clerical vows.

To visit and relieve the sick; to circulate and read Holy Scripture; to search out cases requiring pastoral attention; to invite attendance at public ordinances; to act as pioneers and helpers of the clergy;—all these are offices clearly within the province of lay members of the Church; and in which they may render valuable assistance, without in any way overstepping their own sphere, or trenching on the clerical office.

But when the lay agency is a *paid* one, there may be a question as to the desirableness of employing it. Practically, good and wise men amongst us are

---

[a] Romans xvi. 1, 2, 6, 7, 9, 12.

found to entertain different opinions on the subject (53). And in any case, while its admissibleness, as auxiliary and supplemental to clerical functions, may be pleaded for,—to urge it as preferable to these is hardly consistent with the principles of churchmen, or with reverence for a divinely instituted order.

There is, however, an argument in favour of enlisting laymen as Evangelists in the cause of the English Church, even if their services are not gratuitously rendered, which in the consideration of this subject must not be overlooked.

It will have force with many—and these persons not disposed to sacrifice principle to expediency—by whom it has long been felt that our Church has suffered much, and in many ways, from rigidity of system; and that she needs both elasticity and expansion.

I mean, that lay agency affords occasion for the exercise of gifts which might otherwise not only be lost to the Church, but even employed against it. There is many a man who has had no regular training for the ministry, whom circumstances debar from taking Holy Orders, who has nevertheless an incontrollable impulse to labour in the Christian vineyard. Rome has at all times known how to use such men in subordination to her system (54). Dissent affords them ample scope and encouragement. The English Church, hitherto, has neglected, if not wholly discouraged such candidates for employment. And in her present circumstances, with the many, and loud, and pressing claims on her attention; with a clerical agency confessedly numerically insufficient to cope with the difficulties and compass the work before her,—to continue to do so, would, in the judgment of many, be to prefer ecclesiastical routine to the interests of souls.

Moreover, it seems to be sufficiently established, that certain objections which have been urged against the agency pleaded for have no existence in reality. Thus experience proves that the lay agent does not, as was by some anticipated, develop into the dissenting preacher (55). On the contrary it would appear that he is generally helpful and subordinate,—that he carries out instructions with zeal, and exactitude, and docility,—that he renders to the parochial clergyman much useful service, by informing him where his ministrations are most needed, and obtaining for him entrances before inaccessible. The testimony of many of our most experienced and zealous parochial clergy goes to prove all this.

No agency, however, whether clerical or lay, can be vicarious,—it exonerates no man from personal efforts in the cause of God. As baptized members of Christ's body the Church, we have all of us trusts, as we have privileges in common. "The foot cannot say, because I am not the hand, I am not of the body,—nor the ear, because I am not the eye, I am not of the body." It is only by the cordial and concurrent efforts of both clergy and laity, that the cause of the Church can be maintained, and the work of Christ can be done.

I shall resume this topic on a future occasion.

In my next Lecture I purpose to consider a subject of general and increasing interest at the present day —the requirements of the Christian ministry, and the special training of the Clergy.

LECTURE V.

2 Timothy ii. 15.

"*Study to show thyself approved unto God, a workman that needeth not to be ashamed, rightly dividing the word of truth.*"

Σπούδασον σεαυτὸν δόκιμον παραστῆσαι τῷ θεῷ, ἐργάτην ἀνεπαίσχυντον, ὀρθοτομοῦντα τὸν λόγον τῆς ἀληθείας.

It will be admitted, that of the Church's agencies the most important is that of its ordained ministers. The nature of their office, and the relations into which it brings them with all sorts and conditions of men, necessarily afford the clergy means and occasions of usefulness peculiar to themselves. It is, therefore, hardly possible to over-rate the influence for good or evil, which they must exercise on the religious life of a community: and "like priest, like people," has passed into a proverb.

It will likewise probably be admitted, that at no period were the character and qualifications of the clergy of more moment than the present,—when prescriptive and traditionary claims of every kind are comparatively lightly regarded — and the deference once accorded to station must be in great measure earned by personal qualities. Few will dispute the observation of an eminent statesman, that " it is by influence, and by influence only, that our clergy can be really powerful in these days" (56).

The Church is, therefore, bound to do its utmost to maintain a high clerical standard, and to adopt all possible precautions against the intrusion of unfit persons into Holy Orders. A sufficient period of probation, an inquiry into antecedents, a scrutiny, as far as may be, into the motives and qualifications of candidates for her ministry,— such are steps which no Church with common wisdom or decency could neglect:— and it may therefore be presumed they are not overlooked by our own.

Now it would be difficult to suggest a greater wariness, than is prescribed, if not always exercised, by the English Church in this particular.

She requires every candidate,

To make a written application to the bishop six months before the time of ordination, stating his age, college, academical degree, and the usual place of his residence; together with the names of any persons of respectability, to whom he is best known; and to whom the bishop may apply, if he thinks fit, for further information concerning him.

To be furnished with a title, and ordinarily a nomination to a particular cure.

To present letters testimonial from his college;

and, in case of his having quitted the University, a certificate from three beneficed clergymen, countersigned by their respective bishops, to the effect that they have known and observed his conduct and are satisfied that he has lived piously, soberly and honestly, and is sound in the faith;—and that they believe him in their consciences to be, as to his moral conduct, a person worthy to be admitted to sacred orders.

Further, a notice must be published in the church of the parish where the candidate usually resides, that he intends to offer himself for ordination; and if any one knows any just cause or impediment why he ought not so to be ordained, he is, then and there, to declare the same, or to signify it forthwith to the bishop.

Lastly, candidates are subjected to an examination, of some days' duration, in their scholastic and theological attainments, and religious principles and creed,—varying, of course, in strictness, according to the requirements of individual bishops and chaplains, but generally in our day sufficient—and from which they are not unfrequently turned back.

That, notwithstanding these precautions, unfit candidates do present themselves, and even at times gain admittance into the orders of our Church, cannot however be denied. Without personal piety, without religious earnestness, without any aptitude or liking for sacred functions—even with a conscious distaste for these—it may be with loose habits, and a damaged reputation,—persons sometimes intrude themselves into our ministry.

. Such is, indeed, a matter of painful and public notoriety. It has drawn the attention, and called forth the remonstrances of the laity; and lately elicited a protest which was brought before Convocation, and received due attention from the prelates of our Church (57). Antecedently to this, it suggested a caution recorded in one of the reports of the Lower House, as to the granting of testimonials (58). And it must be added, that the exposure of some recent cases of clerical delinquency has given point and emphasis to both remonstrance and suggestion. The subject is universally felt to be one, which affects more nearly than any other the honour of the sacred order, the interests of religion, and the cause of God throughout the land.

It will, I believe, be gratefully acknowledged by both bishops and examining chaplains, that in respect of testimonials, the Universities for the most part exercise due caution. And it is to be regretted that the example of these learned bodies is not sufficiently followed by others, to whom on these occasions an appeal is made. Certainly it is impossible to overrate the responsibility incurred by those, who on false or insufficient grounds, furnish testimonials for Holy Orders; or who, if cognizant of charges against candidates, do not report these in the proper quarters. But a system is not to blame, however it may suffer, because its prescribed rules and regulations are neglected. The necessary precautions have been taken by the Church. It has delegated trusts which, if duly discharged, would guard its ministry; has vested a solemn charge in its bishops and examining chaplains; has exacted pledges from its candidates, which cannot without impiety be disregarded; has lodged a power of protest in lay hands. Even in the Ordination Service which separates her future pastors to their mission, before the imposition of hands the Church makes a solemn pause, and addresses a forcible appeal to her congregation (59).

I would ask, what more could be exacted in the way of precaution? And though it is impossible for any of us to read the heart, and none can detect unworthy motives or moral unfitness in those who wear a mask,—yet if, in every case, the trusts reposed by the Church were duly discharged—if parents, and tutors, and college authorities, and the parish clergy, and the Christian laity were, severally, to fulfil, as in the sight of God, what is required of them—who can doubt that the Church would be preserved from many an incapable and many an unworthy pastor?

Else, why appeals made too late,—and that by persons who, it may be, have neglected their own duty in the matter; and then, after ordination, write to bishops and examining chaplains, and whisper charges,—about which, when appealed to by the Church, they were mute (60)!

A point, in which our Church is more vulnerable, is that of Clergy Discipline.

Every day more clearly establishes the fact, that we need, not only protection against unworthy candidates, but also more stringent and ready remedy for misconduct in ordained persons.

Instances, indeed, of immorality, or systematic neglect of duty, or gross incapacity on the part of the clergy, are now, we may hope, rarely to be heard of. The sons of Nimrod and of Jehu, we may trust, have also run their course. But where clerical delinquencies do occur, they inflict the deadliest wound upon religion. They bring contempt on the sacred office. They damage the Church in a parish for a generation. They alienate an entire neighbourhood. They make sad the hearts of the righteous, and strengthen the hands of the wicked.[a]

What must it be to reside where the parochial clergyman is not a pattern, but a warning to his flock; to attend the services and hear the sermons of a man, whose own conduct is an outrage on public decency; even to have religion lowered in the eyes of one's children and dependants, by the performances of an ignorant, uncouth, or careless clergyman!

To talk of the duty of parishioners, when the pastoral office is thus disgraced; or to resent their forsaking the parish church, or even seceding from our communion, is to very little purpose in these days. And for the sake of the Church, and the cause of religion, a speedy and effectual remedy for such scandals is devoutly to be wished for.

[a] Ezekiel xiii. 22.

That there ought to be prompt and easy means of dealing with misconduct in a clergyman cannot be disputed. Existing methods are found both cumbrous and expensive, and to afford facilities for defeating justice, and perpetuating scandal. So that cases of gross immorality have been left unpunished, and criminous clergy been allowed to retain their cures for years, to the almost irreparable injury of religion, by reason of the inadequate provisions of the law and the difficulty and cost of prosecuting offenders to conviction.

Under such circumstances, it is unfair to blame authorities. The doctrine of the Church is indeed plain and peremptory. It declares that "it appertaineth to the discipline of the Church that enquiry be made of evil ministers, and that they be accused by those that have knowledge of their offences; and finally being found guilty, by just judgment be deposed." [a]

But is it to be expected that parishioners will impeach, or churchwardens present, or bishops call offenders to account,—when the result may only be a ruinous expense to themselves, and the evasion of the culprit, through the deficiencies of the law (61)?

But the subject which more especially requires our consideration in this place is not the discipline, but the Education and Training of our clergy.

It is impossible to exaggerate the importance of the

[a] Article XXVI.

duties which await candidates for our ministry. To them will be committed our schools, and our pulpits, and the pastoral care of our people. They are to be the expounders of doctrine, and the guides of conscience in all on which it most concerns men to be instructed — on the will and commands of God — on matters of faith, and conduct — on the conditions of pardon, and peace, and eternal life — themes worthy the tongues of angels. They are to be ambassadors of God, ministers of Christ, shepherds of the flock, stewards of the mysteries of God.

That such a commission should have been entrusted, in any day, to incompetent hands, might have been thought impossible. We might have assumed, that the most promising of our families, the ablest of our universities, would have been reserved for it. And if in a former generation the taunt of the historian — that the least gifted, and the least capable, were assigned to the cure of souls, was justified — what wonder that the religious life of the nation had sunk so low? For to commit the sacred office to unworthy hands can, humanly speaking, lead to no other result.

As, therefore, our Church would retain its hold on the national mind, and maintain the cause of God amongst us, its clergy must be duly qualified for their mission. They must be conversant with the themes they undertake to handle, and apt to teach others also. Meagre attainments, a bad address, want of rhetorical power, are not compatible with their position as public instructors in days like these.

The laity complain of the bad elocution of many of our younger clergy, of their inexperience in pastoral duties, of their mediocrity in the pulpit, of their want of breadth of view, and grasp of mind,—of their inability to catechise a class in the national school, or to take a part in parochial details, or to address an audience with the freedom and force which might be expected from a well-educated gentleman, much more from "a scribe instructed unto the kingdom of heaven." They allege that our newly-ordained curates, for the most part, are mere novices in the sick room, and in domiciliary visitation; and are neither so ripe in attainment, nor so ready in utterance, as the licentiates of dissenting bodies.

They allege, moreover, that in the current literature of the day,—even in the newspapers,—religious topics are handled with a vigour and an ability, rarely to be met with in the discourses of the clergy.

Now it must be admitted by all, who take a practical view of the subject, that the standard proposed to the clergy of this country is not only a high one, but demands qualifications almost incompatible. They are required to be diligent in pastoral duties, and at the same time furnished for public ministrations; "they are to serve tables," and yet to "give attendance to reading, to exhortation, to doctrine."[a]

[a] 1 Timothy iv. 13.

They are to "meditate upon these things, and to give themselves wholly to them; that their profiting may appear to all;"[a] yet withal to be prompt and diligent in practical details.

Other communions recognize in those who minister a diversity of gifts, and admit of a division of labour. And this on the principle laid down by the Apostles, "that having gifts differing according to the grace that is given," "as every man hath received the gift, he should minister as of the ability that God giveth."[b] Thus Rome selects her instruments with regard to their different qualifications; and assigns to each his appropriate work (62). Amongst dissenters oratorical gifts are believed to be chiefly prized; and ministerial energy to be mainly employed in the pulpit. But with us every man in orders — whatever his capacity — whether priest or deacon — is expected to be student, pastor, preacher; to occupy the pulpit, to work the parish, to drill the school, to manage the accounts, to superintend the charities, to take the lead in every beneficent and scientific institution; and to bear a prominent part in the social intercourse of life.

It avails little to cavil at such requirements; still less to take umbrage at strictures which, if sometimes unreasonable, cannot harm us, if we learn from them a more excellent way (63). Our wisdom is to see that, as far as may be, our acquirements and practice as

---

[a] 1 Timothy iv. 15.   [b] Romans xii. 6 ; 1 Peter iv. 10, 11.

clergymen, keep pace with the spirit and standard of our age.

And this pleads forcibly for some formative process, some distinct preparatory training for Holy Orders, such as is insisted on in every other walk of life. Professional training is required in all to whom secular interests are committed. We trust neither our persons nor our property to the ignorant or the inexperienced. We do not consider it enough that practitioners should have good natural abilities, and have received a superior general education: in them we require special preparatory study, and professional practical knowledge.

Who can deny that a like system is demanded in the education of our clergy — that candidates for the ministry require, not only a definite course of study, but also a special practical training?

Persons may differ as to the amount of theological learning to be exacted of aspirants to our ministry. Yet, probably, all will agree, that they ought to be versed in Holy Scripture, and capable of expounding it,— that they ought to know something of ecclesiastical history, of modern as well as ancient controversial theology, of the mind of their own Church — as it may be learned from the Prayer Book — of the writings of our great divines,— of the principles of composition and elocution, in order to be able to discharge the duties of both the pulpit and the reading desk with propriety (64). Further, that they ought also to know something of the manner of life, the modes of thought and expression, even the prejudices and prepossessions of those amongst whom they are to minister. Above all,—that to qualify them for the cure of souls, they ought to be themselves under religious influence; and thus to understand the ailments and necessities of the inner man, and the remedy provided for these in the Gospel. For thus, and thus only, can any man minister to minds diseased, or speak a word in season to them that are weary, or lift up the hands that hang down, and strengthen the feeble knees.

We are, as a Church, without any such special systematic training for the clerical office; and in this respect are unfavourably contrasted with almost every other religious body.

The Church of Rome has its Propaganda, and numerous seminaries for educating its clergy in every part of its obedience. The Protestant communions of Germany, Switzerland, and Scotland are similarly provided. So is the reformed Episcopal Church of America. Amongst the dissenting denominations in our own country also there is regular and systematic preparation for their ministry. Can it then be a matter of surprise, if many of the most practical, experienced, and pious members of the English Church feel and deplore its deficiency in this respect,—and ask for the future pastors of its people that course of study and special training, which the theological students of all other religious communities enjoy?

It will be said, you have already in the Universities, which are the great feeders of our Church, the schools of theology you ask for.

Now of all men, we the clergy are least disposed to undervalue these time-honoured seats of learning; or to speak of them without affection, and the readiest avowal of what we owe them. They are connected with many of our fondest recollections — with the studies, and the friendships, it may be, the laurels of our youth — above all with what has given direction and tone to our future life. We are said to cling to them with a regard only too tenacious and exclusive. And the elder amongst us thankfully acknowledge that since our day, new chairs have been endowed, and ampler and better provision made for the special study of theology.

In any observations, therefore, which fall from me on the subject before us, I may be expected to speak with the utmost respect of our Universities. I know that the training of our clergy has already met with grave and thoughtful consideration in this place, and still occupies its leading minds. I have also read with the attention it demands, the recorded judgment of some whom I address, as given in the Appendix to the Report of the Capitular Commission (65).

Still it is a matter of complaint, that candidates from our Universities are found, not unfrequently, inadequately furnished for the Christian ministry; that they know little of theology as a science; are but imperfectly acquainted with the history, and doctrines of their own Church; and are at times even deficient in the knowledge of Holy Scripture. Nor am I speaking from hearsay, but from personal experience, and as having occupied during the last seven years the office of examining chaplain for an important and extensive diocese.

Now there are certain preliminary points in connection with this subject, on which all thoughtful persons are, probably, agreed.

And first, that the education of our clergy should be as enlarged as possible in its nature and objects; that any attempt to isolate or narrow it would be as injurious to themselves, as it would to the interests of society and the cause of religion. The policy of another Church may require the seclusion of her future ministers in seminaries altogether ecclesiastical. But nothing could be more detrimental to our own. It would generate the exclusiveness, the narrow-mindedness, the uncharitableness, which even under present circumstances are too frequently complained of.

All men of judgment will admit that the association of our future clergy with the laity in our public schools and Universities, is the best possible thing for both. It makes them know, and value one another. It prevents future jealousies and misunderstandings, — which, wherever they exist, work such mischief in our parishes,—but which are not likely to occur betwixt those, who have been on a former footing of equality and mixed up in the friendships and wholesome rivalries of school and

K

college life. And at a time when all wise and large-hearted men are endeavouring, as far as may be, consistently with the arrangements of Providence and the welfare of society, to fuse and weld men together, any attempt to isolate the future pastors of the country from those amongst whom they are to minister, would be as absurd, as it would be disastrous if effected. If in the estimation of some, our Universities are even now too exclusively clerical; what would an education confined to candidates for holy orders be? We shall, probably, one and all endorse the judgment of a distinguished member of this University,—that "the exclusive study of divinity, apart from other literary pursuits, and the isolation of clerical students from the laity, would be the most grave innovations on the English practice; and the results might be very different from anything desired or designed" (66).

As far, therefore, as Theological Colleges are proposed as a substitute for our Universities, there can be, it may be hoped, but one opinion amongst us. Pleas for them may be found in the spiritual necessities of our day, in the alleged expensiveness of a regular academic education, in the facility, thus afforded, for the admission of an humbler and less highly educated class of men into holy orders for the supply of our ill-paid and populous cures; though I have endeavoured to show that such are not the men best fitted for this special sphere of labour. And it must be acknowledged that some of these institutions are ably conducted, and work well; and that their students are at times superior in their acquaintance with certain text books of theology, to the average candidates from our Universities.

Still in moral and mental culture, in range of study and breadth of view, in the principles and tone of feeling which we believe to be essential to the ministry of our Church, they fall immeasurably below our Universities. Nor can anything be conceived more injurious to the position and usefulness of the National Church, than that any large portion of its clergy should have been debarred from the advantages afforded in our great seats of learning.

But it is on institutions supplemental, and represented as ancillary to our usual academic course,— that the question turns. And the fact that such have been recommended, after careful deliberation, by a Royal Commission,—and have the countenance of some of our most distinguished prelates, and of leading members, lay and clerical, of our communion, —is a proof how strongly the want they are intended to supply, is felt (67).

Objections against them are, however, urged,— which coming from men of great experience and sagacity, and of large personal acquaintance with the subject on which they speak, are entitled to grave attention.

It is represented, that theological colleges, distinct from the Universities, will generate and foster party spirit — will create different and adverse schools of theology — will become dangerous instruments of undue episcopal influence — will draw sharper the line of separation between the clergy and the laity; and will multiply and widen divisions which are, even now, the plague spots and scandal of the Church.

It is further contended, that such institutions will expose our clergy to the warping and contracting influence of individual, and probably inferior minds; and will result in a want of unity of purpose and uniformity of teaching, and in a narrowed spirit, and lower tone of theology.

At the same time we are told, that in the Universities we have a security against all this, — in the wider association, the more free exercise of opinion, the greater collision of mind; above all, in the higher tone of instruction enjoyed there. It is argued, that the appointment of the Professors by the Crown, or by independent suffrages, is a preservative against unsound views, and the predominating, and perhaps prejudicial influence of an individual mind.

It may, however, be replied, that the institutions now existing as supplemental to the Universities, are not found in practice to justify the apprehensions entertained of them, — that they are not marked by a contracted spirit, or a debased school of theology — or by sectional prejudices and animosities. On the contrary, that those, who have been trained in them, have both when under examination acquitted themselves to the entire satisfaction of bishops and examining chaplains, and have afterwards approved themselves amongst the most zealous, exemplary, and large-hearted of our parochial clergy.

It may even be alleged, that the danger to our youth from the preponderating influence of individuals, from the fascination of personal character and abilities, from the spirit of party, exist in a much greater degree in the Universities themselves — that the rival theological schools, which are apprehended in different dioceses, are found already concentrated in our ancient seats of learning — that some of their most eminent professors have been suspected by the university authorities, debarred from the university pulpit, placed under episcopal interdict — that it has been fresh from our Universities that some of those, who have disturbed our parishes and created in the country at large a reaction against the Church, have proceeded. Finally, that in consequence of the views indoctrinated and the influence exercised here of late, there has been an unsettling of the youthful mind, which has deterred many of our most promising youths from taking holy orders, and has caused throughout the Church both alarm and distrust.

For myself, I do not participate in such fears; but believe, in the words of a high authority, "that for dispassionate, impartial and comprehensive views of the doctrine and discipline of our Church, there is no school of theology comparable to that which may be found in our Universities" (68). I believe that what is illusory in the teaching of some of note in this place will be corrected by future study and experience; while the independence of thought, the love of truth, the large-hearted charity, the personal holiness inculcated, will bear fruit when the erroneous views, and the misunderstandings they have caused, shall have passed away.

Still, admitting that for all, but exceptional cases, our Universities offer great and special advantages for clerical education — admitting that a system of theological instruction cannot be too much under public notice, or too unreservedly subjected to the free play of public discussion and competent criticism — admitting that the two Universities, comprising numbers of highly educated men of all shades of opinion, in pursuit of all kinds of knowledge, and living together in familiar intercourse, possess advantages which a Provincial theological college necessarily cannot have : — further deprecating, in the fullest sense, whatever might have a tendency to lower the tone, or contract the range of theological instruction,— to isolate the clergy,— or foster party-spirit,— or impair the relations in which the pastors of the Church have hitherto been connected with the mass of our people — what we ask of the Universities,-- with their rare advantages, their large endowments, their chartered privileges, is — to render all these more available to the service of religion.

To discountenance the efforts of others, and supply no sufficient substitute — to refuse a remedy for notorious and admitted wants, when it is in their hands to give — it is not thus that our Universities will deal with the wants of the Church and the requirements of the age, — when we turn to them in a great necessity.

To offer, myself, any definite scheme of clerical training, were hardly within my province. Enough for me, to have given utterance in this place to what I believe is felt by many of the Church's warmest friends, on a question which so nearly concerns her vital interests. In doing so, I have but echoed the sentiments of many, who bear rule in this and the sister University, and of some of our most distinguished prelates.

It is for those, who are in authority, to adopt the measures which they may deem the most expedient. A preacher can but deliver what he has learned, from contact with the world—from perhaps his own deficiencies and miscarriages — is demanded of those, who, in days like these, would discharge their ministry amongst our people with efficiency and acceptance.

The question, as it affects the Universities, it must be admitted, is not without difficulties. There are, of course, objections to the prolongation of the usual academic course, from considerations of the further time and cost which this would involve. There are also cases, in which a longer connection with the University, on the part of a candidate for holy orders, might be undesirable. But it has been suggested, that the attention of those intended for the ministry,—after they have passed their final classical examination,— might be confined to theology and cognate studies; that attendance on the lectures of our divinity professors might be made compulsory; that clerical candidates might be stimulated by the prospect of academic distinction in their special department. Further, that in connection with the studies of this place means should be provided for practical training in pastoral work.

What we,— who know the Church's needs, but bear no rule in this place,— ask of our Universities, is to furnish us with candidates, as far as may be, qualified for their future calling. We ask for "workmen that need not to be ashamed, rightly dividing the word of truth," "scribes instructed unto the kingdom of God." Above all, for men whose hearts God Himself has touched,— who have the anointing and the seal of the Holy Ghost;— who whether they minister in our churches, or labour in our parishes, or teach in our schools, will speak out of the abundance of their own hearts, and of the ability which God has given; who can say with the apostle, "That which we have seen and heard, declare we unto you;"[a] whose words will be not merely "that which man's wisdom teacheth, but which the Holy Ghost teacheth."[b]

Give us such men,— and you will be enhancing the claims which our Universities already possess on the love and gratitude of churchmen, and be helping the Church in its weakest point, and at its sorest need.

[a] 1 John i. 3.   [b] 1 Corinthians ii. 13.

You will be providing a seed to serve God, when the present generation has passed away; and enabling the old amongst us to depart in peace, believing that we have seen the salvation of God.

I have already alluded in this lecture to the theological colleges which have been established in some of our dioceses; and of which I retain the favourable opinion I expressed some years ago, in a sermon delivered at Cuddesden, at the request of the Bishop of Oxford (69).

I am, however, myself mainly in favour of a course of teaching and training supplemental to the Universities, and of a more practical character than can be obtained in the institutions just alluded to; such as may be furnished in a well-ordered parish, under the supervision of an incumbent of adequate ability and experience. And my judgment is confirmed by an opinion recently expressed by a select committee of the House of Lords, appointed to report on the means of divine worship in populous districts (70).

It has always appeared to me, that the insight into pastoral work — the practice in the schools— the domiciliary visitation — the acquaintance with parochial machinery— the contact with the middle and poorer classes — the points, in fact, in which our younger clergy are generally, and under existing circumstances, necessarily so deficient,— would be better attained in this, than in any other way.

I had for some years such a system in operation, in a parish of my own; and I shall always look back to it with pleasure. Candidates for holy orders, when graduates of the University, in such a relation, are rather a help, than a hindrance, to a clergyman. The daily service of the Church, the common course of study, the interchange of thought on subjects of mutual interest, the joint supervision of the poor, are not more profitable to those who are thus initiated into pastoral life, than to their instructor.

It, therefore, seems to me, that the distribution of such groups of clerical students throughout a diocese, would prove of signal benefit to the English Church; and supply its ministry with just the class of pastors, that the exigencies of the country and the character of our people call for.

I have dwelt the longer on this subject, because it is of deep and national importance, and appears to affect more nearly than any other the interests of religion in this land. On the clergy, under God, the character, and efficiency, and future of the English Church mainly depend. It is they who are to uphold the cause of vital godliness amongst us; and to maintain the principles of evangelic truth, and apostolic order, and scriptural moderation, which have hitherto endeared the Church of our forefathers to the English people. Reasons enough, why our future pastors should be duly trained for their mission,— and not sent forth to the cure of souls, raw, ignorant, in every way unfurnished for their work.

A period should, surely, in every case be interposed

between the academic degree and holy orders,—during which candidates may sit down and count the cost, and look their future duties in the face; in which they may apply themselves expressly to the study of theology; and take counsel with wise and pious men; and learn from the lessons and examples of fathers in the ministry, what manner of men they ought themselves to be, as Christian pastors,—before they bind on them irrevocable vows, and embark on duties in which both their own salvation, and that of others will be involved.

There are, doubtless, some present here to-day, who are designed for the Christian ministry,—and ere long will be called on to declare before God and the congregation, that they are inwardly moved by the Holy Ghost to undertake it.

I would not say a word, on this occasion, to discourage any sincere candidate for holy orders. Rather would I invite and stimulate my younger brethren —especially those amongst them on whom God has bestowed his choicest gifts of intellect and speech, and who are fired with a desire to benefit mankind— to offer themselves for what I in my heart believe to be the noblest and happiest of earthly callings. I would repeat to them the words which I once heard addressed by Bishop Corrie to a band of youthful missionaries, on the occasion of his last visit to this country—before he returned to lay his bones in the scene of his life-long labours in the East—" If you give yourselves heartily to this work, and trust in God, and do your best, and live to old age as I have done, you will never say, I repent."

Only when I have tried to elicit an opinion on the training of our clergy, it has been said to me, and that by elder members of this University—What you propose may be all very well for candidates who have led careless and idle lives at college.

Young men, I have exercised my ministry in the Church of England nearly forty years. It is long since, as an under graduate, I sat in those galleries, and attended the lectures of a divinity professor, and faced for the first time, as one "separated to the Gospel," the actual conditions of clerical life. I have, perhaps, no right to expect from you who are yet inexperienced, and whose pulse beats high, to feel in this matter exactly as I do. There is much in every path of life that can be learned only by personal experience.

But I know what it is to have been ordained, and to have undertaken clerical vows; to have said, when the Lord of the Vineyard came to hire labourers, and the Captain of the Host to enlist soldiers, Here am I, send me — I have nearly finished the course which you are on the eve of commencing. I can look back from the end to the beginning.

And I would affectionately beseech you, for Christ's sake, for the Church's sake, for the sake of those amongst whom you may be called hereafter to minister; for the support, and consolation, and salvation of your own souls, when trials, and troubles, and sickness and bereavement come, and you are in deep waters, and the floods threaten to swallow you up,— to look the vows and the work that are before you, in the face; and to be sure at least of this,—that you are sincere, and in earnest, and yourselves converted men, before you take holy orders.

Ponder, I would say, the qualifications required of one who is to be a Minister of the Sanctuary, an Ambassador of God, a servant and Apostle of the Lord Jesus. And do not encourage, either in yourselves or others, the monstrous and ruinous delusion that an under graduate may lead an idle, reckless, self-indulgent life at the University,— and then without impiety offer himself for holy orders, and imagine, because he has been ordained, that he is at once made fit for the cure of souls.

The time of preparation is short enough for any man, the most diligent and self-restrained. The realities of Christian life will surely prove on what foundation each man builds.

May yours, my younger brethren, be laid in personal religion, in the discipline of your own spirits, in the subjugation of your own passions, in the heart-felt, experimental knowledge of Him whom you are to preach to others,—and whose cause you can never promote, but as you are called and led by Him, and offer Him the sacrifice of your spirits, souls, and bodies, which are His.

LECTURE VI.

PROVERBS II. 10, 11.

"*When wisdom entereth into thine heart, and knowledge is pleasant unto thy soul; discretion shall preserve thee, understanding shall keep thee.*"

In my last Lecture I spoke of an improved system of clerical training, as essential to the efficiency of the English Church, and to the retention of its hold on an intelligent and educated people.

I grounded my arguments on the requirements of the Christian ministry, and on the special demands made on this in the present day. I urged, that the clergy could never adequately discharge their sacred trust, or answer the legitimate expectations of those of whom they are the teachers, unless their own qualifications of every kind kept pace with the spirit and exigencies of their age.

I further stated, that to the Universities the Church and the country looked to supply the necessary training; and enforced this as amongst the noblest services which they could render to religion.

In the present Lecture I propose to consider what is often treated as an ecclesiastical, and even as a clerical, rather than as a national question — I mean the Education of our people.

To prove that the Church of England is in favour of this, and heartily engaged in it, can hardly be required of me. Whatever may have been the deficiencies of churchmen in this respect before the Reformation, to accuse them in the present day of indifference or obstructiveness in the cause of mental enlightenment and progress, is not only an injustice, but an anachronism. Our Church owes its own liberties and ascendency to the enfranchisement of the national mind. It has nothing to fear, and everything to gain, from the increase and diffusion of knowledge. And it is the desire of every one of its intelligent members to impart the blessings of education to the greatest possible number of their countrymen, and to the greatest possible extent. There is, probably, not one of us who would deny, that the education of our people is the first of duties; and that to train an immortal spirit is to make, or mar the noblest work of God.

By Education, however, as Churchmen we do not mean mere mental cultivation, or physical training, or any specific adaptation of teaching to a future calling in life. We mean by it the leavening the mind and the heart with truth, with principle, with law — the enthroning God in the soul of the nation, and in the soul of the individual man — the making the will of God, as revealed in His Holy Word, the rule of every man's conduct, and the principle of every man's life (71).

With Churchmen the basis of all education is the Bible. This I maintained in a former lecture to be the foundation of our system, and of the claims of the Church itself to the confidence and affection of our countrymen.[a] It may be safely affirmed that no other religious body displays such love and reverence for Holy Writ; or makes such copious use of it in its service; or takes such pains to impregnate with it the hearts of its people.

We therefore deem ourselves bound to see that the education of our people is a religious one: and consequently mere secular teaching — the separation of religion from other branches of instruction — the exclusion, on any pretext whatever, of the Scriptures, or of the clergy, or of the Church formularies from our schools, cannot be entertained. For the Church to adopt a neutral attitude, or an ambiguous utterance on such a point, would be in the face of its most solemn obligations, and in neglect of all experience. The result of such an experiment, wherever it has been tried, has proved to be destructive of both religion and morality.

"Dissever religion from education, and you make men clever devils," was the saying of the great Duke of Wellington; while Washington's dying injunction

---

[a] Lecture II.

to his countrymen was, "never allow education to be divorced from religion."

On this point the history of secular education in America, as set forth in the late able and forcible charge of the Archdeacon of Middlesex, is conclusive (72). On the testimony of both churchmen and dissenters in that country, the Archdeacon demonstrates that the system prevailing there—to quote the report of a committee appointed in Philadelphia to inquire into the subject—"has been not only injurious to the character of the rising generation, but a benevolent fraud on the public bounty."

Thus a preacher before the Synod of the German reformed church at Baltimore—whose sermon was published at the request of that body—observes, "the patrons of this system forget that educated mind without religion is educated vice."

Thus a speaker at an aggregate meeting held at New York in 1855—which included Presidents and Professors of colleges, and Directors of county and city high schools from different parts of the Union—insisted "that a great change must be adopted in the educational system of America; for that from the midst of its schools depravity is growing up, and the State must be shaken to ruins under the present training of its youth. "There is not," he maintained, "one in ten of its teachers, to whom the moral training of a child could be entrusted."

Another speaker declared "that he knew of thirteen young men, who came from one school,—and every one of them had rushed headlong to destruction." A teacher had made to him the following declaration: "I think I must somewhat change my system of teaching, and give a little more moral instruction, for already two of my scholars have been hung for murder."

A learned professor on the same occasion maintained "the necessity of daily religious culture in a school." "Separating religion from the daily work of a child, and confining it to the Church," he said, "is like taking all the salt that should be mingled with our daily food, and eating it alone before breakfast. If religion could not be taught in schools without sectarianism, then let sectarianism be taught." He added, "I would much prefer my children to be instructed in sectarianism than be sent to schools where there is an indifference to religion."

Lastly, the retiring President of the Educational Association concluded his address upon the improvements which the American system requires, with these significant words:— "I have reserved the most important thing for the last, that which must be at the bottom of our whole system, *religious education.* The religious man is everything, the intellectual man without religion is nothing" (73).

In short, the concurrent testimony of churchmen and dissenters from the other side of the Atlantic — and it borrows a dismal significance from what is now passing there — is to this effect — "Hear the conclusion of the whole matter, and the sum of what we need and ask. Give us Christian schools, schools which have a God, a Saviour, a Holy Spirit, a Bible, a hymn-book, a catechism and prayer, a pastor and a pious school teacher—a school between the family and the Church,—a school which will carry forward the education of children in the same spirit in which it was commenced by pious parents —a school that will be a nursery to the Church,— a school so entirely under the control of the Church, that it may carry out the spirit of its great commission, in reference to its own children—" Feed my lambs."

Such we believe to be the education approved and adopted amongst ourselves;—and we can never, as a Church, abandon this without a surrender of our duty and a falsification of our trust.

Moreover, it seems essential that the teaching of our schools should be in accordance with our own formularies and confessions of faith; and thus that the Prayer-book should be taught, as well as the Bible. Call it sectional, or sectarian, or denominational, or what you will;—in no other way can you expound doctrine, or explain the Scriptures. Persons talk of essential and non-essential tenets in religion. But who is to pronounce what is essential or non-essential;—what we are to teach, or to leave untaught;—what are the positive truths of Christianity;—what we are to eliminate? Is it to end in adopting the rule proposed by one of the earliest and most forward advocates of exclusively secular instruction : " Let any teacher who shall utter a single word either for or against religion, be liable to immediate dismissal" ?

How far we are to impose on the children of dissenters the use of formularies which in their case are inapplicable, is quite a different matter (74). All that is contended for is, that the children of the Church should be taught in its elementary schools the distinctive doctrines of the Church, should learn its Catechism, and have this and its Liturgy explained. It is undeniable that this is not merely a matter of principle but also one of finance. "The moment," says Archdeacon Sinclair, "that religious teaching is restricted or abolished, the zeal of educationalists will grow cold, and subscriptions will die away."

It is a gratifying proof of the interest at present felt by our country in the cause of elementary education,—that its annual expenditure on this behalf amounts to two millions. It is also encouraging to know that the percentage of children under education, which, at the beginning of the present century was one in seventeen, has now increased to one in seven,—in rural districts to nineteen in twenty. It is further satisfactory to be assured that the Church, as in duty bound, has been ever foremost in this work,—although the contributions of the clergy have been, in proportion, largely in excess of those of even our wealthiest laymen (75).

We gather all this from the recent valuable report of Her Majesty's Commissioners on Education. We are also informed, that the general system of inspection which is still on the increase—the introduction of a superior class of teachers—the judicious and salutary stimulants supplied in various ways by Government—the sympathy and help rendered by influential persons of both sexes in the support and management of schools, have all acted beneficially.

But the main obstructions which we have to contend with in National Education are still the same. Amongst the commonest and most prominent are, the brief period spent by the children of the working classes in our schools — their broken and intermittent attendance — the early age at which for the most part they are withdrawn—and the bad example in many instances afforded them at home.

We must receive as authenticated facts, that the great majority of the children leave our schools at eleven years of age—in populous districts, four-fifths of them before they are ten, the general average being three-fourths at that age — that only about a fourth of those nominally under education pass half the year at school,— that of those educated in church schools a great majority are lost sight of when they leave school— that when brought again into contact with the parochial clergyman, at the time of confirmation, they are found to be in any thing but a satisfactory condition as to mental culture, or to morals (76).

And the conclusions which, in the view of those by whom they have been most carefully considered, these facts establish, are:—

First, the necessity of making the very most of the period which the children of the operative class pass at school (77).

Secondly, the importance of retaining a hold over them after the school course has ceased.

I. What is needed above all things in our schools is a teaching and a training, which will endear the doctrines, the services, and the ties of the Church to the children of our people. We want a hearty, genial, loving system; we want to interest the minds, and gain the affections of the young. The teaching the Catechism by rote—the hard, dry enunciation of dogmas—the employing religion as a mere exercise of intellect—all these, if not absolutely pernicious, are of comparatively small avail in the training of a spirit (78).

What we really want, is to have truths instilled and imbibed as living realities, and influential rules of life. We want the meaning of our services, their adaptation to the wants of the inner man, the deep personal interest which they ought to have for each, to be understood and to be felt by the young.

To use the Bible as a task book for teaching letters or lessons in reading and dictation—and the Prayer-book as an exercise of memory—and the House of God as a place of confinement on the Lord's day;— in other words, to associate the doctrines and the services of religion with what is irksome and repulsive to the young, to make the day of rest one of extra drudgery to them, and to compel attendance on what they neither relish nor understand, is surely not the way to rear a pious and church-loving population (79).

But to make both Scripture and Service-book intelligible and attractive to children; to cause our doctrine " to drop as the rain, and our speech to distil as the dew, as the small rain upon the tender herb, and as the showers upon the grass"[a]—to deposit truths in the intellect, and implant principles in the hearts of the young—this is to educate. For this is to make God Himself, and His truth, and His law, and His service, and His people dear to them.

And if we have hope for the future of both the Church and the country, it is because we believe that such is the education which is gaining ground, and will soon be universally adopted in our elementary schools. Because we believe pastors and teachers are learning more and more the nature of their holy work,—and what they must themselves be to discharge it; how truthful, and earnest, and sympathising, and exemplary—if they would really feed Christ's lambs, and train souls for eternity (80).

And here there is a point which demands the special attention of those who are preparing for Holy Orders. It is this—that the interest, or absence of interest,

[a] Deuteronomy xxxii. 2.

manifested by the parochial clergyman in a school may, we are assured by our inspectors, be seen at once in the whole mental, and moral, and religious tone of the children.

It is, therefore, the more to be regretted that the management of a school, and the faculty of either communicating information to children, or eliciting what they know, are matters in which, as has been already observed,[a] our younger clergy are for the most part extremely deficient. Very few of them know how to interest the young: and fewer take the necessary pains to acquire the power of doing so. And yet teaching is a science; it does not come by intuition. And in days in which so many of our schools have trained masters—who do understand what teaching is—it is more than ever necessary that the clergy, with a view to their own usefulness and credit, should be "apt to teach." It were therefore well, that a practical acquaintance with the system pursued in our training colleges should be pressed upon candidates for Holy Orders, as an essential branch of education.

II. Another, and important subject for the consideration of the Church is, how to retain its hold upon its youthful members at a most critical and perilous period of their lives — when the discipline of the daily school has ceased.

I question whether there is a parochial clergyman

[a] Lecture V.

in the land who does not find, that the most impracticable subject he has to deal with is a youth of the working classes, when emerging from boyhood into manhood, who mistakes rudeness for independence, and vice for manliness,—and regards the schoolmaster and the clergyman as his natural enemies (81). Who is not tempted to say of him, what St. James does of the tongue, "that every kind of beasts and of birds, and of serpents, and of things in the sea, is tamed, and hath been tamed of mankind:^a but" this one "can no man tame?" Like the "deaf adder he stoppeth his ears"—like the "wild ass's colt he escapeth clean away."

The difficulty is to overcome his shyness, to gain his confidence, to discover how to interest and attach him. Hitherto the Sunday school has been the only way of reaching him. And most of us know how dull, flat, and unprofitable—as generally conducted—this has been. What was urged by Dr. Hessey on this subject, in his closing lecture, is fresh in the memory of most of us. We do not deal wisely, he observes, with the children of the higher classes on a Sunday;— much less so with those of our poorer brethren (82). And every man of sense must admit, that if school on the Lord's Day is to be rendered really serviceable to the Church, and to attract rather than to repel the working classes, there must be more of life, and interest, and novelty infused in it—more of sympathy

^a 1 James, iii. 7.

and of companionship, and less of restraint and of task-work (83).

By many it is now thought, that our main hope for the children of our poorer classes lies in Evening Schools. And the Educational Commissioners in their recent Report call attention to these, and urge the importance of giving to them more perfect organisation and wider extension (84).

A new and deeply interesting field of labour is thus opened up to churchmen. May hands and hearts be found to till it! To supply these we look to our younger clergy and to our gentry who have leisure and ability for the work. Zeal, and courage, and physical energy, are all wanted here: yet no nobler enterprise was ever set before man. It is to civilise with a view to christianise those who have been neglected, till they have become embruted—and are then pronounced irreclaimable.

Ours, happily, are days in which examples to stimulate and instruct are never wanting—in which the first in rank and station are often found to be the foremost in the work of God—in which even women, despite the shrinking delicacy of their sex, have assayed and performed tasks from which manhood hitherto had shrunk (85). And this is the lesson they have taught us—that the dullest minds can be enlightened, and the rudest natures changed, —that no heart is inaccessible to kindness, and that nothing is impossible to them that believe.

And yet the humblest class of our countrymen is

not the only one that has claims of this nature on the Church. On the contrary, there are perhaps none to whose education its attention requires more to be directed, than to that portion of our Middle class, on which, more than any other, the welfare of the bulk of our population depends.

It is impossible to exaggerate the importance of this section of our countrymen. It consists of the chief employers of labour, the principal owners of our cheaper tenements, the persons who are in close and constant contact with our labourers and artisans. They are the men who fill our municipal and parochial offices, who control our vestries, who return our representatives to Parliament; who thus have more influence than any others, in promoting or preventing improvement. As guardians of our poor, as wardens of our churches, as mixed up officially in many ways with the clergy, they ought to be the stay and life of the English Church. But in numerous instances they are the men who uphold and feed dissent.

The reason is, they are just the class to whose education the Church for long has paid the least attention. It educates the poor; it educates the aristocracy; it does not educate the class of which I speak. And therefore in all that really constitutes education —in moral culture, in knowledge of Scripture, in religious training, in depth and breadth of view, in sense of duty—they are, it may be feared, as far as the Church is concerned, the most neglected part of the community. And in the conviction of many more conversant with the subject than myself, their education is the most unsatisfactory of all. Certain branches of instruction, mainly prized by the trading community, it of course imparts. But in other respects it is pronounced by competent authority to be inferior to that which may be obtained in many of our national schools (86). It is utterly wanting in the elements which distinguish our public schools. Its religious teaching and training are radically defective. While on matters affecting the principles and interests of the National Church, it is more wanting than in any other particular.

And hence the defects by which the class of which I speak, is commonly characterised—its inadequate information and prejudice on religious subjects—its vulgar worship of wealth as wealth—its depreciated standard of commercial morality—its self-sufficiency in judging of important questions, and yet the facility with which it is duped by shallow pretensions, and religious and political impostures—its want of power to appreciate depth of thought and real superiority in a teacher—while it is caught by sham and glitter, by a loud voice, and an imposing manner, and a fluent tongue.

There are, doubtless, private schools for the middle class, which are well and ably conducted. But it is to be feared, that the most pretentious and the least efficient are generally most in vogue (87). And the fact that these schools are in many instances the speculations of persons utterly unfit to be entrusted with the education of youth, and mere educational adventurers, is undeniable. Added to which, they are without the guarantee afforded by the inspection of either the Government or the Church.

The matter, it will be admitted, is one of very great importance, and affecting in many ways the social and religious interests of this country. And happily it is beginning to attract general attention. Some good Middle schools have been already founded; and in these, at a moderate expense, the best education is afforded, and gratifying reports as to their acceptance and success are received (88).

I cannot quit this portion of my subject, without adverting to the little benefit conferred by many of the old Educational Foundations on the class, for whose use they were primarily intended. The decay and practical inutility into which many of these have fallen is, indeed, alike deplorable and disgraceful.

Thus it is in evidence, that many of our Endowed Schools are utterly ineffective for the purposes of education: that they are characterised by general dulness and want of life: that they are almost without exception, more or less abused: that they are obstacles to advance and improvement in education. A well known Dean, when under examination before a Parliamentary Commission, described the endowed schools with which he was acquainted, "as generally speaking, unmitigated evils." A Bishop under similar circumstances, declared "that they are the curse of his diocese." An Inspector of Schools represents the masters " as too frequently appointed with no regard to their qualifications for the duties they have to render, and as, in every sense of the term, unfitted for the situations which they hold,— as in some instances, the halt, the maimed, the drunken, the idiotic" (89).

Even when not so abused, many of the Endowed Schools in England have been diverted altogether from their original intention, and rendered lucrative to the few, rather than beneficial to the community at large. They have not been made, as they should have been, good Middle schools; they have effected next to nothing for the education of our yeomanry and tradesmen; they have not leavened, as they might have done, the commercial mind of the country. And it has been with many a matter of regret, and been used by others as an argument against the principle of educational endowments,—that foundations with such important trusts and such large capabilities should, through neglect and mal-administration, have generally proved so inefficient, and productive of so little good.

It must, of course, be admitted, that there are not wanting honourable exceptions; and that some of our endowed schools have proved in every day seminaries of sound and useful learning. And it is gratifying to know that efforts are at present being made in many places to resuscitate and restore them to their original and proper use,— in which endeavour it is to be hoped the Charity Commissioners will render their valuable assistance,—as the Universities, as far as in them lies, seem disposed to do (90).

But I would urge on any of my younger brethren who may be disposed for a time to undertake the duties of tuition — whether the revival of these old foundations might not be an object having claims upon themselves.

That the work of education is one to which those who have an aptitude for it may legitimately consecrate their gifts, will be denied by no one. Yet it behoves men to look to their motives for selecting this particular field of labour. It undoubtedly has baits for the ambitious and the worldly. It offers a more easy and direct path than parochial services to the highest dignities of the Church,. and is much more lucrative than the cure of souls. To a cultivated mind it is also more attractive than ministrations amongst the poor and illiterate. And therefore in our marts of commerce, and crowded districts, and remote rural hamlets, the clergy are crying out that help is not to be had from our Universities, —that the best educated, and the best bred of our youth shrink from spheres where they are most wanted, and prefer lighter and more profitable work.

I would, therefore, ask of any who are disposed to exercise their gifts in teaching—whether to educate the lower rank of our middle class; to raise the intellectual, moral, and religious tone of our agricultural and trading community; to make of our future tradesmen and farmers,—intelligent, thoughtful, and God-serving men, and attached members of the English Church,—would not be a work most worthy of their efforts? For, surely, there is none more called for,—or in which young men of ability and Christian principle could do more good. And knowing, as I do, the spirit which prevails at this time in our great public schools, and the exertions which so many who come from them are making to benefit all classes of the community,—I cannot believe that labourers will long be wanting in the field to which I point.

I have alluded to our Public Schools; and it is not possible to reflect upon the work in which these institutions are engaged, without admitting the mighty influence they must exercise, in a future generation, on the life of the Church, and on the life of the Country.

With some, the question of public or private education may be still an open one. And when we remember the neglect of Scripture and of moral and religious training, and the cruel and vicious practices, by which public schools in a former generation were disgraced,—we cannot wonder if parents hesitate to trust their children to an ordeal, of which they themselves retain such painful recollections.

Happily, these things are in great measure of the past. And if it be true that even now young men come up from public schools to the Universities, ill grounded in the Bible, ignorant and careless about religion, without any knowledge or sense of their duties as churchmen or as Christians,—we may hope that such instances are rare; and must regret that they are possible. And knowing the antecedents of the men who now conduct our best public schools, and the character of their teaching, we cannot doubt that there is a work going on, and a seed growing up under their direction, which will be the blessing and the safeguard of our land, when we are in our graves.

These men tell us, that the aim in education ought to be to inspire diligence, heartiness, and self-control; to implant a sense of duty; to teach practically the great lesson of corporate life. They proclaim that with a view to this the main object of the master ought to be, to enforce Christian principle, and make the word of God the standard of opinion and the rule of conduct (91).

It was thus that a great man, who passed from this earth too soon for his friends—but not too soon for the accomplishment of the work which God had given him to do—earned for himself the glorious designation of the Apostle of Christianity to our public schools. His endeavour was to set God always before a boy; to enthrone the word and will of God in a boy's soul; to make these in every case his standards of right and wrong. They were the lever with which he himself sought to sway the world. His own love of truth, his abhorrence of what was false, and base, and cruel—his resistance to what he thought evil in any shape, sprang from this.

To do your duty; to do it heartily; to do it cheerfully; to do it as well as it could be done—whether it was great or small; above all, to do it as to God Himself—such was the school teaching of Dr. Arnold. His aim was to make the boy what the man should be; to make him, whatever his station or his calling, true, and earnest, and generous, and straightforward—a lover of God, a lover of man, a lover of duty, a lover of work.

And this is the way in which Dr. Arnold's teaching should be tested—not so much by a few celebrities, more or less, which it produced—but by the ordinary type of man it reared—by the number of hard-working practical men whom it taught to do their duty, whether in public or in private life—as schoolmasters, as parochial clergymen, as missionaries, in the senate, at the bar, in the counting-house, in the trench, in the battle-field (92).

Who can doubt that there are lessons to be taught and learned in the πολις of a public school better than any where else? If, for instance, the hope of the Church lies, as is often said, in the next generation,—how important it must be that boys should understand what the Church really is—what its corporate life consists in—what its privileges and its duties are. And this, not that they may learn party words, and be versed in party questions, and carry church terminology even into their sports, and become narrow-minded, and disputatious, and pragmatical; but that they should know how true, and how pure, and how exemplary a churchman, as a member of Christ's body, should be.

And where so easy to teach this, as where everything in school-life symbolises and foreshadows it; where the relations and interdependencies, and the responsibilities and duties which spring out of these, are all full of a corporate being; where the very designation by which schoolboys are distinguished implies that, as fellows, they are all members one of another? How easy to convey, that as school-life is a common life, so is Church-life a common life,— that as the condition of the school, and the success of the school depend on each member realising his own work, and doing it; as each owes a duty to the other; so is it in that great commonwealth, the Church,— of which every boy in the school is a living member, and the school itself is a component and a living part!

To quote the words of one who speaks from experience, " Who ought to have a higher sense of duty, who ought to have a more living spirit within him, who ought better to understand the ties that bind men together,— than those who in the higher forms of a public school have learned, what delegated trusts and mutual obligations are; and what influence, for good or ill, every one may exercise on his brother man?"

At school a boy feels and acts, does this, and

leaves that undone,—because he is part and parcel of a body,—and the corporate sense may be said to pervade his being. The old become young again, when they describe how at any period of life, in any climate, after however long an interval, "to have been at the same school, and under the influence of the same traditions, to have studied in the same classroom, and knelt in the same chapel, is a link which binds together old and young, great and humble; which makes strangers at once familiar, by common topics and the same associations. So that Wellesley, the stately and puissant governor of millions, and Metcalfe, the lad unknown, but just commencing his course from Eton, meet first on the banks of the Hooghly, and feel themselves the sons of the same mother" (93).

And in a degree this applies to our Universities. Yet the lessons and influences are different. And one conversant with both school and college life lately described from this pulpit, the marked and critical transition from one to the other; how a youth is suddenly thrown on his own resources; and in respect of loneliness, in respect of his real inner life, his real self, he finds himself, as it were, on passing from school to college, his own master and alone (94).

And in this, doubtless, lie both the dangers and the benefits with which the Universities are fraught.

The discipline which at school is gregarious, is here individual. The influences of companionship, of example, and, to a great extent, of suasion are relaxed. All, in fact, that the two first decades of a man's life are meant to serve, is now to be tested, and digested, and inwrought into the moral and mental being. Principles are to be proved; powers to be ascertained; the man must walk alone. The independence for which, perhaps, he pined, is come, And in most cases it will be acknowledged, as the writer just alluded to observes, that it is very different from what had been looked for.

Now it is for all who wish well to our Universities — more especially for college authorities, and undergraduates—to bear this in mind: for on it the course of the academic life, and the making or the marring of the individual turn. Self-training, self-discipline, self-improvement, the education and formation of the man, the fitting him for the conflicts and the business of life, and for its final awards,— this will be admitted to be properly and specially the work of the Universities.

They are the great schools of the nation. We have been told to-day to pray for them, as seminaries of sound learning and religious education. They were recently described by an eminent man reared here, as among the greater lights and glories of Christendom. The Country looks to them for its leading minds, for its great characters — for its scholars, its statesmen, its divines—for the ornaments of its senate and of its learned professions—for its examples in public and in private life—for the type of the accomplished Christian gentleman. And unless it sends forth such, its system is denounced, and its education declared to be a failure.

It is to be feared, that by not a few belonging to both the leading and commercial classes of this country, the teaching and discipline of our Universities are distrusted. The one is viewed as almost exclusively classical, and as such unsuited to persons intended for the more stirring professions, and the actual business of life (95). The other is believed to be lax and ineffective. And if the descriptions of youthful idleness and dissipation, which have recently appeared in certain popular periodicals, are accepted as genuine pictures of student-life, we cannot wonder that any one should hesitate to trust those in whose welfare he is interested, in such scenes of contamination. Are these things, it may be asked, permitted in England's seats of learning, and sanctuaries of religion? Is such the training of the future statesmen, and gentry, and clergymen of England — of the men who are to form the mind and influence the destiny of the next generation?

It may, indeed, be replied, that such representations, where not altogether false, are grossly overdrawn. They are certainly not our own recollections of college life. And we have reason to believe that since our day, the moral and religious tone of the Universities, instead of deteriorating, has sensibly improved; while the system of education, far from being of the exclusive nature supposed, has been of late both popularised and extended in its course of study (96).

Still it would appear that our Universities are not,

as formerly, frequented by the younger members of our aristocratic families,—and are wholly neglected by our commercial classes. And though no institution should be judged by occasional excesses,—which the most vigilant authority may fail wholly to suppress, —yet unquestionably, whenever they do occur, they not only damage the Universities, but through them the great religious body with which these are so closely connected,—and whose cause is by many identified with theirs.

The actual faults of student life, however, confessedly are, its frequently aimless and desultory habits, its want of motives, and its waste of time. The words lately heard within these walls, and the stirring appeal grounded on them, indicate the true and prolific source of mischief here. " Why stand ye here all the day idle?" (97) Why the vapid, self-indulgent, objectless life, too often witnessed at the university— the lounging in chamber and quadrangle — the vacuity and dreariness of what ought to be the most golden of life's golden seasons—a time all too short for the seeds to be sown, and the foundations to be laid in it—which must be to so many the turning point of their existence? Why the confession which I lately overheard from an under graduate —'that he did not know why he was sent to the university?'

Not know why you were sent to the school which Alfred founded, where Wickliffe taught, which trained a Canning, and a Peel, and a Dalhousie,— and where so many of the good and great now living, laid the foundations of their usefulness and eminence!

You were sent to the University to develope your faculties, to form your mind, to cultivate your heart, to fit you for the battle and the work of life, to acquire the spirit of application and the power of saying no. So that whether your future station be a high or an humble one—whether you have to earn your livelihood, or only to inherit it—you may learn to live, not for yourself, but for others,—for others that you may live for yourself :—that, this life ended, you may inherit life everlasting.

It has been truly said, that failures in early education are as often caused by a bad home as by a bad school. And so doubtless with academic life. If men are sent to college for the mere sake of society; if no check is put on their extravagance; if the parental example can be pleaded in excuse—why blame the University?

It is when a father has himself improved the advantages offered here — when his own review of college-life is not of misspent hours, and wasted talents, and frivolous and vicious habits,— when he found the university himself, and can paint it to his son, as a school of learning, as a sanctuary of religion, as the seed plot of intellectual feats, as the nursery of the intellect and the heart,—that as he has sown, he may look to reap.

And if there be exceptions to this law,—and the example, and the pleadings, and the sacrifices and privations of home, at times yield no fruit,—let us hope that such instances are rare—and that, as in former days—there are now not a few students in this university with whom, next to the desire of pleasing God, home example and home affection are the mightiest incentives to diligence and virtue.

To one looking from without, a special danger of academic life seems to be, to isolate men, to limit their attention to their own thoughts and pursuits,— and thus to render them unpractical, and tempt them to deal with matters even of deep religious interest as subjects of barren speculation, rather than as calls to strenuous personal exertion.

This will also account for that want of intercourse between the junior members of the university and those to whom they should be looking for direction, which is with many a subject of complaint. Be it admitted, that the special work of the Universities is self-education; that men are to learn here to converse with themselves, to analyse for themselves the motives and the end of life, to decide upon their future course.

Still it is in learning this, that they want help. It was so with ourselves when we were under-graduates. We longed for some one to take an interest in us, to speak a word in season, to lead us by the hand, to exercise an influence over us, half brotherly, half paternal. And all who desire the welfare of our Universities must feel, that were the relation between the governing and the under-graduate body more unreserved and more cordial—were the advice, and sympathy, and encouragement afforded, which the one requires, and the other, perhaps, longs to give,—the connection would be much more healthy, and mutually profitable. Half the estrangement that mars, and at times embitters it, is the result of misunderstanding: and this, in the great majority of cases, is caused by shyness. A look or word of sympathy, a passing smile, even a reproof administered in love, may be all that is required to establish the mutual confidence which would be the happiness of both tutor and pupil.

It is this that has been of late days the making of our Public Schools:—and the attachment of so many of our young men to the place of their early education and to their former teachers, is one of the most hopeful and exhilarating features of the age. But it is the result of the frank, hearty, genial relation between the master and the boy that prevails there.

May I be permitted, in conclusion, to say a word on another influence which has wrought so much of late for our public schools; which is felt so powerfully from week to week within these walls; which might, with the blessing of God, effect so much in every college chapel?—I mean the influence of the pulpit.

Ought it, I would ask, to be possible for any member of the collegiate body to pass his whole academic course, or even a single term, without listening to the exhortations of a preacher?

It will, of course, be replied,—there are the sermons

every Sunday at St. Mary's. Nor can the value of the religious instructions there imparted be easily overrated. But then, unhappily, as is well known, numbers of the under-graduates habitually absent themselves from the University sermons: and it seems impossible to enforce their attendance. Under these circumstances, I would ask with all humility, whether it would not be well to send the message to those who will not seek it; and to afford, at least occasionally, to every under-graduate, in his own college chapel, the all-important lessons which otherwise would never reach him?

Such privilege has been long afforded in the chapel of the college to which I myself belong. And even now, after an interval of many years, I can recall instructions delivered there, of which I hope the impressions may never pass away. "The lips of the wise disperse knowledge, and a word spoken in due season, how good it is!"[a]

Why should not every student in this University enjoy like advantages, and be able hereafter to bear like testimony? There are few such opportunities of sowing seed unto life eternal, as every college chapel might afford.

[a] Proverbs xv. 7, 23.

LECTURE VII.

1 CHRONICLES XXIX. 1.

"*For the Palace is not for man, but for the Lord God.*"

THE religious life of a community may be not unfairly tested by the characteristics and accessaries of its worship. Mean and dilapidated buildings, a neglected ritual, slovenly and unfrequent services, inadequate spiritual provision and church accommodation, are unmistakable signs of a lethargic state of religion. The more so,—when contrasted with lavish expenditure and material progress in all that affects the interests of this world.

No one denies that the condition of our parish churches, in the early part of the present century, was most discreditable to us as a people. We need not revert to days when our Liturgy was abolished, and our sacred buildings were profaned,—when "they hewed down their carved wood-work with axes and hammers," and defaced their ornaments, and desecrated fonts, and altar tables, and tabernacle work:—when not only their furniture was prosti-

LECTURE VII.

tuted to the commonest of domestic purposes,—but consecrated buildings themselves were converted into dwelling-houses, and even receptacles for cattle.

I allude to mutilations and disfigurements, in which the age immediately preceding our own indulged; in which some of the elder amongst us may have borne a part,—and with which all present have been more or less familiar. "If there can be anything," says Archdeacon Hare, "meaner, more graceless, more spiritless, than the theology of the last century, it is its churches; which were thus aptly fitted for the doctrines proclaimed in them. And not content with its own inability to produce anything excellent, it was restlessly busy in spoiling what it had inherited from its ancestors. One can hardly enter an old church without being saddened and shamed at seeing how it has been disfigured by repairs and alterations, dictated by the parsimonious ignorance of the 18th century" (98).

Those were days when they filled our churches to the door and to the ceiling with pews and galleries, and blocked up, or modernised the tracery of their windows; and shrouded roof, and monument, and arch, and column in whitewash; when—worst of all—they relegated the poor to distant, and dark, and damp, and draughty corners, if they did not drive them out of church altogether.

That these things had their source in forgetfulness of God, can hardly be disputed. Men could not have disfigured, and desecrated, and neglected our sacred fabrics; or been guilty of the encroachments and exclusiveness, of which so many of these furnish evidence, had they possessed any true idea of worship, or any real awe of God.

The revival of religion necessarily changed all this. It imparted reverence, and therefore respect for holy things and holy places. It recalled how "God is greatly to be feared in the assembly of His Saints, and to be had in reverence of all those who are round about him."[a]

It also taught that God is "no respecter of persons"[b] — that the soul of Lazarus is as precious in His sight as the soul of Dives.

The recovery of Christian art, the restoration and multiplication of churches, increased facilities for public worship, greater accommodation for the poor, the vindication of equal rights in the House of God, an abatement of the pride, and selfishness, and exclusiveness, which mar worship, and mock God,— all followed as a matter of course—though not immediately, nor simultaneously.

When Wesley sounded the note which woke the English Church from its death sleep; when Whitfield reasoned of righteousness, temperance, and judgment to come; when the fathers of the great modern religious movement stirred everywhere the national mind in the beginning of the present century,—these men took comparatively little thought of the Church's

[a] Psalm lxxxix. 7.   [b] Acts x. 34.

material structures and outward forms. For they were the pioneers of a religious revival,—and had to resuscitate dry bones, and to breathe life into an effete and almost extinct theology, and to impart elementary lessons in religion.

But the effect of their preaching was, as might have been anticipated. Both Church and nation awoke to a sense of their responsibilities. Parliament gave a million, and afterwards half a million, for the erection of churches : private benefactions flowed in the same channel. More sacred buildings were erected in this country in the course of a few years than during the whole preceding century. And though from ignorance of the true principles of church-construction and even of the nature of Christian worship, great architectural enormities were committed, and much public money wasted, the effort in itself was a noble one, and as such doubtless acceptable to God (99).

Only men had to learn that we go to church to pray,—that preaching is not the sole, or even the chief end in view,—that praying is the end of preaching,—that a building is designated a church, because it is the House of God; and that the want of comeliness and decency therein, the making the comfort of the worshipper the primary consideration, the encroachment on common rights, and especially on those of the poor, were wholly inconsistent with the proper ends in view. Above all, that the jealousies, and feuds, and animosities,—by which our churches have been so often profaned,—ignore the very end for which we erect and frequent them. They needed to call to mind the words of Jacob, "How dreadful is this place:"[a] to remember how Moses put off the shoes from his feet[b], how Joshua fell upon his face, how Daniel retained no strength[c], how St. John was as one dead, in the felt presence of God.[d]

That men professing godliness should have tolerated—far more that they should have perpetrated what we have witnessed, and still witness in many of our churches—will, we may hope, with another generation be a matter of amazement. For that such things will soon be of the past can hardly be questioned.

And in my further remarks upon the fabrics of our Church, I shall point out what appears to me essential for rendering them available for the purposes of religious worship and of Church extension.

I. First, that we should realise ourselves, and teach others, what churches really are — why we are to frequent them — how we ought to use them — how, unless they promote in worshippers reverence, and awe of God, and lowliness of mind, and brotherly charity,—and cause them "to esteem others better than themselves," and "in honour to prefer one another," they altogether fail in their design.

II. Consequently, that we should ourselves respect, and seek to recover in our churches rights, which are

---

[a] Genesis xxviii. 17.   [b] Exodus iii. 15.
[c] Daniel x. 8.   [d] Revelation i. 17.

the inheritance of all,— which are common to all,— and which ought to be shared by all.

What we, in this matter, as a Church, mainly require,—is to vindicate in God's House the common rights of worshippers, more especially the rights of the poor.

"We cannot abstain"—I quote the report of the Lords' Committee in 1858—"we cannot abstain from expressing an earnest hope, that some plan may be devised by which every church in the land may be made, what it ought to be, a common sanctuary in which the rich and poor meet together" (100).

On this point there ought to be no difference amongst religious men. The Word of God proclaims, that if "in our assemblies we say to the rich man in gay clothing, Sit in a good place, and say to the poor, Stand thou here, or sit here under my footstool, we have respect of persons, and are partial in ourselves, and have become judges of evil thoughts."[a]

The law of the land declares, that our parish churches are inalienable and common; that they are for the use freely, and in common, of all the people. It imposes rates, and enforces them upon this distinct understanding (101).

And if, unhappily, in this particular the practice in this country has long been at variance with both the Bible and the statute book, all who are practically acquainted with the subject—and know the offences,

[a] St. James ii. 2, 3, 4.

and the jealousies, and the feuds, and the litigations, and the deceptions to which it leads—are aware that it has tended, more than anything else, to secularise and denationalise the Church, to estrange and exclude worshippers, to neutralise clerical efforts, and to impede and frustrate the Gospel (102).

There, therefore, seems no room for compromise. To reclaim and attach to the Church the great body of our countrymen, we require freedom and equality in worship. What we ask is not *free seats*, but *free churches*. We want the area of the House of God unincumbered and unappropriated: for nothing short of this will satisfy either the demands of Christianity or the necessities of the Church. Every other scheme is defective, and open to abuse; and is habitually abused. It even leads to imposture:—as when the spiritual destitution of a neighbourhood is set forth, and subscriptions are raised for the purposes of church extension; and grants are secured from charitable societies, on the express condition that ample accommodation is provided for the poor; and the seats so obtained, are described as free and unappropriated for ever,—and then allotted to persons of the middle and upper classes, who perhaps seldom use them (103).

We are indeed told, that different ranks will not sit together in the House of God; that even operatives prefer paying a small rent to secure a sitting for themselves (104); that freedom and equality of worship are unsuited to our ritual, and to the tastes and habits of Englishmen. And on pleas like these, we are required to sanction what God forbids, and what is in direct violation of the common rights of Christian men.

And yet, is it not hypocrisy to profess to build churches for common use, and then to appropriate them to a class; to bemoan the ungodliness of the poor, and then to deny them the means of religious instruction; to prate about the Gospel, and then to exclude those who have most need of it; to make our boast of Scripture, and profess to believe every tittle of it to be the word of God, and then to ignore some of its plainest precepts?

To perpetuate this abuse on any plea, is to neutralise our parochial system, and to abrogate our claim to be a National Church,—nay, to make religion itself appear in the eyes of many an imposture.

As respects our Fabrics, therefore, the first practical step in Church Extension is to utilise existing accommodation. We can do this, only by reclaiming our parish churches for the common use of the parishioners; and by sweeping away the partitions which mar their architecture, and diminish their accommodation, and destroy their character as Houses of God, and places of Common Prayer.

We have no alternative but to abolish private ownership in what is legally public property; and to restore to the people of this land their indefeasible privileges as Christians, their inalienable rights as citizens. All appropriation in parish churches,—

whether by faculty, or purchase, or prescription,—is indefensible; and ought not to be tolerated in a free land, or by a Christian people. We cannot humanise the masses; we cannot preach Christ's gospel to the poor; we cannot discharge our functions as clergymen; we cannot maintain our Church as a National Communion, if private and exclusive claims are allowed in parish churches.

But besides this—to meet the immediate demands for church accommodation in this country, we have great need of Temporary Fabrics,—which may be of moderate dimensions and modest in their architectural character.

Buildings of this description were recently recommended in the Report of the Lower House of Convocation on Home Missions; have been sanctioned by several of our church-building societies (105); and are already in use in different parts of the country.

They may be erected at a very moderate cost; and are especially suited to the sudden up-growth, and shifting character of our population.

One designed by an eminent architect for a former parish of my own, has been for some years in use as a School on the week-days, and a Chapel on the Sunday; and has been adopted as a model by several of our colonial bishops (106). Similar structures, though of a more temporary character, will be shortly erected in out-lying parts of the diocese to which I belong,—of an ecclesiastical type, but at a cost of only £1 a kneeling,—and so contrived as to admit of being moved to a different site, at a comparatively trifling expense (107).

As Missionary Stations, such structures are invaluable; and were first suggested to myself by the late Dr. Arnold (108),—not as substitutes for more permanent erections, but for the purpose of gathering in a congregation, preparatory to a more suitable and permanent building. Had they been generally adopted years ago, they would have averted much of the spiritual destitution under which we are at present suffering; and they offer a prompt and easy remedy for it now (109).

Suffer me to remind you that in this respect an example was set us by the Jewish Church, more than two thousand years ago. The law of Ezra covered Palestine with synagogues. Comparatively few of his countrymen could statedly attend the Services of the Temple. But all had the means of religious worship and instruction provided at their own doors. Wherever a congregation of ten persons of years of discretion could be gathered together, there might the ordinances of religion and the means of grace be enjoyed. It is computed that in Jerusalem there were nearly five hundred such supplemental places of religious resort. Every trade and fraternity amongst the Jews had its own. While in the later days of the old dispensation, in districts inhabited by the disciples of Moses,—in scattered hamlets, on mountain brows, by river sides, on the sea shore, in upper chambers, on housetops,—the synagogue, or the proseuche, or the private oratory, afforded to sojourner and to traveller, the means of social or of solitary prayer (110).

In advocating, however, cheap and unadorned structures for religious worship, I speak of them only as supplemental and exceptional—as temporary expedients, necessitated, and therefore justified by the present pressing and appalling exigencies of our spiritual condition. To adopt them as a substitute for permanent churches—and that in a rich and luxurious age like ours,—were not to follow the example of him, who if he extemporised the Synagogue, also restored the Temple. Neither ought it to be questioned, that places of worship to be frequented even by the poorest, ought to be, as far as possible, in form and material worthy of the purpose to which they are devoted. On the other hand, that buildings in which the humblest classes are exclusively to worship —ragged churches, and poor men's churches—are essentially wrong in principle. They are at variance with the spirit of the Gospel: they also imperil our social security. "England," observes an able writer, "is one vast mass of superficial splendour, covering a body of festering misery and discontent. Side by side appears in fearful and unnatural contrast, the greatest amount of opulence and the most appalling amount of misery."

Now, one main object of religious worship is, to sink for a while the outward distinctions of this world and its glaring contrasts, to humble the rich and exalt the brother of low degree. And while we have redundant wealth and extremest poverty, the palace and the hovel, Dives and Lazarus, in close and terrible proximity,—we have need of at least one place on earth, in which both rich and poor may contemplate what the one perhaps is tempted to idolise, and the other to envy, in connection with something higher and better than this world:—in which the one may forget his grandeur, and the other his destitution; and both may anticipate the state, "where the wicked cease from troubling, and the weary are at rest— where the prisoners rest together, and hear not the voice of the oppressor; and the small and great are there; and the servant is free from his master; where light is given to him that is in misery, and life unto the bitter in soul."[a]

It is a painful and perilous contrast which Foreign lands present to our own in this particular. Go to Italy, or Germany, or the Netherlands, or France,— and compare the usage of these countries with what obtains at home. In foreign lands you pass at once from dirty streets and the haunts of poverty into stately and magnificent churches,—where the glories of art, and the achievements of decorative skill, and all that is most highly esteemed amongst men, combine to "beautify the sanctuary of the Lord, and to make the place of his feet glorious;"[b] and where without distinction of age, or sex, or rank, or personal ac-

[a] Job iii. 17—20.   [b] Isaiah lx. 13.

commodation, all, like one family, and with one voice, on their knees, worship God (111). Is it unreasonable, if we ask that here at home, in a land consecrated to freedom, and distinguished by a pure and reformed faith, "rich and poor may meet together in the presence of Him who is the maker of them all,"[a] and our churches may supply what may elevate the poor man's mind and recreate his spirit, and be to him palace, refuge, home?

In one sense the poor have more need and more appreciation of what is beautiful and true in church architecture, than the rich who are satiated with grandeur in every form. To a poor man, especially in cities, a church may present the only type, and convey the only idea of the beautiful. To him a beautiful church may be everything. And the more the House of God, and the worship of God lift him out of himself, and the vulgar and depressing atmosphere in which he commonly dwells,— the more they will have attractions for his heart. The discomfort in which he ordinarily lives, his habitual and oppressive sense of confinement, render a vast and dignified building—such as our cathedrals and larger churches, into which pews have not intruded —to him indescribably attractive. Thus we see how the people swarm to the churches abroad, how they congregate in our own cathedrals,— how they appreciate the space, and the freedom, and the majesty, and the music, which such large and noble

[a] Proverbs xxii. 2.

edifices afford them. The narrow, cramped, free seat would have no attraction for the operative classes abroad; nor have they for such men amongst ourselves.

And all schemes for comprehending the masses within the Church, which stop short of putting them on a perfect equality with richer Christians when within walls consecrated to religion, must fail. They are not Christian-like. They fall short of that great principle which the lowly rank of our blessed Lord, while on earth, plainly inculcated. They fall short of all apostolic spirit and teaching.

The only way to win the operative classes, and to elevate the poor, is to place them, at least in the House of God, on a level with yourselves. You have outraged and debased them,—and this in Protestant England,—by excluding them in many of our great towns from this freedom and equality of worship. You shrink from coming into close and familiar contact, even in the House of God, with those whose manners and habits would be equal to your own, if refined by real Christianity. The only really revolting person is one who has been debased by evil passions, and sordid habits, and grovelling after wealth; and such is more frequently to be met with in a class, which in this country is daily forcing itself into power and importance,—and then tramples on the rank from which it has emerged, and would monopolise our churches to the exclusion of the poor.

But when we have recovered our churches for the

people, the next thing will be to fill them. To do this we must render our Services interesting and attractive, and remove stumbling blocks out of the way.

And this, we are told, can only be effected by alterations, or at least modifications in the doctrine, and discipline, and devotional formularies of our Church—in other words by a Revision of the Liturgy. Nor are the arguments by which this is contended for, to be contemptuously or summarily disposed of, —but on the contrary are such as require the most earnest and careful consideration on the part of churchmen.

For first, we have dissent in its rapid growth, and numerical strength, and political antagonism,—of which the bare existence in any shape may well be a source of distress and disquietude to churchmen.

Secondly, we have the fact that of those ministering in the Church itself, numbers reconcile themselves to conformity by putting a forced and non-natural construction upon the language of its Offices; while by a great majority of the clergy most of its canons and some of its rubrics are systematically disregarded.

To which must be added, that not a few of our young men of high intellectual promise, and lofty spiritual aspirations, are said to be deterred from taking Holy Orders by inability to accept portions of the Church's teaching.

Lastly, we are assured that by the laity in general portions of our Liturgy are neither relished nor accepted.

LECTURE VII. 187

Now unquestionably it is the duty of a Church, more especially of one established and professedly national, from principles of equity and policy, and with a view to comprehension, to conciliate to the utmost admissible extent, consistently with principle and truth. The basis of a National Church ought, as was lately urged in the House of Lords, to be as broad as possible (112). And as our Church puts the Bible into the hands of all its members without note or comment, it especially becomes her to deal tenderly with the individual conscience. It can never be her true policy to eject or exclude, where she can possibly retain.

Few, in our day, it may be hoped, will be found to justify the narrow and reactionary policy of the dominant Church party on the occasion of the last revision of our Liturgy. On the contrary, probably most of us, deplore the intolerance which, for the sake of an enforced uniformity, then ejected from their cures two thousand of the Church's most gifted and exemplary pastors. And after an interval of two centuries some may be found ready to concede, and even to prefer, not a little of what was then roughly and contemptuously refused (113).

Certainly no calm and practical man will deny, that our Liturgy admits of improvement; that it is within the province of the Church to effect this; that for the work of revision, there are divines as competent in the reign of Queen Victoria, as there were in that of Charles the Second or of James the First.

It is expressly declared in the preface to the Prayer-book, "to be but reasonable, that upon weighty and important considerations, according to the various exigency of times and occasions, such changes and alterations should be made therein, as to those that are in place of authority should from time to time seem either necessary or expedient." With, however, this proviso, "that it is the wisdom of the Church to keep the mean between the two extremes, of too much stiffness in refusing, and of too much easiness in admitting of any variation."

Probably few of us are not prepared to endorse this. We shall admit it to be one thing to stifle inquiry, or to force tender consciences,— and another thing to encourage an undefined agitation, and indulge a restless love for change: one thing to relax unnecessary barriers, to alter ambiguous or obsolete expressions, to eliminate whatever may perplex or encumber, to rearrange or abbreviate what we still believe to be both scriptural in its tenets and unrivalled in its structure,— with a view of bringing our Liturgy more into harmony with present habits and prevailing wishes;— and another, and altogether different thing, under the guise of liturgical revision, to aim at a revolution in our services, and a radical change in the doctrine and discipline of our Church. The one we may admit to be a question of expediency, while we feel bound to reject the other at once as an absolute sacrifice of principle.

LECTURE VII.

Now, on some points it would seem that there is little difference of opinion in our day, among thoughtful and moderate churchmen. All are probably agreed, that the Calendar of lessons and of Saints' days is susceptible of improvement — that the Psalter and Table of Lessons might be so arranged as to provide, without repetition, for a third service on the Sunday—that without in any way discrediting the Athanasian Creed, as one of the Church's noblest confessions of faith, there are objections to using it in mixed congregations,—that the Rubrics and Canons require careful revision.

It may even be thought that certain words in the Order for the Burial of the dead, by which some consciences are wounded, might be modified without impairing that glorious and consolatory Service (114),—while in the Office of Matrimony there are portions which might with propriety be omitted.

By some whom I address, even such modifications might possibly be deprecated,—while there are others who believe, that to promote unity in creed and community in worship, our Formulas of faith and Forms of devotion require to be still further simplified and abbreviated.

By none, however, can it be denied that were all possible liberty and latitude allowed, and a royal commission appointed, and licence given to Convocation to deliberate, and the Legislature appealed to, to-morrow,—it could not be to initiate a new system, but only to deal with one that is established; not to compose a new Liturgy, but to treat of doctrines and devotions which have come down to us from remote antiquity,—which have been sealed with the testimony of our confessors and the blood of our martyrs,—which are the accredited and accepted deposit of the national faith,—which most of ourselves have over and over again subscribed,—and which are interwoven with the language, and the habits, and the affections of our people.

It may also be questioned, how far any practicable changes in our Liturgy would reconcile the great body of Dissenters; whereas, on the other hand, the palpable danger of alienating, and even driving from our communion many of its most valuable members stares us in the face. To conciliate dissenters by the sacrifice of churchmen—to incur a certain loss in hope of a contingent gain—could be justified on no principles of justice or expediency; while by altering our doctrines,—besides other and insurmountable objections,— we should really exclude, on the plea of comprehending, and narrow what is now catholic and wide.

We are further assured by an eminent Congregationalist minister,— whose sympathies with the Church have even subjected him to suspicion, — that "attempts to resuscitate schemes of comprehension, plans for the coalition of different bodies, will be in vain. That the divisions into sections of the Christian Church, the existence of distinct Protestant evangelical denominations, must be

LECTURE VII.

accepted as a great fact. That sectional divisions on the ground of forms and modes of administration and discipline, are most likely inseparable from the condition of the Church in the present world. That if it were possible for all Protestant evangelical denominations to be fused together in one Church to-day, and as such to have a fresh start, it would be split into innumerable divisions to-morrow. That it is too late for any particular Church to seek to absorb all others into itself—you might as well discuss the restoration of the Heptarchy " (115).

On the other hand, it is contended by a writer of our own communion,—that the difficulty lies with the dissenting ministers,—that these, if questioned as to the grounds of separation, would probably bring forward ecclesiastical, rather than theological or liturgical objections — the sole headship of Christ, the voluntary principle, the parity of Christian ministers, the independence of Church and State. But that on the minds of dissenting laymen, questions about the ideal constitution of a Church, abstract theories of Church government, have little hold; that certain definite objections to a few phrases in the Prayer-book, probably, weigh more with them than all the Ecclesiastical theories in the world. These,—which he considers the practical gravamina of dissent,—he urges us to remove; and promises that if we do so, though the visionary dissenters, the ecclesiastical doctrinaires, the political agitators, might not conform,—yet that the religious dissidents, the calm, the moderate, the sensible men, would mostly join the Church. Above all, that though in our own day we may not see the full effect of wise liturgical concessions, yet that the children of the present generation of dissenters would be won (116).

Whichever of these views is the correct one,—it will be admitted that the duty of the Church is the same,— and this is to do what is right, because it is right; to alter and amend whatever needs to be altered and amended,—not with a view of attracting others,— but from a desire to be in harmony with truth. Not but that the Church, as a national communion, is bound to give no avoidable offence, and to consult, as far as may be, the interests and wishes of every portion of the community.

Irrespective of what we owe to those without, our present position would appear to be in some respects neither a creditable nor a safe one. We have a rule of Discipline which is not in accordance with general practice, Canons which have fallen into desuetude, and Rubrics which are not generally observed and in some cases are self-contradictory,— which · not unfrequently are an occasion of offence if carried out, and a burden to scrupulous consciences where they are neglected.

It may be difficult to amend these things,—nor may the present be exactly the time to attempt it. But to deny, or to ignore them is impossible; and inasmuch as they are a source of weakness, and a cause of offence, they cannot but be regretted.

LECTURE VII. 193

But the means of attracting to our Services, and attaching to our Communion, we have already. No need of extensive alterations to secure acceptance for a Liturgy, which men of all times and all religious bodies — Dissenters as well as Churchmen — have pronounced unrivalled amongst human compositions,— and which those who separate from our communion confess they can seldom join in without being moved to tears (117).

Some of the changes which under peculiar circumstances, and for special occasions, are required, may be made at once by permission of the Ordinary; and when tried are found to work well both in town and country congregations. A trifling modification, a partial re-arrangement will effect what is desired. We need no royal Commission, no canon of Convocation, no enactment of the Legislature for this purpose (118).

Are our Services too long, at hours inconvenient to a portion of our flocks, not sufficiently varied in their character? We have but to separate Offices originally distinct — though now blended together — to adapt the time of service to the convenience of worshippers,— to curtail our own sermons. I was once informed by a clergyman that he found our Liturgy wearisome, only when he was debarred the pleasing excercitation of preaching: it was one in which he himself copiously indulged. Were the laity consulted, they would probably tell us that the tedium

o

complained of is to be traced rather to the pulpit than to the reading-desk.

What we really want, is not so much to alter our Services, as to do them justice; to imbibe the spirit of them; to administer them with propriety and unction; to reflect them in our sermons and our lives.

The true corrective of error is earnest truth; and by action, rather than by either controversy or concession, must the Church do her work and win her way,—" by pureness, by knowledge, by long-suffering, by kindness, by the Holy Ghost, by love unfeigned, by the word of truth, by the power of God, by the armour of righteousness, on the right hand and the left." [a]

What we need is more of energy, more of homeliness, more of sympathy with every rank, and age, and condition of life—good music, stirring hymns, congregational psalmody, earnest preaching, hearty prayer — far more than changes in the constitution of our Church, or alterations in its Prayer-book.

We want to be able to say with truth, and to make it felt,— that we are journeying to the place of which the Lord said, "I will give it you: Come thou with us and we will do thee good: for the Lord hath spoken good concerning Israel." [b]

---

[a] 2 Corinthians vi. 6.   [b] Numb. x. 29.

LECTURE VIII.

---+---

Acts ix. 6.

"*Lord, what wilt Thou have me to do?*"

Κύριε, τί με θέλεις ποιῆσαι;

In bringing these Lectures to a close, it may be advisable shortly to recapitulate the main points which I have advanced.

I drew attention to the nature, office, and mission of the Church, as God's kingdom upon earth, founded and furnished to impersonate the mind and life of God, and thus to manifest to the world that it comes from Him.[a]

I maintained that the Church recognises as its standard and pattern, humanity as revealed in Jesus Christ:—that it is founded, not on force, not on prescription, but on Christ's sovereignty and divine appointment.[b]

I showed that its instruments were, the Ministry,

[a] Lecture I.   [b] Ibid.

the Sacraments, the Scriptures, the Church's Forms of devotion embodying its Creeds, and corporate Fellowship and Action.[a]

I further maintained, that the religious body in this country, designated the Church, answers to these conditions, and is by principles and organisation qualified for the office assigned it.[b]

I pointed out its difficulties and obstructions, its shortcomings and failures[c]; and drew attention to its need of increased agencies and resources, and further development and improvement, and more cordial, energetic, and combined efforts on the part of its members.[d]

I have wished to exaggerate nothing, to extenuate nothing, to keep back nothing; but to admit blemishes and deficiencies, candidly and explicitly; and to put forth remedies, as they have been suggested to my own mind during a varied pastoral experience of many years.

My aim has been to stir churchmen to inquire what can be done to supply the needs, to remove the defects, to increase the efficiency, to promote the welfare of the body with which they are themselves incorporated,—in whose trusts and privileges they participate,—whose interests they are bound to foster and to further.

Such questions may be overlooked,— they may be stifled,— they may be evaded; – or, when taken

[a] Lecture I.
[b] Lecture II.
[c] Lectures III. IV.
[d] Lectures IV. V. VI. VII.

up they may be dealt with as a man's own affairs when they get into disorder. Many will not look at them at all — some begin, but get bewildered and disheartened, and close the inquiry. Others look difficulties in the face, determine to know the worst, and set themselves resolutely and earnestly to retrieve.

To not a few in our day the condition and prospects of the English Church have caused only disquietude and despondence. Such persons have bemoaned its shortcomings, but never tried to redress them. Or they have forsaken the communion whose vows were upon them, and which they were bound to stand by till the last. Or they have even taken up a railing proverb, and joined the assault against it.

Others have been chiefly concerned to know what is expected of the Church; what it is pledged to; where its weakness lies; where it may have erred; how it may amend.

There has been a long breathing time allowed to the Church of England. It has had warnings many and portentous, both from without and from within. Our prelates were told by a leading statesman thirty years ago, to put their house in order. There has been no want of stir in the opposite camp. Assaults have been made on both the constitution and the standards of the Church. State protection has been diminished, and in some instances withdrawn. It is a staff that often fails in time of need. Woe to the Church whose dependance is on acts of uniformity, and bills of pains and penalties, and political and religious tests; rather than on the truth of its own principles, and the attachment of its own members, and the strength of its inner life, and the help that cometh of the Lord!

Under these circumstances, some, as I have said, have gone to sleep, some have forsaken our camp, some have gone over to the enemy; some, taking counsel of God, and of their own true hearts, have set themselves to look to their own foundations, to strengthen their own outposts, to polish their own weapons, to do their own work.

If there is one lesson more than another that these men have been taught by recent events,— or which they have learned on their knees, and in their own personal conflicts,— and which has been thus inwrought into their hearts,— it is belief in the principles of the English Church, and reliance on the blessing that is sure to attend on the honest, earnest, genial, and courageous discharge of its mission.

We know its faults, we know its wants, we know its weaknesses,— we know where it has faltered, and where it has failed; we know where it requires help, and where it needs amendment.

When we review the past, the wonder ought not to be, that the English Church has a great work still to do and much ground to recover,—that there are numerous dissidents from its fold,—that there are multitudes ostensibly belonging to it, baptized with its baptism, called by its name,—whose spiritual condition is a scandal and a snare to it. If it had not been a true branch of Christ's Church, and planted on the Rock of Ages, it must have come to an end long ago. When we recall its somnolency, its unfaithfulness, its repose on an arm of flesh — what has been called the dreariness of political Anglicanism—how, for long, its dignities, and emoluments, and the trusts these involved, were bestowed — how its cures were served —how its parochial offices were filled—what was the condition of its fabrics, and the manner in which its services were performed,—we must feel that but for its Liturgy, and its seminal principles of life, and the truths of which it is the depository,—and above all, the infinite forbearance of God,—its light must have been quenched, and its candlestick removed out of its place.

But then, to invalidate its claims as a Church, you have to prove that its system is to blame; that its principles are erroneous; that it fails, when the conditions of success are complied with.

There is no question about the lethargy, and the nepotism, and the shortcomings, and the wrong doings of so-called churchmen in days gone by,—any more than there is about their imperfections and failures now. But these are attributable to a neglect of the true principles and actual mission of our Church. They occurred because its rule was disobeyed, and its observances were neglected, and its truths were kept back, and its offices were improperly filled — because what it enjoined was set at nought, and what it forbade was done. Had its spirit been understood, and its requirements complied with, the religious life of those who belonged to it would have been altogether different. We should have had devotion in the reading-desk, and light in the pulpit, and exemplary holiness in the parish.

To establish the Church of England in the heart of the nation — to recover those who have forsaken its fold — you must embody its principles, exhibit its doctrines, and exemplify its teaching.

It asks for greater freedom, and for fuller development — to have its parochial and diocesan system carried out — to have its offices properly filled, and its ordinances duly administered. It needs more bishops, more clergy, more abundant and more efficient ministrations, more co-operation on the part of its members, more systematic religious training, more places of worship. It needs to have its property secured, and rightly dispensed. It needs to have the means of manifesting itself to every man's conscience, and carrying its message to every man's door.

The national Church cannot adequately discharge its mission, — but is misrepresented and misunderstood — if it is cramped, and crippled, and badly served; if it is shorn of its strength; if you deal with it as the Philistines did with Samson.

Give it greater liberty, and greater scope; give it a due supply of the weapons of its spiritual armoury. Let its apostles, and its teachers, and its helps, and its governments, and its administrations, be such as are enjoined in Scripture, and are proportioned to the exigencies of the day. Give it rulers and pastors according to God's heart. And then see if it will not approve itself as the Spouse of Christ, and the spiritual mother of your people.

The main ground of hope in any Church, of course, is, that it is a kingdom planted by God Himself — organised, and furnished, and sustained by Him — and entitled to our homage, and our trust, and our energetic personal help, because it is not a human, but a divine institution.

The experience of eighteen hundred years may surely teach us this,—and that no permanent blessing waits on efforts unauthorised by God, which are necessarily desultory, disjointed, and spasmodic. "If a counsel or a work be of man, it will come to nought; but if it be of God, ye cannot overthrow it; lest haply ye may be found to fight against God."[a] For whatever originates in man,—and depends mainly on the zeal, and ability, and eloquence, and administrative powers of a merely human agency,—necessarily contains in it the elements of dissolution.

How — it may be asked — has Romanism stood its ground for so many centuries, and held its sway over so large a portion of Christendom, in spite of its manifold corruptions, and transparent impostures? And how, though the marks of decrepitude and the

[a] Acts v. 38, 39.

tokens of decay are upon it, does it seem still to renew its youth, and recruit its strength? Is it not because it is a branch of Christ's Church, though a recreant, and a fallen one?

And why is it, that forms of Protestant nonconformity never permanently thrive: that the society which boasted of a Watts and a Doddridge, and other eminent names, has in so many instances decayed and died out, or become Unitarian?—but that the very principle in which dissent originates, involves its disruption and extinction.

Again, why is it that the successive assaults that have been made on the Church of England seem only to rectify, and consolidate it?—but because these show where it has failed,—and thus serve to resuscitate some dormant grace or latent principle, and cause it to bring forth from its spiritual armoury and furbish some weapons that have been allowed to rust.

Who can question that it was the want of religious earnestness, of evangelical truth, of spirituality in its ministers and members, of sympathy with pious minds, which some years ago constituted the weakness of the Church, and the strength of its assailants?—Or that it was in greater danger from sectarian efforts then, than now when dissent is arrayed against it as a party and political combination?

No sooner did the doctrines which had been unheeded in the Church's Prayer-book, reappear in its pulpits, and its ministry was characterised by the spirit of its formularies,—than the strength of the Church returned, its hopes revived, its houses of prayer were filled with devout and attentive worshippers; and the interest, and the trust, and the attachment of its members were restored.

Again, when it had lost sight of its characteristics as a Church; and its orders, and its sacraments, and its discipline were neither understood nor valued,— the danger which menaced it from an opposite direction apprised it of its error. It reverted to its principles, it recovered its equilibrium, it proved its foundations — and in the strength of these it stood.

The men that went out from it, distrusted its orthodoxy, questioned its vitality, predicted its decline. Where is it, and where are they? They are gone, their place knoweth them no more;—but the vacancy they created is supplied. Are they happier, more established, more useful, more in favour with God and man, than they were of old? Is the prayer that we breathe for them not this,— that they may "remember the kindness of their youth, the love of their espousals,"[a] and see their error, and return: — and the word that we send after them not this, "What iniquity have ye found in me, that ye are gone far from me, and have walked after vanity, and have become vain?"[b]

And so, doubtless, it will be with the danger which more immediately menaces us now—and which seems to some, to be the most insidious and deadly

[a] Jeremiah ii. 2.   [b] Ibid. ii. 5.

of all. It is but the return of the pendulum, the reflux of the swell, — or the spray upon the reef, that warns that peril is nigh. For all error is but an exaggeration or perversion of truth, and, as a great writer observes, "the first step in resisting error is to understand the truth at which it aims." "No mere negation,—but the full liberation of the truth, which lies at the root of error, can eradicate error" (119).

As members of the English Church we maintain the truth to lie between bondage and licentiousness— between superstition and rationalism—between a blind and ignorant acquiescence in what we have never investigated, implying a surrender of judgment and an abdication of conscience, on the one hand — and a defiance of authority, and a rejection of truth, on the other.

And because we believe that our Church holds this even balance, and preserves this golden mean,— and that in her case, as I have said, whatever stimulates inquiry, only leads to self-correction, recalls some principle that has been overlooked, revives some light that has burned dim,— our persuasion is, "that no weapon formed against her shall prosper, and that every tongue that shall rise in judgment, she shall condemn."[a]

Next to our confidence in the principles of the Church itself, is our reliance on the sound sense and

[a] Isaiah liv. 17.

right judgment of the English people. We believe our national church to be the expression of the preferences, and the exponent of the mind of our countrymen: that it commends itself to their judgment, and is in harmony with their spirit.

The English are a real, a practical, and a homely race. They mislike pretence, they suspect extravagance, they have no sympathy with transcendental spiritualisms or with mooning mysticisms,—they are averse to both superstition and fanaticism. They approve the sound and scriptural principles, the sober and masculine piety of their national Church. They rely on the great, grand, enduring principles, on which it reposes,—and which it is its business to proclaim and embody.

It is only when they think that they have cause to suspect the piety, or the soundness, or the good faith, or the good sense of their religious teachers, that they are estranged. The history of every religious excitement, of every disruption and secession that has tried and torn the Church since the Reformation, seems to proclaim this.

Manliness, faithfulness, discretion, consistency of life and doctrine, strict attention to practical duty, are the qualities which the English people prize in their spiritual guides. It therefore behoves all who love the Church, and seek its peace, and its extension — and would have it rooted and established in the hearts of our people — in their teaching, in their mode of celebrating worship, in the arrangement of their churches, in their personal conduct and demeanour,—even in their dress,—to give no offence in anything, that the ministry be not blamed. And all who understand the temper of our countrymen must pray, that the Church's doctrine, and its discipline, and its ritual, may be such as to secure respect, and inspire confidence,—and that the desire and aim of all its members may ever be to heal sores, and compose differences, and promote peace, and unity, and goodwill, and practical godliness, in every parish, and in every dwelling.

Experience shows that wherever the Church is fairly represented,—that is, wherever its doctrines are faithfully proclaimed, and its principles truly carried out, and its clergy and laity heartily combine,—a blessing rests upon its efforts, and it grows at once in favour with both God and man. Interest is awakened, religious life revives, the fruits of the Spirit flourish and abound. The very aspect of external nature undergoes a change. "They build the old wastes, they raise up the former desolations, the desolations of many generations."[a] "For as the earth bringeth forth her bud, and the garden causeth the things that are sown in it to spring forth; so the Lord God causeth righteousness and praise to spring forth."[b] The Spirit of the Lord is upon our Church, and His words are in her mouth, and it may be said of her,—"Arise, shine; for the light is come, and the glory of the Lord is risen upon thee."[c]

[a] Isaiah lxi. 4.   [b] Ibid. lxi. 11.   [c] Ibid. lx. 1.

In the Lectures now drawing to a close, my aim throughout has been to enforce at once the corporate life, and the individual trusts and accountableness of churchmen. I exposed, at the commencement, the mistaken and pernicious opinion which restricts the Church to the Clergy,—and which in proportion as it has prevailed has impaired the religious life of our communion. For its tendency is to discourage on the part of the laity, that co-operation in counsel and practical effort, without which no religious body can thrive. It has caused them in many instances to resign altogether to the clergy the practical labours of religion; and thus excluded them from functions which belong to them as members of the household of faith. And yet a pious layman, if he be so minded, may in his sphere do as much for the conservation and extension of the Church, as the most energetic and exemplary of clergymen. And there is an increasing conviction, that the Church needs the aid of its lay members, in some more definite position and practical share in the administration of its affairs, than they have been hitherto called to. Other religious bodies have known how to avail themselves of lay co-operation :— and amongst them the laity exercise an important voice and agency.

In saying this, I am, of course, not unmindful of the services rendered by the laity in an office assigned to them in the constitution of our Church, to which distinct and important duties are attached — I mean the office of Churchwarden. Nor can it be doubted that were this always filled, as happily in these days it often is, by men who appreciate its importance, and heartily and conscientiously discharge its duties, an abundant blessing would rest upon their labours. Were all our wardens men of devout and earnest minds, and as they should be, regular communicants; did they always zealously and intelligently co-operate with the clergy in works of charity, and second their efforts for discountenancing vice and immorality in their respective parishes; it is impossible to over-rate the good which might result, from a firm yet conciliating discharge of their office. And a very solemn responsibility rests with those who appoint to, or who accept it on light or unworthy grounds, and without a due sense of its trusts. To intrude a careless or irreligious man into the clerical office is felt to be an outrage: how is it that the same standard is not applied to one hardly less sacred in its character and duties? To minister about holy things, to be the guardian of God's house, to have the custody of its goods, to keep order during divine service, to seat the parishioners, to assist at the administration of the Lords' Supper, to protect the rights of the poor and the interests of morality, to make presentments at Visitations,—what sacred, and what solemn trusts are these! For one indifferent to religion, or hostile to the Church to undertake them, is nothing less than impiety. And though such cases in these days, we may hope, are comparatively rare, yet they ought to be impossible. And so they would, were the nature of the appointment duly considered, and persons always elected to it for their moral worth and religious fitness, and their approved attachment to the Church.

But besides this, there are numerous points on which the judgment and feelings of the lay members of the Church ought to be consulted, on which they are at present debarred from any legitimate means of expressing these. The character, the usefulness, the continuance of the Church as a national establishment, are imperilled again and again on matters affecting the details of public worship and the ministrations of the clergy, where its lay members have no voice, and are viewed as intermeddlers if they interfere.

From how much that has not only disturbed the peace of parishes, but agitated the public mind, and prejudiced the cause of the Church, would it have been preserved, had our pious and leading laymen possessed some legitimate method of remonstrance!

In saying this, I am not proposing any organic change in the constitution of our Synods. These are essentially a clerical convocation. To introduce the lay element would be to change their character. Even to open up the question, it is thought, might endanger their existence: for no change, it is obvious, could be made without the sanction of the Legislature; and many, at the present time, would object to appeal to this.

But the fusion of the laity with the clergy in

Diocesan, and Archidiaconal, and Ruri-decanal Conferences is an altogether different question. It has been tried with the happiest effects in our Colonial Church, and in some of our Dioceses at home; and its general adoption has been recommended by a committee of Convocation, and has the sanction of some of our most exemplary prelates. No man can deny the great and manifold blessings which might result to the English Church, were the sympathies, counsels, and personal efforts of the laity more enlisted and exercised in its behalf (120).

But if the hope of the Church lies—as it truly does—in its corporate fellowship and action, it is only by the recognition and discharge of individual duty that this can be attained. The question for every one of its members to consider, is suggested in the words of my text; and the answer in every case would be—to do your duty in that state of life in which God's Providence has placed you.

Men dream away life, thinking what they would do, if they were what they are not. A man says, if I were a prelate, if I were a statesman, if I were a great landed proprietor, if I were the head of a college, if I were in this or that position,— if I had this man's intellect, or that man's purse, or that man's gift of speech—if I were anything but just what I am—what a work I would achieve! I would resuscitate the Church, I would reorganise the State, I would reform the Universities, I would regenerate society!— And while he is thus constructing theories, and building castles in the air, his own duties are forgotten.

Neglect of present work, waste of passing moments, want of resolution to face the drudgery and overcome the temptations of daily life,—it is this that renders the existence of so many men barren and unprofitable.

And hence the unavailing regret, when men would give the world to live over again. 'If,' they will say, 'I had practised more self-denial in my youth — if I had studied more when I had time and opportunity — If I had not contracted those debts, and wasted those golden occasions — if I had resolved from the very first to discharge the duties that devolved on me from day to day! Oh! for ten years back again, with the added experience of age!'—Such are their lamentations over the irreparable past.

"Lord, what wilt thou have me to do?" Men not unfrequently ask this question only to exonerate and exculpate themselves. But the true answer of one who knows life, would be in almost every case,—What might you not do? the youngest, the least gifted, the most isolated, the most obscure — whatever your position, or your faculties, or your sex.

May we not learn what might be done, from what is neglected? Ask college authorities,— ask men of practical experience,—ask those who know the needs of the Church, and the needs of the nation, — what our religious, and educational, and social, and political requirements are.

They tell us of the unprofitable lives many of our young men lead, of their frightful waste of time, of their recoil from duty, of their want of manliness to prepare themselves for the duties of future life — that they do not study, do not improve their minds — that they neglect lectures — absent themselves from religious services — take no hearty, honest interest in anything.

Yet these young men are the hope of England,—the owners of its property, the inheritors of its titles, the future occupiers of its most important positions!

The authorities of this place will even tell us of some who mean to be clergymen — or, as they say, to go into the Church — as if they were not in the Church already — and no doubt intending to be pattern men when they have taken orders—who meantime neglect what they will have hereafter to inculcate and press on others—who are not even regular at chapel—who absent themselves from the Lord's table—as though ordination were to operate as a charm, and of itself change the whole tone and habit of life!

In like manner we hear of men with a large stake in the country—the representatives of great families, inheritors of noble names — who from descent, and revenue, and position, ought to take a lead, to guide opinion, to be the foremost promoters of improvement, —and like some — of whom it has been said, that if they had been born in the humblest condition they would have raised themselves to the highest — make what they inherit but a starting-point, and eclipse the fame of their ancestry by their own,—who are personally without either credit or influence. They neglect their estates, their tenants, their dependants. They leave everything in the hands of agents,— whereas such trusts as theirs can be delegated to no man. They waste time, and health, and substance in frivolous and vicious indulgences,—and of all this the report comes back to scandalise the neighbourhoods of which they ought to be the patterns and the boast. They do nothing for education, nothing for Church extension, nothing for the improvement of those for whom they are responsible; and then resent the interference of better men who endeavour to effect what they have neglected.

Need we wonder at the prevalence of ignorance, and discontent, and crime,—at the separation of the classes—at the increasing cry for social and sanitary reforms?—Or need we be surprised if our institutions are undervalued, and should the cause of those who would destroy them make way?

"Can any man amongst us," observes a leading journalist, "say he has no work, when if he goes into the nearest mews, or back lane, he will find multitudes of stray sheep, whom no pastor ever sought out, with whose hearts no man of God ever communed?" (121.)

Contrast districts where humanising and sanctifying influences are withheld, with others where they are in operation. Can we not all tell of clergymen who have reformed parishes, of employers who have elevated the condition of a community, of laymen who have changed the cha racter of a district, of noblemen who have infused life into a county, of ladies who have planted Churches, of bishops who have regenerated dioceses, of statesmen who have saved an empire, of sovereigns who furnish an example to the world? (122) And simply because all these realised God's claim upon themselves—and sought the help of His Holy Spirit to fill the post His providence assigned.

Are not these things for examples? Are they not to show us what might be done? How every waste place might be redeemed, and every rude nature reclaimed. How England might be christianised, and the world evangelised, and humanity redeemed, and God glorified, and earth and heaven break forth into jubilate,—if each one amongst us would put forth his own strength, and do his own work!

Tell not those who have had experience of life, that any one is too humble, too obscure, too meanly gifted, to exercise influence for good or evil on a fellow-creature.

Is not Example contagious? Is it not all-powerful? Has it not wrought many a time with ourselves in what we have done, or what we have foreborne—in exciting us to good, or encouraging us in evil. And may not this teach us how efficacious it must be with others; how every act of a man's life, every word that falls from him, every stroke of his pen provokes imitation,—and may involve the happiness or the misery of a fellow-creature?

Believe me, there is not one of you, my younger

brethren, whose indolence, whose self-indulgence, whose waste of time, whose extravagance, may not spread infection;—not one of you, whose diligence, whose manliness, whose self-control, may not infuse life, and vigour, and principle into a brother's soul. The hopes of the country, the hopes of the Church rest on you. You will colour for good or for evil the future of both. Think how many, whose names are now on every tongue, whose praise is in all the Churches, — to whom nations turn in every emergency, or whom they mourn as prematurely taken away,— were, a few years ago, like yourselves, students at a university (123). It may be for some of you to furnish the example, to guide the councils, to promote the religious welfare, to influence the destiny of the land that gave you birth. You may, every one of you, be the pattern of a neighbourhood, of a parish, of a home. Will you disappoint these hopes, and neglect these trusts, and waste the inestimable boon of life,—till you come to wish that you never had been born? Or will you henceforth give yourselves, in the strength of God's Holy Spirit, to fill the position, and to do the work which He has assigned to you?

And now may I be permitted to direct a special appeal to some present to-day, not often addressed from a university pulpit.[a]

"Tell me," said a lady, to one of her own sex on

---

[a] This Lecture was delivered on the Sunday in Commemoration Week.

her death-bed, "what word of instruction you will leave behind you for the world you are quitting?" —"That my sex has its mission — that there are thousands of women in England, now wasting life in listlessness or frivolity, who might be happy and useful, if they would only be like those of whom we read in Holy Scripture, as servants of the Church, helpers in Christ, labourers in the Lord. If they would humbly and unostentatiously—without in the least stepping out of their own sphere, or neglecting domestic duty—do something to teach the ignorant, to console the afflicted, to relieve the sick, to succour the distressed, to raise the fallen, to help the helpless to help themselves."

It may indeed be asked, has not the name of woman been associated with such ministries in every age, and throughout the world? Where has sickness, or pain, or privation, or calamity been ever found, where she has not relieved it? Do we not owe to her the noblest impulses of life? What would the Gracchi have been without Cornelia? What son amongst us has not mainly owed what is good in him to a mother?

And yet, till of late, services of which other communions have long known how to avail themselves, amongst us have been almost exclusively confined to private life, or to the cottages of the poor. It was not so in apostolic and primitive times,—nor is it now with continental Christianity. Woman had of old her recognised office in the Church. The Deaconess was an accredited order in early times (124). Rome has its Sisters of Charity, as have Protestant Communions in France and Germany. Half a century ago, Southey wrote, "There is work enough for us all—it is of women I am now speaking, who feel in themselves the strength of heroic virtue, and aspire to its rewards, and shrink from no scenes into which its exercise would carry them. Such women you have among you: there are such, and there ever will be such in every generation. Why have you then no Béguines, no Sisters of Charity? Why, in the most needful, the most merciful form that charity can take, have you not yet followed the example of the French and the Netherlanders? No Vincent de Paul has been heard in your pulpits, no Louise le Gras has appeared amongst the daughters of Great Britain. Piety has found its way into your prisons; your hospitals are imploring it in vain;—and oh! what a want is that,—and how different would be the moral effect which these medical schools produce upon the pupils educated there, if this lamentable deficiency were supplied. I know not whether they, or the patients, suffer most from its absence. Many are the lives that might be saved by it, many are the deathbeds to which it would administer a consolation that is now too often wanted, and many are the young hearts which would be preserved by its purifying and ennobling presence, from an infection worse than that which affects the life alone. A school of medicine ought to be a school of humanity:

when it is not so, the profession which of all others ought most to soften the heart, tends sureliest to corrupt and harden it." He adds, " that this blessed spirit of charity might not only reform our hospitals by its presence, but lessen the pressure upon them, by seeking out the sick, and attending them in their own habitations." And he concludes in words which were prophetic, — " the Protestants were formerly reproached for making no exertions to spread the Gospel among heathen nations. That reproach has been done away. Thirty years hence, this other may also be effaced, and England have its Béguines and Sisters of Charity. It is grievously in need of them. There is nothing Romish, nothing superstitious, nothing fanatical, in such associations; nothing but what is righteous and holy, nothing but what properly belongs to that religious service which the Apostle James, the brother of our Lord, has told us is pure and undefiled before God and the Father. They who shall see such societies instituted and flourishing here, may have a better hope that it may please the Almighty to continue his manifold mercies to this island, notwithstanding the errors which endanger, and the offences which cry to heaven " (125).

The answer has since been given from the battle fields of the Crimea, and the slopes of Scutari. Elizabeth Fry had unlocked to her sex the cells of Newgate. Florence Nightingale opened to them our hospitals and our fever-wards; Mrs. Chisholm, the holds of our emigrant ships; Miss Carpenter our reformatories. A woman has found for us the "Missing Link." A woman has given us "Light upon the Line." A woman has taught Christian ladies "Ploughing and Sowing" in the Wolds of Yorkshire. A woman has taught them "what Life is, and what to do with it." Prisons, asylums, penitentiaries, ragged schools, the garrets and cellars of our great cities—all know now the soft step, the gentle hand, the soothing voice of her, who once ministered to our Lord Himself, and succoured His Apostles,—and of whom it has been truly said, that "if religion were everywhere else exploded, it would retain its hold in the heart of woman." In words written long ago by one who ante-dated much of the charitable effort of the present day by both precept and example, "Happy if she can shed a ray of comfort on the bed of sickness, or relieve an erring child of sin, or direct a wanderer to that open door from which no suppliant is ever turned away" (126).

One word, and I bring these Lectures to a close. My subject has necessarily led me to speak chiefly of the Church's active life. It indeed best became me to handle topics with which I am myself familiar.

But am I, therefore, unmindful of the labours of men of more sedentary lives and recondite pursuits —of the services which students and scholars have rendered to Biblical criticism and exegetical theology, Ecclesiastical history and Christian science — of the erudition which has established the text, and explained the meaning of Scripture, exploded error, supplied links to evidence, reconciled the deductions of philosophy with the truths of inspiration,— and thus furnished weapons for others to wield, and bulwarks beneath which tempted souls may find a shelter?

Am I unmindful of what the Church of England owes to those who preside, and those who teach in these ancient seats of learning — the men who train the future scholars, and statesmen, and divines, and gentry of this country, — whose lessons in the pulpit or the lecture-room not only store the minds and stir the hearts of youth in this and kindred institutions,— but of which the sound is gone out into all lands: and their words unto the ends of the world?[a]

Am I unmindful of the work done for God and for His Church by men with no vows of ordination upon them,— whose example and active co-operation afford such help and stimulus to the ministers of religion, — or whose writings are redeeming the literature of our day, and strengthening, and refreshing, and bettering the hearts and souls of thousands?

Every age, and every sphere of life has its proper gift of God. Every one of us may do the work, and advance the cause for which our blessed master gave Himself:—clergymen and laymen, male and female, those of us whose sun is going down, and those on whom a long course of usefulness is opening.

[a] Psalm xix. 4.

May the language of one and all be: "We offer and present unto Thee, O Lord, ourselves, our souls and bodies, to be a reasonable, holy and lively sacrifice unto Thee." Then, whether our path be through sunshine or through shade—whether we share the prizes of this life,—or only lay the foundations on which others shall build, and sow the harvest, which others shall reap,— our labour shall not be in vain in the Lord. And when we all meet again — as we shall never do, till the graves are rent, and the books are opened, and the names are rehearsed, and the crowns are distributed at the last, — it will be seen — that no effort in Christ's cause has been forgotten, nor has any labourer in His vineyard missed his reward.

NOTES

NOTES.

LECTURE I.

NOTE (1), page 3.

SINCE these Lectures were delivered, suitable replies to the work more especially alluded to, have appeared from the pens of writers of reputation and ability. It is to be hoped that the antidote will circulate as widely, and be imbibed as eagerly as the poison.

In confirmation of the opinion expressed by myself at page 3, I transcribe with pleasure the following extract from a distinguished and lamented writer :—" Read a work on the ' Evidences of Christianity,' and it may become highly probable that Christianity, &c. &c., are true. That is an opinion. Feel God: do His will, till the absolute Imperative within you speaks as with a living voice— Thou shalt, and thou shalt not; and then you do not think, you *know* that there is a God. That is a conviction and a belief. Have we never seen how a child, simple, and near to God, cuts asunder a web of sophistry with a single direct question? How, before its steady look and simple argument, some fashionable utterer of a conventional falsehood has been abashed? How a believing Christian scatters the forces of scepticism, as a morning ray, touching the mist on the mountain side, makes it vanish into thin air? And there are few more glorious moments of our humanity than those in which faith does battle against intellectual proof: when, for example, after reading a sceptical book, or hearing a cold-blooded materialist's demonstration, in which God, the soul, and life to come, are proved impossible — up rises the heart in all the giant might of its immortality to do battle with the understanding, and with the simple argument 'I *feel* them, in my best and highest moments, to be true,' annihilates the sophistries of logic.—" Obedience the Organ of Spiritual Knowledge."—*A Sermon by the late Rev. F. W. Robertson.*

Note (2), page 6.

The scandal here alluded to is urged with much force in the address of a Ruri-decanal Board, which appeared some months ago in a leading Church journal. It constitutes, in fact, one of the greatest blots in our present police regulations. In no foreign city are such scenes to be witnessed, as every night disgrace the principal thoroughfares of London. To whatever extent vice may prevail in other countries, it does not there obtrude itself as with us.

Note (3), page 7.

The following testimony, borne by Bishop Selwyn, is extracted from his sermons preached before the University of Cambridge during his recent visit to this country:—" In the course of a long journey in almost every part of England, I seem to have observed in the great majority of the clergy a desire to give up controversial bitterness, and to devote themselves with earnestness to the great work that lies before them. It has pleased God to awaken a zeal among us, which our elder brethren in the ministry speak of with astonishment, when they compare it with the indifference of former times. A great and visible change has taken place in the thirteen years since I left England. It is now a very rare thing to see a careless clergyman, a neglected parish, or a desecrated church. The multiplication of schools may well be made a subject of special thanksgiving to Almighty God. The teaching of our public schools and universities has risen to a far more religious character. Even our cathedral system, the last to feel the impulse of the spirit of the times, has put forth signs of life, while many were predicting its extinction."— *The Work of Christ in the World*, Sermon I. p. 7.

NOTE (4), page 9.

The Declarations of Charles II. for liberty of conscience, were invariably opposed. The non-conformists were as adverse, as the Church, to toleration: they declined accepting it for themselves, when coupled with the condition that the Roman Catholics should share in it. "Toleration," observes the late Dr. Cardwell, "in any extensive application of it, was a thing impossible. The presbyterians were as unwilling to accept it now at the hands of the conformists, as they had resolutely withheld it from others, when they themselves were in a condition to bestow it: and if the Independents came forward in its support, they only created a tempest of bitterness and scorn, by invoking the recollection of that period of confusion, when their principles had prevailed, the only period when it was ever known that toleration had been carried into practice."—*History of Conferences on the Book of Common Prayer*, by E. Cardwell, D.D., p. 268.

NOTE (5), page 10.

The state churchmanship alluded to is well described by Mr. Maurice in the following passage:— " Such was the new tone which the character and patronage of George III., and the dread of French disorganization, rendered popular. One cannot call it a very elevated tone. So long as the war lasted, it was mixed with much that was generous and patriotic in the upper classes of laymen; the portion of the clergy who shared in it became active magistrates, careful of their domestic and relative duties, zealous in defence of that which seemed to them old and English. With these useful dispositions were connected a tendency to maintain customs and practices, simply because they did exist, and could allege some moderate prescription in their favour: an acquiescence in the maxims of society, even when they seemed to be at variance with the higher morality; a great impatience of enthusiasm and mysticism, and all that cannot be at once brought under the rules of existing convention, or obvious expediency; a suspicion of any great efforts of active virtue and self-sacrifice; a feeling that the Church is bound to sympathise with the aristocracy, and to overlook its sins, for the sake of preserving good order among the people; a strong sense of the service which subjects owe to their rulers, without any corresponding sense of the service which rulers owe to their subjects; an inclination to assert the privileges of clergymen, chiefly by treating it as a rudeness that any infidel notions should be broached in their presence; great anxiety for a State encouragement of religion on the ground that otherwise it was not likely to thrive, or to enlist fashion and opinion of the world on its side; a vehement dislike of dissenters, as disturbing the quietness and regularity of society, and as introducing something of vulgarity into religion; a certain anger and restlessness at the discovery of any new doubts respecting the English Church or Christianity, which could not at once be removed by an application of the arguments used on behalf of establishments in Paley's Moral Philosophy, and of the Gospel in his Evidences." — *Maurice's Kingdom of Christ*, vol. ii. p. 498.

Note (6), page 10.

The correspondence alluded to will be found in a work entitled " Lights and Shadows of Church Life in Australia, including Thoughts on some things at Home," by T. Binney. London, 1860.

Note (7), page 11.

That John Wesley had no intention to create a schism is proved by words written by him in 1789, shortly before his death. " I never " says he " had any design of separating from the Church. I have no such design now. I do not believe the Methodists in general design it, when I am no more seen. I do, and will do, all that is in my power to prevent such an event. I declare once more, that I live and die, a member of the Church of England; and that none who regard my judgment or advice will ever separate from it." This passage bears date December 1789, and is signed, John Wesley. A like protestation may be found in the Arminian Magazine 1790. " Two young men sowed the word of God, not only in the Churches, but literally by the highway-side. They were members of the Church of England, and had no design of separating from it, and they advised all that were in it to continue therein, although they joined the Methodist Society; for this did not imply leaving their former congregation, but only leaving their sins. As long as the Methodists keep to this plan, they cannot separate from the Church, and this is our peculiar glory. It is new upon the earth. Revolve all the history of the Church from the earliest ages, and you will find that whenever there was a great work of God in any particular city or nation, the subjects of that work soon said to their neighbours, 'Stand by yourselves, for we are holier than you.' But with the Methodists it is quite otherwise; they are not a sect or party. They do not separate from the religious community to which they at first belonged. They are still members of the Church, such as they desire to live and die. I believe one reason why God is pleased to continue my life so long, is, to confirm them in their present purpose not to separate from the Church." See " the opinions of the Rev. John Wesley with regard to continuing in the Communion of the Church," Netherton, Truro.

These extracts are made from a speech delivered in the Lower House of Convocation of the Province of Canterbury on Saturday, March 2, 1861, and entitled Prayer for Unity, by the Rev. F. C. Massingberd, M.A.; and no one who heard that speech will forget the spirit in which it was delivered, or the impression which it produced. Mr. Massingberd quotes some words contained in a representation drawn up by a considerable number of the members of Convocation, and which show sufficiently the desire for unity entertained by them. "In the earnest hope and trust that all the deliberations of the Synod may tend, under God's blessing, to the removal of mutual misunderstandings, and thereby to the healing of differences and the promotion of peace and charity, and may prepare the way for gathering to the bosom of the Church those who are not now of her communion, they proceed to submit to your Grace and your Lordship, in detail, certain principal points, &c."

NOTE (8), page 16.

See the Life and Correspondence of Thomas Arnold, D.D., by Arthur Penrhyn Stanley, M.A., 3rd edit. p. 222. Dr. Arnold's view of the nature of the Church, which he describes as "a society for the purpose of making men like Christ, — earth like heaven, — the kingdoms of the world the kingdom of Christ," is thus stated in a letter to his friend Dr. Hawkins, Provost of Oriel, dated November, 1830. "In one sense, and that a very important one, all Christians belong to one society; but then it is more like Cicero's sense of 'Societas,' than what we mean by a society. There is a '*societas generis humani*,' and a '*societas hominum Christianorum*;' but there is not one '*respublica*,' or '*civitas*' of either, but a great many."—*Life of Dr. Arnold*, 2nd edit. vol. i. p. 271.

NOTE (9), page 23.

This subject is treated with his usual truthfulness and power by the Rev. F. W. Robertson in a volume of sermons delivered by him at Trinity Chapel, Brighton. See second series, containing amongst other able discourses, sermons with the following titles — "Christ the Son;" "Christ's estimate of sin;" "The sanctification of Christ;" "The Good Shepherd;" "The restoration of the erring."

NOTE (10), page 27.

The effects of Baptism when rightly administered and received is thus described by Dr. Heurtley in his volume of

LECTURE I.   231

Bampton Lectures on Justification, delivered in 1845. "From that moment, he, who before was spoken of as a subject of Satan's kingdom, as dead in trespasses and sins, as having no part or lot in Christ, is regarded as regenerate, and grafted into the body of Christ's Church, as washed from all his guilt and sanctified by the indwelling of God's Spirit, who has now vouchsafed to take up His abode in Him." The following passage from Bede, quoted by Jer. Taylor, " Works," vol. ii. p. 243, is given in a note in the same work:— " The catechumen descends into the font a sinner, he arises purified; he goes down the son of death, he comes up the son of the resurrection; he enters in the son of folly and prevarication, he returns the son of reconciliation ; he stoops down the child of wrath, and ascends the heir of mercy ; he was the child of the devil, and now he is the servant and the son of God."

NOTES.

LECTURE II.

NOTE (10), page 40.

SEE an article on "the Churches of the British Confession," in the October number of the Christian Remembrancer, 1861, in which this subject is discussed with much learning and perspicacity.

NOTE (11), page 43.

The Rev. E. Harold Browne, in his "Exposition of the Thirty-nine Articles, Historical and Doctrinal," supplies the authorities for these statements. See Article 23rd, section 1st, p. 556, &c. &c.

NOTE (12), page 46.

"But, of the many beautiful histories in which Fox abounds, none is more beautiful than that of Rowland Taylor, Rector of Hadley. We will not enter," says Professor Blunt, "into all the details of this thrice-told tale of sorrow;

his pastoral faithfulness — his successful teaching, so that his parish was remarkable for its knowledge of the word of God;—his efforts to introduce to each other rich and poor, by taking with him in his visits to the latter some of the more wealthy cloth makers, that they might become acquainted with their neighbours' wants, and thus be made to minister to their relief; — his bold defiance of the Roman

Catholic priest whom he found in possession of his church, surrounded by armed men, and saying mass; — his reply to John Hull, the old servant who accompanied him to London when he was summoned there before Gardiner, and who fain would have persuaded him to fly; — his frank and fearless carriage before his judges; — his mirth at the ludicrous apprehensions he inspired into Bonner's chaplain, who cautioned the bishop when performing the ceremony of degradation not to strike him on the breast with his crosier staff, seeing that he would sure strike again; — his charge to his little boy, when he supped with him in prison, before his removal to Hadley, not to forsake his mother, when she waxed old, but to see that she lacked nothing, for which God would bless him, and give him long life on earth and prosperity; — his coming forth by night to set out upon his last journey; his wife, daughter, and an orphan foster-child, watching all night in St. Botolph's church-porch, to catch a sight of him as he passed; — their cries when they heard his company approach, it being very dark; his touching farewell to them, and his wife's promise to meet him again at Hadley; — his taking his boy before him on the horse on which he rode, John Hull lifting him up in his arms; — his blessing the child, and delivering him again to John Hull, saying, 'Farewell! John Hull, the faithfulest servant that ever man had;' the pleasantries, partaking, indeed, of the homely simplicity of the times, with which he occasionally beguiled the way; — the joy he expressed on hearing that he was to pass through Hadley, and see at once before he died the flock whom, God knew, he had most heartily loved, and truly taught; — his encounter with the poor man, who waited for him at the foot of the bridge with five small children, crying, 'God help and succour thee! as thou hast many a time succoured me and mine;'— his inquiry, when he came to the last of the alms houses, after the blind man and woman that dwelt there; and his throwing his glove through the window for them, with what money in it he had left; — his calling one Soyce to him out of the crowd on Aldham Common, to pull off his boots and take them for his labour, seeing that 'he had long looked for them;'— these and other incidents of the same story, combine so many touches of tenderness with so much firmness of purpose,— so many domestic charities with so much heroism,— such cheerfulness with such disaster, that if there is any character calculated to call forth all the sympathies of our nature, it is that of Rowland Taylor. God's blessing is still generally seen on the third and fourth generation of them that love Him; and if Rowland could have beheld the illustrious descendant which Providence was preparing for him in Jeremy Taylor, the antagonist of the Church of Rome, able after his own heart's content,— the first and best advocate of toleration, the greatest promoter of practical piety that has ever, perhaps, lived amongst us,— he might humbly have imagined that God had not forgotten this His gracious dispensation in his own case; and had approved his martyrdom, by raising from his ashes a spirit more than worthy of his name."—Blunt on "The Reformation," 20th edition, p. 274.

Note (13), page 47.

See Jer. Taylor, "Dissuasive from Popery," part II. lib. ii. c. 47, lib. iii. 2, 1; Tertull. adv. Hermogenem; Origen, Homil. v., in Levit.; Athan. ex Festali Epistola, xxxix., Tom. ii. p. 39, Edit. Colon.; Basil, Hom. xxix. adv. Calumniantes S. Trin.; Ambros. Offic. lib. i. c. 23; August. De Doctrina Christ. lib. ii. c. 9.

Note (14), page 48.

We are indebted to Queen Elizabeth herself for the authority thus assigned to the Church in Article XX.

Note (15), page 50.

See "England and Rome," or "A Discussion on the

principal Doctrines and Passages of History in common debate between the Members of the two Communions," by W. E. Scudamore, M.A. Rector of Ditchingham, Letter 1. sect. 4; also Harold Browne's "Exposition of the Thirty-nine Articles," Art. vi. p. 178.

Note (16), page 50.

"In the interpretation of the Articles, our best guides must be, first, their own natural, literal, grammatical meaning; next to this, a knowledge of the controversies which had prevailed in the Church and made such Articles necessary; then, the other authorised formularies of the Church; after them, writings and known opinions of such men as Cranmer, Ridley, and Parker, who drew them up; then the doctrines of the primitive Church, which they profess to follow; and lastly, the general sentiments of the distinguished English divines, who have been content to subscribe the Articles, and have professed their agreement with them for now 300 years. These are our best guides for their interpretation. Their authority is derivable from Scripture alone."— Introduction to Harold Browne's "Exposition of the Thirty-nine Articles," p. 10.

Note (17), page 53.

The remarks of the Rev. F. D. Maurice on this subject in his important work entitled "The Kingdom of Christ," and elsewhere in his writings, demand the gravest attention of Churchmen, especially of the clergy.

Our Church, as is well known, requires of its *lay* members no confession of their faith, except that contained in the Apostles' Creed.

Note (18), page 54.

"Church Life in Australia," &c. &c., by T. Binney, Preliminary chapter-- "The two Pictures," p. 27.

NOTE (19), page 55.

I quote with pleasure the following passage from the late S. T. Coleridge on "The Constitution of the Church and State:"—" Amongst the numerous blessings of the English Constitution, the introduction of an Established Church makes an especial claim on the gratitude of scholars and philosophers; in England, at least, where the principles of Protestantism have conspired with the freedom of the government to double all its salutary powers by the removal of its abuses. That the maxims of a pure morality, and the sublime truths of the divine unity and attributes, which a Plato found hard to learn and more difficult to reveal,— should have become the almost hereditary property of childhood and poverty, of the hovel and the workshop; that even to the unlettered, they sound as *common-place;*— this is a phenomenon which must withhold all but minds of the most vulgar cast from undervaluing the services even of the pulpit and the reading desk. Yet he who should confine the efficiency of an Established Church to these, can hardly be placed in a much higher rank of intellect. That to every parish throughout the kingdom there is transplanted a germ of civilization; that in the remotest villages there is a nucleus round which the capabilities of the place may crystallise and brighten; this unobtrusive, continuous agency of a Protestant Church Establishment,—this it is, which the patriot, and the philanthropist, who would fain unite the love of peace with the faith and progressive amelioration of mankind, cannot estimate at too high a price—'it cannot be valued with the gold of Ophir, with the precious onyx, or the sapphire. No mention shall be made of coral or of pearls: for the price of wisdom is above rubies.'— The clergyman is with his parishioners and among them; he is neither in the cloistered cell, nor in the wilderness, but a neighbour and family man, whose education and rank admit him to the mansion of the rich landowner, while his duties make him the frequent visitor of the farmhouse and the

cottage. He is, or he may become, connected with the families of his parish or its vicinity by marriage. And among the instances of the blindness, or at best of the short-sightedness, which it is the nature of cupidity to inflict, I know few more striking than clamours against church property."
—Pp. 79, 80.

NOTE (20), page 60.

The view on this subject maintained by a great living statesman is thus given in the report of a speech delivered by the Right Honourable B. Disraeli at the annual meeting of Oxford Diocesan Societies in 1861. "I should grieve," he says, " to see this great Church of England, the centre of light, and learning, and liberty, sink into a position, relative to the nation, similar to that now filled by the Episcopal Church of Scotland, or possibly even subside into a fastidious, not to say finical, congregation. I hold that the connection between Church and State is one which is to be upheld and vindicated on principles entirely in unison with the spirit of the age, with the circumstances with which we have to deal, and with the soundest principles of political philosophy. The most powerful principle which governs man is the religious principle. It is eternal and indestructible, for it takes its origin in the nature of human intelligence, which will never be content till it penetrates the origin of things and ascertain its relations to the Creator — a knowledge to which all who are here present well know that, unaided and alone, the human intelligence can never attain. A wise Government, then, would seek to include such an element in its means of influencing man; otherwise it would leave in society a principle stronger than itself, which in due season may assert its supremacy, and even, perhaps, in a destructive manner. A wise Government, allying itself with religion, would as it were, consecrate society and sanctify the State.

" But how is this to be done? It is the problem of modern politics which has always most embarrassed statesmen. No solution of the difficulty can be found in salaried priesthoods and in complicated concordats. But by the side of the State of England there has gradually arisen a majestic corporation — wealthy, powerful, independent — with the sanctity of a long tradition, yet sympathising with authority, and full of conciliation, even deference, to the civil power. Broadly and deeply planted in the land, mixed up with all our manners and customs, one of the main guarantees of our local government, and therefore one of the prime securities of our common liberties, the Church of England is part of our history, part of our life, part of England itself.

"It is said sometimes that the Church of England is hostile to religious liberty. As well might it be said that the monarchy of England is adverse to political freedom. Both are institutions which insure liberty by securing order. It is said sometimes that the Church in this country has proved unequal to its mission, and has failed to secure the spiritual culture of the population. It is perfectly true that within the last fifty years there has been a vast and irregular increase of our population, with which the machinery of the Church has been inadequate to cope. But the machinery of the Church in that respect was incomplete only; it was not obsolete. It is said that the Church has lost the great towns; unhappily, the Church has never found the great towns. They are her future, and it will be in the great towns that the greatest triumphs of the Church will be achieved, for the greater the population and the higher the education of the people, the more they will require a refined worship, a learned theology, an independent priesthood, and a sanctuary hallowed by the associations of historic ages.

"Here, then, is a common ground on which, dismissing all unsubstantial and illusory feelings of perplexity, distrust, and discontent, all sections and parties of Churchmen may unite and act together in maintaining the religious settlement of this realm."

NOTES.

LECTURE III.

NOTE (21), page 67.

So stated in the Report of the Registrar General to the Viscount Palmerston, then her Majesty's Secretary of State for the Home Department, intitled " Census of Great Britain, 1851; Religious Worship, England and Wales." Objections have been made to the manner in which this conclusion was arrived at, *vide* " Prayer for Unity," a speech delivered by Rev. F. C. Massingberd. But the habitual neglect of worship by multitudes in this country cannot be disputed. In the Rev. Dr. Hume's evidence before the Lords' Committee on Church Rates, p. 134, he says, "In Southwark there are 68 per cent. who attend no place of worship; in Sheffield there are 62; in Oldham 61½; in Lambeth 60½; in Gateshead 60; in Preston 59; in Brighton 54; Tower Hamlets 53½, Finsbury 53, Salford 52, South Shields 52; Manchester 51½; Bolton 51½; Stoke 51½; Westminster 50; Coventry 50. I have taken 34 of the *great towns* of England, embracing a population of 3,993,467; — and 2,197,388, or 52½ per cent. of the population of those towns *attend no place of worship whatever*. The population is growing very rapidly in our large towns, and religion ought to grow with at least *equal* rapidity, but it is not doing so. In 1851 we had 9,000,000 in towns of 10,000 people and upwards, and only 8,000,000 in smaller towns, in villages, and in rural districts; and at the close of the present century, I believe that 70 per cent. of the gross population will be seated in large towns. Therefore, if our large towns are left to themselves practical heathenism must inevitably soon outgrow Christianity."—*Report.* P. 134.

NOTE (22), page 67.

The united Committee for providing special religious services for the working classes, especially in the Eastern and Southern parts of the metropolis, give as one of these reasons for opening theatres for the purpose, " the deplorable spiritual condition of the working classes in London, as shewn by the estimate that only about two in every hundred of the working men are found to attend any place of worship."—Circular dated Sept. 17, 1859, and signed by Lord Shaftesbury and others.

Again in a sermon preached before the University of Oxford on the feast of Epiphany 1860, by the Rev. R. Gregory, M. A. one of the Incumbents of Lambeth, entitled " What is the Spiritual Condition of our Metropolis?" we read as follows: " What is the spiritual state of the inhabitants of our poor London parishes? They are in a state of practical heathenism; religious observances of every kind are neglected; the form and the spirit have alike fled, there is little avowed unbelief, but nearly universal indifference; it is no question of Church or Dissent, or of religious opinions by which we are assailed (though differences have helped to produce the result over which we mourn), but whether there shall be any religion or none! An immense majority of the people — certainly not less than four out of every five—never enter any place of worship from year's end to year's end; and very few indeed of those who neglect worship, I have reason to know, ever kneel down to say a prayer, or, so far as we can judge, have any real sense of awe of a higher Power. They live like the brutes, a mere animal life; their thoughts are bounded by what has relation to this world; they rarely commit great crimes; they make no profession of unbelief: but the only creed in which they really believe, and by which they act, is, 'Let us eat and drink, for tomorrow we die.' 'The poorer the place, the fewer the people who enter any place of worship.'"

Note (23), page 68.

I quote the following from an able article on "Spiritual Destitution" in the Quarterly Review of April 1861 :—" It is a fact well known to the police, and not to the police only, but to every man who has had an opportunity of observing the state into which the masses are falling, that there never was a time when the temper of the lower orders in this country was less satisfactory than it is now. There are whole streets within easy walk of Charing Cross — there are miles and miles of lanes and alleys on either side of the river below London Bridge — where the people live literally without God in the world; where there seems to be no knowledge of the difference between moral right and moral wrong; no belief whatever in a future state, or of man's responsibility to any other authority than that of the law, if it can catch him. We could name entire quarters in which it seems to be a custom that men and women should live in promiscuous concubinage —where the most frightful debauchery goes on night and day in the lowest public houses — where the very shopkeepers make a profession of atheism, and encourage their poor customers to do the same. Nor are other, and, to the mere politician, more alarming signs of the times wanting. Socialism, in one form or another, is making prodigious progress among our work people generally. It has its teachers, who know exactly how to adapt their language to the feelings and capacities of those to whom they are sent; and they are indefatigable in their endeavours to make converts. To the rude, the old doctrine of indiscriminate confiscation is preached; to the more thoughtful, a different view of the case is presented. In private rooms, in the dwellings of journeymen and mechanics, small social meetings take place, which attract no attention from without, but within which dangerous and enticing themes are continually broached and enlarged upon. . . . Of this we are quite sure, that no merely fiscal arrangements, however excellent in themselves, will touch the root of an evil so insidious and so full of peril to society. They may suffice to keep the surface of things smooth till times of trouble come; but woe to the nation which in time of trouble has not been taught to look higher than to the decrees of earthly sovereigns or the enactments of earthly legislatures."

Note (24), page 69.

Numerous instances confirmatory of the above remark will at once occur to the reader's mind:—and these unhappily not confined to the trading and commercial classes, but compromising persons whose position in society used to be regarded as a guarantee for honour and integrity. Never perhaps has the *auri sacra fames* more predominated than in the present generation; while the dishonest speculations and disgraceful bankruptcies which have tarnished so many hitherto unblemished reputations, and spread ruin far and wide, are a terrible confirmation of the Scripture, "The love of money is the root of all evil."

Note (25), page 69.

"Now I think it is undeniable that the signs of an awakened feeling to the importance of religion, and to its paramount claims to attention, prevail extensively among all ranks of our fellow countrymen, and especially among the intelligent orders of society in the middle and higher classes. Many unchristian usages have gone into desuetude; many habits, at which our forefathers would not have blushed, have been laid aside; decencies are more respected, inconsistencies are less tolerated; many are less ashamed to declare themselves on the Lord's side and to confess Christ openly."— A Charge delivered to the candidates for Holy Orders at an

LECTURE III. 243

ordination at Farnham Castle on December 17th, 1859, by Charles Richard Bishop of Winchester.

NOTE (26), page 70.

See "Liturgical Purity our rightful Inheritance," by John C. Fisher, M.A. of the Middle Temple, p. 496; a work of much research and ability, and of equal candour,—and of which it is justly observed by one who, it may be presumed, in the main agrees with its writer, that, "when a man has made himself master of it, he will probably find out what revision means."

NOTE (27), page 70.

In the work quoted above, p. 437, the words are, "a recognised and established institution." See also, "The Liturgy and Dissenters," by the Rev. Isaac Taylor, written in a fair and earnest spirit. Mr. Taylor, however, takes his statistics from the attendance at public worship on the Census Sunday, March 30, 1851, which is generally admitted to have afforded a very fallacious test.

"It cannot," observes the Archdeacon of London in his recent Charge, 1861,—"it cannot be too much known and considered, that if all the non-conformist worshippers, *including* Roman Catholics and Jews, but *excluding* Methodists, were united together, they would be but a small portion of the people, not more than one-fifth the population of England and Wales. I found this statement on the calculations made by Dr. Hume of Liverpool, which were grounded upon the data furnished by the official Report upon the Census of 1851, and laid before the House of Lords' Committee in the last year. I have very recently made inquiry of him, whether he has had any reason to doubt the accuracy of his calculations, and find that, having been in controversy with various opponents, he has maintained his ground."

Mr. Taylor expresses a hope that the religious census of 1861 would give a domiciliary, as well as a congregational return;— but this was objected to by the dissenting bodies in this country. " The Dissenters," says Mr. Taylor (p. 6.), "are already dangerously numerous and powerful. They are conscious of their strength, and are prepared to use it."

NOTE (28), page 71.

In " The Nonconformist's Text-book," by Mr. Miall, from which the following passages are extracts, we have an index to the animus of political Dissent. " The Clergy are men who of necessity, are inimical to all reform, abettors of every abuse; united, organised, and therefore formidable opponents of every progressive improvement." (p. 72.) " They have been invariably the deadliest foes of liberty civil and religious." (p. 74). " The education of the people owes nothing to them. The point-blank unscriptural, or rather anti-scriptural, character of this national Church is no less a marked characteristic of it, than its pitiful vacancy of all significance. As nothing more stupidly unmeaning can be conceived, so nothing more flatly contradictory of Christianity can be devised. One is amazed at the blindness of men who could ever have mistaken *this thing* for a Christian Church." (p. 246.)

But for a full exposition of the dangers with which our Church is threatened, and of the plans for its overthrow which have been deliberately formed, and are openly avowed, the reader is referred to an address delivered to the clergy of the archdeaconry of London, at the annual visitation, May 23, 1861, by W. H. Hale, M.A. Archdeacon of London. It is entitled " Designs and Constitution of the Society for the Liberation of Religion from State Patronage and Control."

In this able and vigorous address, written under the deepest sense of dangers, political and religious, with which the State, as well as the Church, appears to be threatened, the Archdeacon states, " that he has tried to express his opinion in terms, as free from offence as they can possibly be, when truths are to be spoken and facts mentioned in opposition to other men's sentiments or interests."

As indicative of the sentiments thus alluded to, take a passage quoted by the Archdeacon from the Report of the Conference of the Liberation Society. "After all, the Church of England is a political structure, an ecclesiastical corporation based upon Acts of Parliament; and it will be through the medium of the legislature that it will be overthrown. The benumbing, deluding, destructive influence it exerts on society, in its arrogant pretensions as the representative of the Christian religion, may be more or less counteracted by the exertions and influence of voluntary Christian societies. But for these, the Establishment would long before this have been developed in all its terrible proportions, and indeed, the whole nation would at this hour have been prostrate at the feet of a ruthless and besotted superstition, as in the case of the kingdoms of western Europe, and in the powers cursed by the domination of the Greek Church."

NOTE (29), page 76.

See "Report from the Select Committee of the House of Lords appointed to inquire into the deficiency of means of spiritual instruction and places of divine worship in the metropolis, and other populous districts of England and Wales, &c. &c. July 1858."—"Before quitting the metropolis generally, it is right to state, that according to a return of the Bishop of London's secretary, the churches in that diocese having a population of more than 5000, are 163, being one Church, on the average, for 11,000 of the whole population, 1,768,656; the number of clergymen is 373, one, on the average, to 4800. Bearing in mind that 2,000 are as many as can be tolerably well visited by a single clergyman, it appears that the number ought to be at least 900; that there is, therefore, a want of not fewer than 527 more parochial clergymen in that portion of the metropolis which is within the diocese of London. But adding to it those portions which are in the counties of Surrey and Kent, the deficiency can hardly be estimated at less than 600." (p. vii.)

Note (30), page 77.

Since the spiritual destitution existing at Bradford was brought prominently before the notice of the public, in the evidence given before the Committee of the House of Lords, noble and truly Christian efforts have been made to redress the frightful state of things then existing. From information kindly supplied by the esteemed Vicar of Bradford, the Rev. Dr. Burnett, it appears that a society has been formed for the erection and endowment of ten new churches, of which three have been already consecrated, a fourth is almost ready for consecration, and the fifth and sixth have been begun. One of these churches is erected at the sole expense of Francis Sharp Powell, Esq., of Horton Hall, at a cost of 10,000*l*.

Note (31), page 80.

See the luminous and important evidence of Dr. Hume, of Liverpool, as given before a Select Committee of the House of Lords, appointed to inquire into the question of Church rates, in 1860.

Note (32), page 82.

See a sermon preached at the annual meeting of the Church Extension Society for the archdeaconry of Coventry, by Walter Farquhar Hook, D.D., then Vicar of Leeds, 1857, from which the following is an extract.

"It is a misfortune, but a fact, that the best educated of our clergy are not to be found where they are most required; and consequently while the upper classes in our rural districts are almost universally churchmen, we find in our towns the influential opponents of the Gospel, those who deny the fundamental truths which relate to the divinity, the incarnation, and the atonement of our blessed Lord and Saviour Jesus Christ, the scheme of salvation and the doctrines of grace. The cause of the evil is obvious. From a variety of circumstances,— our town livings, with few exceptions, are the worst endowed livings in the Church. The more highly educated of our clergy, therefore, remain at the universities until they retire to country parishes, where their work might be as effectually done by men of inferior mental ability and power. And this being the evil complained of, instead of applying a remedy, we are actually increasing it by the formation of our Peel districts. By the formation of Peel districts we are creating an additional number of pauper benefices, and by so doing we are retarding the extension of the Church among the upper, the middle, and the more influential classes of society. We are sending forth into our towns a class of clergy not sufficiently educated to meet the exigencies of the times.

" What the real remedy should be, this is not the place to determine: but in addressing a Society for Church Extension, it may be permitted even here to remark that *the evil would be met, if every Peel district were regarded as a missionary station and a temporary appointment.*"

See also a letter from W. F. Hook, D.D., to the Right Rev. the Lord Bishop of Ripon, printed in the appendix to "Minutes of Evidence given before the Select Committee of the House of Lords," already referred to (p. 592), on which it is observed in the Report, " This leads to the consideration of the great importance of providing generally, so far as may be practicable, for the better endowment of livings in large towns, in order that there may be a greater inducement to clergymen of ability and experience to accept the charge of populations so circumstanced."

NOTE (33), page 84.

I refer particularly to the disgraceful scenes recently enacted at St. George's in the East, London, about which there can be but one opinion entertained by unprejudiced and Christian men. It was well observed by a venerable and distinguished member of the House of Lords, Lord Brougham, when the subject was referred to in Parliament, " That however persons might differ about the questions in dispute, such outrages should have been at once put down by the strong hand of the law."

NOTE (34), page 84.

See a sermon entitled "the Church's duties and the Church's opportunities," preached in the nave of Wells Cathedral on Thursday, October 4, 1860, at the annual meeting of the Diocesan Societies, by Charles John Vaughan, D.D., vicar of Doncaster, &c.

NOTES.

LECTURE IV.

NOTE (35), page 86.

It is impossible rightly to estimate in our own day the service rendered to the cause of Christianity in this country by the "Inquiry into the deficiency of means of spiritual instruction and places of divine worship," called for by the Bishop of Exeter, and the valuable Report in which it resulted. To the indomitable perseverance and profound sagacity exhibited by the venerable Prelate who acted as chairman of the committee by which the inquiry was conducted, our present meed of admiration may indeed be rendered. But the value of such an effort in the cause of God can be fully appreciated only by those who in future generations shall reap the fruits thereof.

NOTE (36), page 90.

Evidence of the Rev. John E. Kemp, Rector of St. James's, London, as given in Minutes of Evidence taken before Select Committee, p. 258, a. 393.

NOTE (37), page 90.

See Evidence of the Rev. W. Ackworth: Minutes, 104—113. This case is especially alluded to in the Report, p. xv., and is commented upon with great force by the Rev. Edward Hawkins D.D., Provost of Oriel College, in a striking and exhaustive sermon on the subject of "Spiritual Destitution at Home," preached before the University of Oxford, on Sexagesima Sunday, 1860. See note p. 31, from which I venture to extract the following passage. "Unhappily, even the Government, when it is itself a proprietor and an employer, sometimes sets a most unworthy example. I find, indeed, instances to the contrary at p. 230, where the Government proposed, and the House of Commons voted, 10,000*l*. to the London Diocesan Building Society, on the part of the Woods and Forests, as they are very large landed proprietors in London; and in p. 112 we have an account of a grant of 8000*l*. for the erection of a Church in Woolwich Dockyard. But consider such a case as that of Plumstead, 'which contains the Woolwich Arsenal,' where about 12,000 souls have been added by the Government Works in eight years to an old parish with a church holding 350, and that a mile and a half distant from the bulk of the population. One incumbent, endeavouring to meet the urgent demand for a new church, offered 1500*l*. himself, and raised 250*l*. in the parish; but this being all he could effect, he returned the money and retired from the parish. To his successor the Government promised a grant of 100*l*., when he himself offered 1000*l*. and the sacrifice of two years' income. It also granted 1000*l*. for the erection of schools; and these being opened for divine worship on Sundays afforded some, but very inadequate, relief. Application was therefore made to the Government, 'the claims of the parish having been strongly urged, both at the War Office and in Parliament,' and a grant of 1500*l*. was made on condition that the vicar also raised 1500*l*., which he only effected by contributing himself a third of the amount; and when a further sum of 500*l*. was found absolutely requisite for the work, he sought in vain to obtain it from the Government which had 'created the population,' and whose officers had represented that, 'to do what was recommended, not to say anything of moral considerations, would be a matter of extreme economy.' Doubtless it would have been so; but there were higher considerations which should have prevailed. The case may well be described 'as scandalous to a Christian nation;' whilst the people 'came and laboured like beasts of burden, no man caring for their souls; and so died, not knowing whither they went.'—Report, pp. xv. xvi., Evidence, pp. 104 — 113. Such was the history of this sad case in 1858. In 1860 it runs thus: — 'By continuous importunity the additional grant of 500*l.* has been obtained. The Church has been built; it is not yet paid for, though the incumbent has drawn very largely upon his private means; and he is solely responsible for the debt. Even now, in consequence of the larger extension of the Government Works, he fears that his parishioners have less accommodation for public worship than when he first appealed to the War Office; yet he cannot command the time and labour which would be consumed by a second appeal.'—What right have we, under such circumstances, to expect a blessing upon our public works?"

Note (38), page 91.

So stated in a Pastoral Letter addressed by the present Bishop of London to the laity of his diocese in 1860. See leading article in *Times* newspaper, April 16th, 1860.

Note (39), page 93.

" Teeming populations often now surround half-empty churches." " The grand requirement of the case is a multiplication of the various *agents*, by whose zeal religion is disseminated, not *chiefly* an additional provision of *religious edifices.*"—Census Report, p. 161.

Note (40), page 98.

The following are the regulations respecting grants out of the Common Fund issued by the Ecclesiastical Commissioners for England, May 1861. " The Ecclesiastical Commissioners for England are prepared to receive applications for grants, out of the Common Fund under their control, towards making better provision for the cure of souls. These grants will be made only on condition that they be met by benefactions from other sources. A benefaction from trustees, or from any diocesan or other society or body of contributors, as well as from any individual, whether such benefaction consist of money, land, house, site for a house, tithe, or rent charge, any or all, may be met by a grant from the Commissioners; but neither a grant from Queen Anne's Bounty, nor a charge upon the revenues of any ecclesiastical corporation, aggregate or sole, ' *except as undermentioned*,' nor any endowment, bequest, gift, or benefaction already secured to a benefice or church, can be met by a grant from the Commissioners. The grant will not in any case exceed the amount of the benefaction, and as a general rule it will not exceed 1000*l*. Grants will be made to *existing* benefices. Districts *proposed*, but not *actually assigned* by Order in Council, will not be eligible to receive grants except in cases where the amount of benefaction offered would, with the Commisioners' grant, be sufficient to provide 150*l*. per annum. In selecting cases, priority will be given to those which, having regard to income, either taken by itself, or combined with population and area, or either of them, shall appear to be the most necessitous. A benefice held contrary to the provisions of the Plurality Act as applicable to new incumbents will not be considered eligible for a grant, except in the case where the object is the immediate provision of a parsonage house. A benefice which has received a grant is not disqualified, on the offer of a further benefaction, from receiving a further grant in any subsequent year. The grant and benefaction may at any time, with the consent of the Commissioners and the Bishop of the Diocese, be laid out in the purchase of land, or tithe rent charge within the parish or district, or in the purchase or erection of a parsonage house. Applications must reach the Commissioners' office before the 1st of December in each year in order to obtain a grant in the following spring; and in the event of a grant being made to a benefice, the be-

LECTURE IV. 253

nefaction, if in money, must be paid to the Commissioners on or before the 1st of June, or the grant will be rescinded. The Commissioners reserve to themselves the power of altering these regulations from year to year as they may deem expedient. All communications to be addressed to the Secretary, Ecclesiastical Commission, 11, Whitchall Place, London, S.W."

NOTE (41), page 98.

The principle on which the Salop in Lichfield Poor Benefice Fund is conducted is thus stated in an appeal published in 1860.

"Our Diocesan Church Extension Society, so long as funds shall be supplied to it, will meet 400*l.* raised in augmentation of an endowment below 200*l.* a year, with 200*l.*

"In 1860 the Ecclesiastical Commissioners met 100*l.* raised for Albrighton next Shrewsbury, with 100*l.* 500*l.* for Grinshill with 500*l.* 600*l.* for Preston Gobalds with 600*l.* 900*l.* for Bayston Hill with 900*l.* 1500*l.* for Ash with 1000*l.* (maximum grant).

"In the Archdeaconry of Salop there are fifty-three benefices below 200*l.* per annum.

"It is proposed to raise 800*l.* per annum, for aiding four of these benefices each year with 200*l.*, to be met with 200*l.* from local resources. The resulting 400*l.*, when increased to 600*l.* by our Diocesan Church Extension Society, to be offered to the Ecclesiastical Commissioners for a grant, thus securing probably 1000*l.* or 1200*l.* for investment for the permanent increase of the endowment of such poor benefices."

NOTE (42), page 100.

In an age so distinguished for Christian liberality it may seem invidious to select names for notice; but those of Miss Burdett Coutts, and the Misses Monck,—of Archdeacon Bentinck, of the late William Egerton, Esq. of Tatton Park, of the Messrs. Whitehead at Rochdale, of Mr. Arkroyd, of Baroness Windsor, Mr. Hubbard, Lord Derby, and the Duke of Northumberland will occur to every mind. The last mentioned nobleman, who is lay rector of the parish of Tynemouth, having offered to give a sum of 15,000*l.* provided the Ecclesiastical Commissioners would contribute a like sum, towards the establishment of district churches in that parish—which proposal, owing to circumstances, the Commissioners did not think themselves able to accept—has now contributed the munificent sum of 30,000*l.* for the purposes of endowment only ; and it is expected that the Commissioners will build the new churches and parsonage houses. The whole expense of carrying out this important scheme will be further defrayed by the noble duke.

There are of course numerous other instances of similar, if not equal, liberality, of which the amount will never be known, but of which an account is kept before God.

NOTE (43), page 102.

See "The Offertory, the most excellent way of contributing money for Christian purposes," by J. H. Markland, D.C.L.; "The Use of the Offertory," by the Rev. Richard Seymour, M.A.; also "The Offertory," in a volume entitled "Parochialia," p. 311. "Such an act of general oblation," observes Bishop Blomfield in his Pastoral Letter, 1843, "is calculated to remind every separate congregation, and every individual worshipper, that they are all members of one spiritual body, of which Jesus Christ is the Head." "The practice of giving will create habits of bounty," observes Archbishop Howley. Our bishops, it is believed, are now unanimous in favour of such a method of collecting alms.

The Bishop of Lincoln, in his last Charge, 1861, urged it "as a wholesome, a liturgical, and a scriptural method of almsgiving, in which rich and poor are encouraged to unite in the fulfilment of a plain duty." He further suggests that "in all cases where the Holy Communion is administered, the alms of the whole congregation might be collected, as there seems no reason why those who deny themselves the privilege of communicating, should be deprived also of that of giving alms."

In a former parish of my own in which this practice was observed, the alms thus collected increased from 20*l*. a year to an annual amount of 156*l*.

NOTE (44), page 103.

The following extract is given from a tract on "Church Extension," by an able and exemplary incumbent of my Archdeaconry. "If the real 'tenths' of the Ecclesiastical nett incomes were now paid, and 'first-fruits' left out entirely, the actual product would be not less than 300,000*l*., per annum. In lieu of this, a new and fair assessment of the nett income, and a rate graduating upwards upon all livings above 200*l*. yearly, beginning with sixpence in the pound, would, without hurting any one, raise a nett yearly sum of 120,000*l*. and provide for the endowment of 70 or 80 churches yearly, at 1500*l*. average each. What but such an honest and Christian, and, let it be added, really conservative effort as this, is required to call forth the hearty co-operation of the laity of every rank from the peer to the labourer? It would be a glorious day for the Church of England, and for the cause of Christianity itself, when some such measure should be cheerfully embraced by the patrons and beneficed clergy of the Established Church. It would open a door of hope to crowded and increasing places, and would make many a heart to leap for joy."

NOTE (45), page 106.

"Your episcopate remains at this moment, in point of numbers, exactly where it was at the time of the Reformation,—notwithstanding your clergy have immensely increased; notwithstanding your population is actually quadrupled; and notwithstanding the duties discharged by the bishops, both in Parliament and in their dioceses, have been doubled and trebled in amount." (Speech of the Right Honourable the

Secretary of State for the Home Department, as reported in the *Times* newspaper of June 10, 1852.)

" The people of *America* have seen their episcopate increased from *one* bishop to *thirty-two* in less than *eighty* years; but the people of *England* have had no augumentation of their episcopate, except by the addition of a single bishop, for the last *three centuries.* Why should England be precluded from that benefit which America so freely enjoys?"—Letter to Viscount Dungannon, entitled, "Proposed Subdivision of Dioceses," by Chr. Wordsworth, D.D., Canon of Westminster.

NOTE (46), page 107.

His Lordship adds in this communication, dated Riseholme, January 10, 1854—"The remedy, as to this diocese, is obvious; to erect Nottinghamshire into a separate diocese, with its see at Southwell. To this should probably be added the Isle of Axholme. I have no means of judging whether the endowment of such a see could be provided by the improved management of the estates of the Chapters of Lincoln and Southwell; but, if not, I have little doubt that it could out of the episcopal estates of Lincoln. Nor is it unreasonable to believe, judging from the analogy of the Colonial bishoprics, —only too closely applicable to the manufacturing districts of Nottinghamshire,—that as much, at least, would be effected for church extension by the presence and concentrated influence of a Bishop, as could be done if the sum appropriated to the endowment of the see were expended in the endowment and augmentation of livings. These remarks will apply, *mutatis mutandis,* to several other dioceses in England."

NOTE (47), page 108.

See the letter already referred to "On the proposed Subdivision of Dioceses," by Dr. Wordsworth.

NOTE (48), page 109.

The objection of the Nonconformists was to Prelacy, not

to Episcopacy. They state, at the Savoy Conference, "that they have no objection to a balanced episcopacy, but complain, 1. of the extent of dioceses, which rendered a personal superintendence impossible: 2. of Bishops deputing their authority to officials who were sometimes laymen: 3. of their occasionally assuming the sole power of ordination, and exercising arbitrary power in articles of visitation." In his Declaration the King professes that " he will endeavour to appoint good Bishops who shall be preachers, and that where the dioceses are large, they shall be assisted by suffragans." Vide " A Sketch of the History of the Church of England, to the Revolution in 1688," by the present Bishop of St. Asaph. Pp. 485, 486.

NOTE (49), page 109.

See the first Report of the Cathedral Commissioners, p. xvi.; also third and final report of the Cathedral Commissioners, p. xxv. 1855.

Recommendation of the Cathedral Commissioners. *Third Report*, p. xxvi.:—

" 1. We recommend, that a permissive Bill should be framed and introduced into Parliament (similar to the Act 31 Henry VIII. c. 9), empowering your Majesty, and your Majesty's successors, to divide any diocese, under certain conditions of territory and population, and with the consent of the bishop where it is proposed to effect the division, before the avoidance of the see.

" That in no case should a new see be erected, unless a sufficient income with a suitable residence be provided."

Third Report, p. xxvii.: —

" We recommend that a general statute be framed enabling your Majesty, after due inquiry by a Commission specially appointed for that purpose, to recommend a person to be elected coadjutor, *cum jure secessionis*, to a bishop, in case of such bishop requiring such aid and relief by reason of advanced age or protracted infirmity, and being ready to

s

surrender a portion of his episcopal income in favour of such coadjutor."

NOTE (50), p. 109.

I subjoin copies of the Declaration and Memorial referred to.

I. *Declaration as to an Increase of the Episcopate in England and Wales.*

"We, the undersigned clergy of the United Church of England and Ireland, thankfully acknowledge the increase of zeal and activity which has of late been shown in the Church of England, but deplore that her energies are greatly hindered by the want of an Episcopate at all adequate to the present spiritual needs of the people.

"Whereas the population of England and Wales has increased during the last three hundred years from about four millions to nearly twenty millions, and whereas the present number of the Clergy is about eighteen thousand, and it is calculated that they are increasing at the rate of three hundred a year, while the number of Bishops has remained the same, with the addition of *one* only.

"We believe that opportunities of more frequent personal intercourse between a Bishop and the Clergy and Laity of his diocese, and the more frequent administration of the holy rite of Confirmation, would tend to infuse new life and vigour into the Church, and to promote unity, consistency, and efficiency in the labours of those who are working for the salvation of souls. And, judging as well from the experience of former ages as from the happy results which have attended the extension of the Episcopate in the British Colonies, we confidently anticipate similar advantages from the extension of the Episcopate at home.

"We desire, therefore, hereby to express our earnest hope that measures may speedily be adopted for the adequate extension of the Episcopate in England and Wales."

II. *Memorial on the Increase of the Episcopate.*—*To the Right Honourable Viscount Palmerston, K. G., M. P., First Lord of the Treasury, &c. &c., the Memorial of the undersigned Lay Members of the Church of England sheweth,*—

" That in the opinion of your Memorialists an increase of the Episcopate in England and Wales is much to be desired.

" The population of England and Wales has more than doubled itself during the last fifty years; but the number of Bishops has been only increased by one since the middle of the sixteenth century.

" In America and the British Colonies, the Episcopate may be increased according to the needs of the population; and it seems to be reasonable and just, that a similar benefit should be enjoyed by Her Majesty's subjects at home.

" Your Memorialists are of opinion, that more frequent personal intercourse than is now practicable between a Bishop and the Clergy and Laity of his Diocese, would promote unity and efficiency in the labours of those who are endeavouring to advance the moral and spiritual welfare of the people.

" The more frequent administration of Confirmation would stimulate the energies of the Parochial Clergy in imparting religious instruction to the young, in those practical duties which would render them loyal subjects and patriotic citizens, as well as good Christians.

" Facilities have been already afforded by recent enactments for the sub-division of parishes; and the application of a similar principle to Dioceses seems to follow as a natural consequence from those legislative provisions.

" In the year 1847 Her Majesty issued a Commission for inquiring into the state of the several Bishoprics in England and Wales, and was graciously pleased to declare therein an ' intention, that a measure should be submitted to Parliament for continuing the Bishoprics of St. Asaph and Bangor as separate Sees, and establishing forthwith a Bishopric at

Manchester; and also, as soon as conveniently might be, *three other additional Bishoprics.*'

" The former part of Her Majesty's gracious intention, concerning the Bishoprics of St. Asaph and Bangor, and a See at Manchester, has been fulfilled; the latter part, which relates to the foundation of three other additional Sees, has not yet been carried into effect.

" It has been found by experience both at home and in the colonies, that, wherever a new Episcopal See has been established, the number of the Parochial Clergy has been much increased, and the efficiency of the Parochial system proportionally augmented, and pious and charitable institutions have been greatly multiplied. Upwards of half a million sterling has been raised by voluntary contributions in the Diocese of Ripon, and expended there in the erection and endowment of Churches, Parsonages, and Schools, within sixteen years from the foundation of that See. The creation of an Episcopal See at Manchester in 1847 has led to similar results.

" Your Memorialists do not contemplate any increase of the number of Bishops in Parliament; and they are of opinion, that an income of 3000*l.* per annum would suffice for the endowment of any new Episcopal See, as long as the Bishop of that See was not called to the discharge of Parliamentary duties; and that, on his succession in course of time to a seat in the House of Peers, an addition of 500*l.* per annum should be made to the Episcopal income.

" Your Memorialists would suggest, that, before any new See were founded, a considerable portion of the requisite endowment should be provided by means of local and other voluntary contributions, which would, if they were forthcoming, constitute a reasonable indication of the desire existing for the erection of the new See. It would, however, appear to your Memorialists, that, where an existing Diocese is capable of division, a part of the endowment belonging to such See may equitably be apportioned for the purposes of the new See.

" Certain Dioceses may be mentioned, which seem specially

to need subdivision, and in which there are resources already available for the foundation of additional Sees.

"The Diocese of London contains more than two millions of souls; that Diocese might be divided, and another See might be formed by converting the Collegiate Church of Westminster into a Cathedral Church, as it formerly was, and by raising the Dean to the dignity of a Bishop.

"Another Diocese which requires sub-division is that of Exeter. It is the most extensive of any in England and Wales; and the Cathedral City of Exeter is distant about 145 miles from the western extremity of the Diocese. The necessary funds for the endowment of a new See might be partly derived from the Episcopal and Capitular Revenues of that Diocese, which will soon be greatly improved in value. The present Bishop of that Diocese has frequently expressed his desire for its sub-division, and has intimated his willingness to resign to a Bishop of Cornwall the Episcopal preferment within that county.

"Another similar instance may be found in the Diocese of Durham. Its population has increased with unexampled rapidity in the last few years. The income of the Bishop is 8000*l*. per annum, which greatly exceeds the average income of other Episcopal Sees; means might thence be derived for the sub-division of that populous Diocese, and for the erection and endowment of an Episcopal See in the town of Newcastle-upon-Tyne; and other favourable local circumstances might be mentioned which would facilitate this result.

"A desire has been manifested in the county of Hertford for the transformation of the ancient abbey of St. Albans into a cathedral church; and it is very desirable, that the Bishop of Rochester should be more nearly connected than at present with his cathedral city; and that the clergy of the Kentish portion of the diocese should have easier access to their bishop than is now the case.

"The Diocese of Lincoln, with its vast area and large number of clergy, is another diocese which, as has been attested by its present bishop, needs subdivision; and a cathedral for a new diocese, to be taken out of that of Lincoln, would be found already prepared in the collegiate church of Southwell.

"Wishes have also been expressed for the restoration of the city of Bristol as an independent episcopal see; and the existence of a cathedral with a dean and chapter in that city would promote the fulfilment of such a design.

"We are also assured, that in the archdeaconry of Coventry, which was annexed to the see of Worcester in 1836, and contains a population amounting to four-sixths of the diocese, there is a strong and general desire for the erection of a separate see on the next avoidance.

"For this there is a prescriptive claim. Coventry was an episcopal see for seven hundred years; and one of the stately churches might suitably serve as a cathedral: and it is believed, that the funds required for endowment, in addition to what could be spared from the see of Worcester, would not be wanting.

"Other dioceses might be mentioned which need subdivision. We consider, however, that the inhabitants of those dioceses are the parties most competent to express an opinion on this subject; and that, if they are desirous of such a subdivision, local contributions would not be wanting, when once the necessary powers may have been given by parliament for the erection of additional sees.

"With this view Her Majesty's Commissioners for Inquiring into the State of Cathedral and Collegiate Churches recommended in the year 1855, 'That a permissive bill should be framed and introduced into parliament (similar to the Act 31 Hen. VIII. cap. 9), empowering Her Majesty and Her Majesty's successors to divide any diocese, under certain conditions of territory and population, and with the consent of the bishop where it is proposed to effect the division, before the avoidance of the see.'

"This recommendation of Her Majesty's Commissioners, among whom were the two Archbishops and the late Bishop of London, and the present Bishops of Durham and Oxford, appear to your memorialists to deserve attentive consideration; and since, as they understand, your lordship on a recent occasion expressed an opinion, in which they entirely concur, that any question of episcopal extension ought to be considered with reference to the country at large, they would earnestly entreat your lordship either to introduce into Parliament or to support such a legislative measure as may enable Her Majesty's subjects, who desire an extension of the episcopate, to profit by such an exercise of the royal supremacy in constituting additional sees at home, as has already been called into action, and is now in operation with very beneficial results, secular and spiritual, in the colonial dependencies of the British crown."

To this memorial were attached the names of many leading members of both Houses of Legislature, and of other influential laymen. It was also signed by all the churchwardens of all the parishes of the city of Coventry, and by nearly all the magistrates, by the Mayors of Newcastle-upon-Tyne, of Tynemouth, of Grantham, &c. &c.

III. *Representation of the Lower House addressed to the Upper House of the Convocation of Canterbury, February* 11*th,* 1859.

" We would respectfully suggest that the large extent of some of our Dioceses, both in population and area, precluding the possibility of sufficient personal intercourse between the Bishop and the Clergy and Laity of his Diocese, together with the want of more concentrated action, furnishes strong reasons for some *Increase of the Episcopate,* which might be obtained without any interference with the number of Episcopal seats in the House of Lords, were the precedent followed which has been already established at the erection of the See of Manchester. By this means each bishop would have fuller opportunities of making himself well acquainted with his diocese, before he would be called to succeed to his legislative duties. We would suggest the expediency of a general enabling Act (similar to the 31st Henry VIII. c. 9.)

to which resort might be had as often as circumstances require, or opportunity offers, for the erection of new Sees. We would further suggest that arrangements should be made for the case of any Bishop who might become wholly, or feel himself partially incapacitated for the effective discharge of his duties; in the one case by some well-considered provision for a retiring Bishop—in the other case by adopting the recommendation of the Cathedral Commissioners with regard to Coadjutor-Bishops. Such an office has existed from the earliest ages; it was strongly recommended by the authors of the 'Reformatio Legum;' it still exists in many parts of Christendom; and has recently been revived in our own Colonial Church, in the case of the Bishop of Jamaica."

Size of some of the dioceses in England, population in 1851, *and area.*

Dioceses.	Population.	Area in acres.
London	2,143,340	246,157
Manchester	1,395,494	845,904
Chester	1,066,124	1,630,988
Winchester	1,080,412	1,598,568
Ripon	1,033,457	1,567,793
Lichfield	1,022,080	1,740,607
Exeter	922,656	2,530,780
York	764,558	2,261,493
Worcester	752,376	1,037,451
Durham	701,381	1,906,835
Lincoln	677,649	2,302,814
Norwich	671,583	1,994,525
Rochester	577,298	1,535,450
Gloucester and Bristol	538,109	1,000,503
Oxford	503,042	1,385,779
Ely	482,412	1,357,765
Peterborough	465,671	1,240,327
Bath and Wells	424,492	1,043,059
Canterbury	417,099	914,170
Salisbury	379,296	1,309,617
Chichester	336,844	934,851
Hereford	216,143	986,244
Carlisle	372,306	901,052
Sodor and Man	52,387	180,000
St. David	407,758	2,272,790
Llandaff	337,526	797,864
St. Asaph	236,293	1,067,583
Bangor	192,964	985,946

"The average population of the Dioceses in England and Wales in March 1851, was about 645,000, and may now be estimated at more than 660,000."—*Third Report of the Cathedral Commission*, p. xl.

While these pages have been passing through the press, the following resolutions have been unanimously carried in the Lower House of Convocation of the Province of Canterbury, February 14th, 1862; that house having been previously desired by the Archbishop and Bishops in the Upper to communicate to them the conclusions at which it arrived on that subject.

"I. That this house is of opinion that some increase in the Home Episcopate is necessary.

"II. This House is of opinion that there are two modes by which an increase in the Episcopate may be effected, viz. :

"(1.) By a subdivision, or re-arrangement, of existing dioceses.

"(2.) By means of the statute of Henry VIII. (26 Henry VIII, cap. 14) for the appointment of suffragan bishops.

"III. This House is of opinion that a general permissive Bill should be introduced into Parliament, enabling Her Majesty and Her Majesty's successors to subdivide dioceses, under certain conditions of territory and population; but that no subdivision of any diocese should take place without the consent of the bishop of the diocese which it is proposed to subdivide.

"IV. That it is desirable that a Committee should be formed, consisting partly of bishops and clergy, and partly of laymen (similar to the Committee for the Extension of the Colonial Episcopate), whose duty it should be to receive and to dispense funds, accruing from voluntary contributions, for the endowment of new sees at home.

"V. That no new see should be erected until a suitable church should be set apart for the cathedral of the diocese, and until an endowment of not less than 1500*l.* per annum, with a house, should be provided for the bishop of the new see.

"VI. That it is also desirable that advantage should be taken of the Act of Parliament above referred to (26 Henry VIII. c. 14), not only whenever, from age or infirmity, a bishop is unable to discharge in person the active duties of his office, but also provisionally in large and populous dioceses with a view to future subdivision."

NOTE (51), page 110.

The following Table shows the result of the increase of the Colonial Episcopate, and the augmentation of the Clergy in the several dioceses.

Diocese.	First Bishop consecrated.	No. of Clergy at Foundation of Diocese.	No. of Clergy at present.
Nova Scotia	1787	. .	72
Fredericton	1845	30	55
Quebec	1793	4	41
Montreal	1850	45	53
Toronto	1839	86	139
Rupert's Land	1849	5	12
Newfoundland	1839	. .	47
Jamaica	1824	. .	116
Barbados	1824	23	80
Antigua	1842	25	35
Guiana	1842	23	30
Calcutta	1814	. .	125
Madras	1835	. .	96
Colombo	1845	22	38
Cape Town	1847	14	59
Sydney	1836	. .	54
Newcastle	1847	17	23
Melbourne	1847	3	25
Adelaide	1847	4	28
New Zealand	1841	12	49
Tasmania	1842	19	75

NOTE (52), page 111.

See letter by Dr. Wordsworth addressed to Lord Dungannon, already referred to.

LECTURE IV. 267

NOTE (53), page 113.

See testimony on this point furnished in the evidence of the Rev. T. J. Rowsell, Perpetual Curate of St. Peter's, Stepney; the Rev. W. Champneys, Rector of Whitechapel; and the Rev. John E. Kempe, Rector of St. James's. Answers 1097, 1099, 1646—1666, 3350—3371.

NOTE (54), page 113.

See the contrast between the policy of the Church of Rome and that of the Church of England in this respect, as described by the late Lord Macaulay in his review of Ranke's " History of the Popes."

NOTE (55), page 114.

I have been assured that no instance of this has occurred among the lay agents employed by the London Scripture Readers' Society.

While this note has been passing through the press, I perceive, to my extreme gratification, that at the last session of Convocation of the Province of Canterbury, which from illness I have been myself unable to attend, the following representation has been carried in the Lower House, February 12th, 1862:

Representation of the Lower House addressed to the Upper House of Convocation of the Province of Canterbury.

" The Lower House having been directed to take into their consideration the Report of the Diaconate Committee, beg leave to lay before His Grace the President, and their Lordships of the Upper House, the following representations, with the respectful request that they will be pleased to take such measures as to them may seem expedient in order to carry their recommendations into effect.

"The questions which have been submitted to us are the following: — 1. Whether the Diaconate might not be extended in such a manner as to mark more distinctly the difference between that Order and the Priesthood, and thus to give increased efficiency to both, by a better adjustment of their several duties, as defined in the Ordinal of the Book of Common Prayer; and, 2. Whether it might not be expedient to revive the ancient order of 'Readers,' as was designed by Archdeacon Parker immediately after the Reformation.

"I. In considering these questions we have assumed—

"(1.) That there is an urgent necessity for additional agencies within the Church of England, adapted to the present circumstances of our country.

"(2.) That there are many persons, in different stations of life, who would rejoice to be employed in the work of the Church under some definite and authoritative commission, but who are precluded by various causes from becoming candidates for Holy Orders.

"II. With these facts before us, we have first of all turned our attention to that part of the subject which relates to the consideration of the best means of promoting the efficiency of the Diaconate, with a special regard to its distinctive and subordinate character.

"III. The distinction between the Second and Third Orders of the Christian Ministry is clearly defined in our Ordinal. This distinction has, however, been very much lost sight of, partly in consequence of the Diaconate being considered merely as a step to the Priesthood, and partly in consequence of the Deacon having not unfrequently been placed in the sole charge of a parish. We think that it would contribute greatly to the efficiency of their future ministry, if Deacons could be placed under the direction of experienced Priests during their Diaconate; and that the difference between the Deacon and the Priest would be marked more distinctly, if the Deacons were encouraged to continue in that Order, whenever practicable, for a longer period than is now usual before they are advanced to the Order of Priesthood.

"IV. We have next considered whether this third and lowest Order of our Church is capable of any extension, so as to admit the persons already alluded to, who may be supposed capable of rendering efficient service under regular appointment. But we regret to say that we find serious obstacles in the way of such extension, and for the following reasons: —

"(*a.*) The indelible character of the Diaconate constitutes one great difficulty; inasmuch as the Church might on this account often lose the help of those who could give the service of a *time*, but not the service of a *life*, to this especial part of her work.

"(*b.*) The amount of literary qualification, as required by the Ordinal and the Canon, presents another difficulty. The persons whose services are sought, could not, for the most part, be admitted, unless the strictness of the examination were relaxed. And, inasmuch as it would be practically impossible to have different degrees of qualification for the same Order, there is too much reason to fear that the whole standard of qualification for admission into the Christian ministry might ultimately be lowered.

"(*c.*) Other impediments present themselves from the provisions of Statute Law, which affects persons in Deacon's Orders.*

"V. From these and other considerations we are of opinion, that, whatever increase may take place in the number of persons admitted to the Diaconate, a supplemental agency is also required, which shall be in accordance with our ecclesiastical system.

"VI. Our attention has therefore been directed in the next place to the expediency of reviving the ancient Office of

---

* For example, Clergymen in Holy Orders are exempt from serving on juries (6 Geo. IV. c. 50, s. 2). They are also precluded from sitting in Parliament (Stephen's Commentaries, vol. ii. p. 391), or from engaging in trade (1 & 2 Vict. c. 106, s. 29), &c.

Readers. We find that this Office, which can be traced back to the third century, or even to an earlier period, was partially restored, for a short time, immediately after the Reformation. The purpose of its restoration at that time was, to secure parishes from being entirely destitute of all religious teaching, through the difficulty of finding a sufficient number of persons duly qualified for admission into Holy Orders. A class of persons is now needed to assist the Clergy of parishes with large or scattered populations in house-to-house visitation, in catechising, and in performing some other ministrations as may be assigned to them by competent ecclesiastical authority.

"VII. Various terms have been suggested as indicative of the nature of the Office which the present necessities of the Church require. But, whatever name may be assigned to the Office, we think that its duties should be so adjusted that it may include persons of all ranks and classes of society; the time of some being given wholly to the work; of others, only in part; some receiving stipends, and others rendering gratuitous services; that those admitted to it should receive their commission, on the nomination of the Incumbent, from the Bishop of the Diocese, after due examination as to their moral character, their religious knowledge, and their efficiency, with the solemnity of a public service in the Church, and by an instrument under the Episcopal hand and seal; and that they should be in all respects under the control and direction of the Incumbent in whose parish they are employed. We further think that they should be at liberty at any time whatever to resign the commission so received from the Bishop, and that the Bishop on the other hand should have the authority to revoke such commission.

"VIII. We make this recommendation with a full conviction of the pressing wants of the Church of England, and of the need of a greatly multiplied agency to enable her to fulfil the purposes of her high and holy calling. Nor would we conclude without the earnest prayer, that whether by these or by some other means, an 'effectual door' may be opened for the piety and zeal of those who seek by a definite mission from the Church, and in hearty communion with her, to promote the temporal and spiritual welfare of their fellow-creatures.

"*Jerusalem Chamber, February* 14*th,* 1862."

NOTES

LECTURE V.

NOTE (56), page 117.

THE words occur in a Letter to the Right Rev. William Skinner, D.D., Bishop of Aberdeen, and Primus, on the Functions of Laymen in the Church, by the Right Honourable W. Gladstone, M.P. for the University of Oxford. I give the context, "The distribution of local power, as between clergymen and vestry, is the irregular, disorderly, and hazardous compensation for the absorption of central power in the clergy at large, as contradistinguished from the laity at large. I do not say, then, that the exclusive prerogative of legislation in the clergy makes them too much our masters; far from it; but I say this: it exalts their power at the expense of their influence; it exalts the shadow at the expense of the substance; it exalts the name at the expense of the thing; it increases what they cannot use, and takes from them what they could. *It is by influence, and by influence only, that our clergy can be really powerful*" (p. 25).

NOTE (57), page 119.

The whole subject is of such importance, and is generally so little understood by the laity, that I give, *in extenso*, both the petition itself and the discussion in the Upper House of Convocation to which it gave rise, February 14, 1860, as reported in the " Chronicle of Convocation : " —

LECTURE V.

"*Ordination of Ministers.*

"The BISHOP OF LONDON.— The Bishop of Lichfield has placed in my hands a petition from certain persons in his diocese, which petition certainly is of great importance — the more important, perhaps, or at all events not the less important, because I believe the statements in it are not really capable of being substantiated, though they represent a state of feeling on the part of certain members of the laity which it is necessary your lordships should know. My right rev. brother not being able to be present, begged that I would, in presenting the petition, make any remarks that occurred to me. The subject is the mode in which we, the Bishops of the Church of England, exercise our discretion in the selection and examination of candidates for Holy Orders. I think I ought to read the petition, not, as I said before, because the statements are true, for I think they are erroneous, but because they express the feelings of a great number of persons.

"The BISHOP OF ST. DAVID'S — Who is the petition from?

"The BISHOP OF LONDON — It is from the Mayor of Derby and a number of influential laymen in that city. The petition is as follows: —

"'That your petitioners desire to approach your venerable house with every feeling of confidence and respect.

"'That your petitioners have observed with deep sorrow and regret several instances which have recently been made public, of offences against religion and morality committed by persons in Holy Orders.

"'That your petitioners thankfully acknowledge the high character which the clergy justly bear, as a body, and which contrasts so pleasingly with that of the clergy of many other countries; but your petitioners cannot conceal from themselves the fact, that the sacred order of the ministry is

T

continually receiving the accession of more persons of careless and ungodly lives, than your venerable house can possibly be aware of.

"'Your petitioners are constrained to set before your lordships the painful fact, that many persons are, from time to time, ordained, whose lives and conversation are notoriously opposed to the solemn professions required from them at their ordination, whereby great scandal is given to all earnest Churchmen, and much ground given for the allegations of Dissenters, that holiness of living is not requisite in the priesthood of our church.

"'Your petitioners desire also respectfully to call the attention of your venerable house to the fact that too many of these persons, on their ordination, do not make any alteration in their habits of life and conversation, but are, notwithstanding their entry into the Diaconate or Priesthood, still so remarkable for carelessness and levity, as to make themselves the subject of remark in all societies; that your petitioners have observed that this is not confined to members of any party in the Church, but may be noticed in persons holding very opposite theological opinions.

"'That your petitioners are quite aware that the certificate of three beneficed clergymen is in theory a sufficient testimony to the moral fitness of candidates: but they venture to submit that these testimonials are frequently given on a very partial acquaintance, and frequently on the representations of interested friends.

"'That your petitioners believe that it will be impossible for your lordships to be certain of the moral fitness of candidates for Holy Orders unless some further inquiry be made by your lordships' directions before admitting them to examination. Your petitioners submit that in the habitual absence of any special inquiries by the diocesan, the whole responsibility of deciding upon the moral fitness of candidates rests with the clergy who are applied to for testimonials, thus placing them in a position of great delicacy and difficulty, but from which they would be relieved were it known that the Bishop of the diocese would probably test the value of the certificates by inquiries of his own.

"' Your petitioners would not venture to intrude upon your venerable house upon a subject peculiarly resting with your lordships, had they not a deep conviction that the evil referred to is much more widely spread than your lordships, burdened with the care of your large dioceses, can be at all aware of.

"' Your petitioners therefore humbly beg that your venerable house will be pleased to take such measures as may seem good to it for the more effectual exclusion of ungodly or careless men from the Holy Order of the Priesthood.'

" The importance of this petition seems to me to consist in this — that it shows a wide-spread ignorance, on the part of the laity, as to the steps taken by your lordships in the examination into the qualifications of candidates for Holy Orders. There are two statements made in the petition to which I would especially call your lordships' attention. One of them is this:—

" ' Your petitioners are quite aware that the certificate of three beneficed clergymen is in theory a sufficient testimony to the moral fitness of candidates, but they venture to submit that these testimonials are frequently given on a very partial acquaintance, and frequently on the representations of interested friends.'

" I wish to remark, that if that be a true statement, it is of great importance that the attention of the clergy generally should be directed to this — that we, in receiving the testimonials of three beneficed clergymen, consider there cannot be a more solemn declaration than that which those three beneficed clergymen make as to the fitness of the person whom they recommend for admission to Holy Orders. In my judgment, and I am sure in the judgment of your lordships, a clergyman who puts his name to testimonials declaring any person whom he recommends fit for Holy Orders, when he has any doubt of his fitness, is guilty of as grievous a sin as can well be committed. The words of the declaration, as I well remember, are most stringent; they not only declare the conviction of the clergyman as to the fitness of the of the candidate, but they declare that from personal acquaintance with the candidate they know that he is fit. Not only does the clergyman say, 'I do not know anything against the man,' but 'I never heard anything against him, and I have had opportunities of judging of his conduct.' And I consider that any clergyman who will attach his name to such a testimonial, as a matter of form, will be most grossly and grievously neglecting his duty. It has been lately stated, in connection with this subject, that we all know that college testimonials are mere matters of form. Now, my lords, it was my lot for many years to be the tutor of a college, and I can safely say that the testimonials in that particular college were by no means matters of form, but that we did most seriously and conscientiously consider whether we were justified in stating that the person whom we recommended was fit to be admitted to Holy Orders. Connected with this, there is another point of some interest. There is very great diversity as to the form in which the different colleges send their testimonials. At Oxford, the form is a very stringent one, but at the sister university it is much more lax; and although I do not believe that it is intended as a matter of form, yet at Cambridge the testimonials are not so rigid and explicit in their expression as I could desire. I will pass on to another statement in the petition: —

" 'Your petitioners believe that it will be impossible for your lordships to be certain of the moral fitness of candidates for Holy Orders, unless some further inquiry be made by your lordships' directions before admitting them to examination. Your petitioners submit that, in the habitual absence of special inquiries by the diocesan, the whole responsibility of deciding upon the moral fitness of candidates rests with the clergy who are applied to for testimonials.'

" Now, I can hardly suppose that the writer of this

petition has the slightest conception as to the steps which are taken by Bishops in respect to the qualifications of candidates for ordination. I have no doubt that what I find to have been the practice of my predecessor in the see of London is, more or less, the practice in every see in England. And in order that this may be ascertained, I will state what was the practice which I found prevailing in London. In the first place, six months before the ordination (and, as I understand, elsewhere three months before the ordination), every person who wishes to present himself as a candidate, must give his name to the Bishop. As soon as possible after this intimation, the Bishop has a personal interview with the candidate, and endeavours to satisfy himself, both by his chaplain and personally, whether, *primâ facie*, the young man ought to be admitted into Holy Orders, judging from sight and conversation and from a slight preliminary examination. The candidate is then required to give the names of three persons, who may be applied to, privately, in the very way pointed out by the petitioners, independently of the public testimonial. These three persons are solemnly required to give their assurance whether they do or do not believe in their consciences the person to be what he ought to be. This private communication sometimes results in the gentleman who has been appealed to, saying that he does not know enough of the candidate to be able to express an opinion. Another reference is then required, and another appeal is made. Thus, by private inquiry, great care is taken to ascertain whether the person is what the public testimonials represent him to be. It is then, I believe, the custom of most of your lordships, as it is the custom in this see, that at the time of the examination we do not delegate another person to carry on the examination, but personal intercourse takes place between the candidate and the bishop, and the bishop endeavours to satisfy himself by all the means in his power whether the candidate is really a person fit to be admitted. I can hardly conceive anything more solemn than the position in which the candidate, the Bishop, and his examining chaplain stand during the examination week; and, anxious as I should be myself in any way to take greater pains to ascertain the fitness of the candidates — willing as I should be to introduce any alteration that tended in that direction, I am not aware how this could be done so as to obtain greater security. The only thing that occurs to me is this: — In the diocese of London there are a great number of candidates, and it has been sometimes suggested that it would be desirable to have four ordinations in the year instead of two, thus reducing the numbers at each ordination. But I have hesitated in taking that step, and for two reasons — first, because I do not think it very desirable for the diocese, that I should be perpetually pouring a number of young men into it. I know that there are many excellent persons desirous of holding curacies, who are liable to be superseded by young men, and I am rather anxious to put a check upon that practice. And more than that, I think that when a large number of persons are engaged on a solemn occasion, the number adds to the solemnity. On this point I should be most thankful to adopt any suggestion of my right rev. brethren or any one else, by which we could increase the solemnity of Ordination, or the securities to be given as to the character of the persons ordained. But the question remains, how can the impression to which I have called your lordships' attention have got into the minds of the petitioners? Now, it is a most melancholy fact, that certainly at this time, when by God's mercy the Church is exerting herself more than in past years, and there is more zeal among clergymen and more regard for the people's souls — at this very time, strange and unheard-of scandals have certainly accumulated more than at any former period. How this is to be accounted for I cannot say. Probably, when good is at work, evil is also at work; and the temptations which beset men are not to be put down by any vigorous system which may be adopted by ourselves or by others, nor even by force of public opinion. It is a subject of deep humiliation to all who are interested in the Church, to think that such scandals should have arisen, but we are bound to consider whether there are or are not any facilities under which they are promoted and encouraged. I wish to draw your lordships' attention, then, to a matter in which I think the clergy generally could fairly assist us in saving the Church from this sort of scandal. I am sure that I speak the sentiments of your lordships when I say that we are all most anxious to do our part; but it cannot be denied that there does grow up in every diocese — most certainly there has grown up in this diocese, and I am most desirous, if possible, that it should be remedied — a mode of calling in the assistance of clergymen for temporary duty, of whom very little is known, but who, by being thus occasionally employed, get a sort of footing in the diocese, and I believe in a great many instances in this way scandal arises to the Church. I was very much surprised the other day to receive from a clergyman of standing and position a letter, in writing which I think he showed great wisdom, asking whether he might safely employ such and such a person, whose name he mentioned. The moment I saw the name, I knew it as one that is familiar to the right rev. bench, and I think it would be well that the public should understand that the right rev. bench have the means of knowing something of the antecedents of the clergy generally, which the public at large, and the clergy at large are not possessed of. I wrote back to my correspondent, stating that I thought he would act unwisely if he employed the curate in question, and recommended him to look carefully to his testimonials, and be certain that they were duly signed and countersigned by the bishop of the diocese. I wish our brethren would remember that for even the temporary employment of a clergyman it is desirable to have testimonials — not printed testimonials, of which I have a great abhorrence — not testimonials from the other side of the water, which come to us in abundance. I generally find that the man about whom the less said the better, can produce many testimonials; and when these volumes of testimonials come to hand, be sure there is something wrong. What we want is simply this — the testimony of three clergymen, countersigned by the bishop of the diocese, that the man applying may be safely employed. The clergyman to whom I have referred, wrote in reply to my letter, expressing surprise at what I had told him, and adding that he had applied to a most respectable registry office in London for a curate, and that they had recommended this gentleman. Now, I have no great opinion of registry offices for clergymen, generally speaking; but there is a registry office connected with the Curates' Aid Society, which I knew something of. It was not the office from which the recommendation had come in this instance; but my attention having been drawn to the subject, I requested the secretary of that society to furnish me with a list of the clergymen on his list. He did so, and I found many names upon it that were familiar to me, and I believe to all your lordships, as persons in whose favour we should scarcely like to give testimonials. I immediately begged the gentleman who conducts that registry to be very careful as to whose names he admitted for the future upon the list, and I believe he at once took steps to make the register more safe than it was at the time I received the communication I have referred to. It should never be forgotten that those who recommend assistants to the clergy take upon themselves a very grave responsibility. I believe things have of late years very much improved in this matter, and that the clergy, when they have occasion to go away for a short time, do generally take care that their places are well supplied. Still, they are not aware of all the difficulties of which we are cognisant, and they would act more wisely if in all cases they referred to us, the Bishops, because we have the means, which they have not, of ascertaining whether the person who offers himself to undertake the temporary charge is such a person as he represents himself to be. In the old times, the practice in London, when a clergyman required assistance, was to send to St. Paul's Coffee-house, where a clergyman could be had for an odd Sunday at any time. Thank Providence, that state of things has passed away; but it is still of importance that attention should be drawn to the subject, and I am sure it would be a great service if a number of names were selected of persons who could be depended upon, for there is always a great number of respectable clergymen who may be safely depended upon available for such duty, and it would be much to be regretted if these most respectable and worthy persons were confounded with others who are in a very different category. I mentioned—I hope not in disrespectful terms—the testimonials which come to us in such abundance from the sister island; and in dealing with them there is a difficulty, not only as regards the clergymen who sign them, but as regards the Bishops who countersign them. Some of my right rev. brethren in that country have a peculiar habit of signing testimonials; and there is one most rev. prelate, for whom I have the deepest respect, and for whom the whole Church has the deepest respect, who will never sign that 'this clergyman is worthy of credit,' but signs—'As far as I know, he is worthy of credit,'—or 'I have no reason to know that he is unworthy.' This places the Bishops here in a difficult position, because we have not that security which we ought to have as to the character of the applicant. Then, there are others of our right rev. brethren on the other side of the water who will not sign any testimonial at all. There is, however, a very easy cure, which is simply to say, that without the testimonials duly signed and countersigned we will not have the men. I have great respect for the laborious services of many of these clergy; but I believe we might gain as well as lose by the discontinuance of that free-trade that has now existed for some time between the two countries on this matter. I think it desirable for us to put before our right rev. brethren there the importance of their signing such testimonials as we do, and then we should have the same means of testing the accuracy of the testimonials which are presented to us from Ireland as we have of testing the accuracy of the testimonials of clergymen in this country. I present this petition, totally disagreeing with it. The Bishop of Lichfield also disagrees with it; but I think it important, nevertheless, as showing the great misapprehension that exists with regard to the care we take to ascertain that the persons on whom we lay hands at ordination are really such as are fit for the sacred office.

"The BISHOP OF WINCHESTER—In common with many of my right rev. brethren, I listened with great anxiety to know whether the memorialists could suggest any rule more stringent than that we are in the habit of exercising in regard to the examination of candidates for the holy office; and in using the word examination, I do not mean to confine it to the literary qualifications of the individual, but to extend it to his moral character, and his ability to teach, and the other qualifications necessary for a person in Holy Orders. I do not scruple to say, that there is no period in the whole year which so heavily weighs on my mind as the Ember weeks for ordination. I have no doubt I share this anxiety with my right rev. brethren, and I should be glad if any of them could suggest some mode by which my mind might be better satisfied with respect to the fitness of the candidates who come before me. I have had occasion publicly to request the clergy in my own diocese to exercise more discretion in presenting candidates than they do at present—not, I believe, from any indifference on their part, but from the belief that the Bishop himself takes care to make a full examination into the qualifications of the candidate, which they have not the means of doing. Now, I think they are mistaken in their view. It is incumbent on them to satisfy themselves, so far as their influence extends, as to the fitness of the candidates they present. It is placing an unfair and undue degree of pressure on the Bishop and the examining chaplain, to leave to them, and to them alone, the painful and always difficult task of ascertaining the fitness of a candidate. The modes of inquiry mentioned by my right rev. brother are no doubt, in their degree, sometimes more and sometimes less, as occasion may require, the modes which all your lordships use. They are such as I myself employ, and I may say that I never admit a candidate as an approved candidate without having first seen him personally, and subsequently remitted him to my examining chaplain, who, in a preliminary interview, satisfies himself as to the extent of the information and the degree of knowledge he has acquired; and by this means I ascertain the disposition of the candidate's mind — a point which I need not say cannot be ascertained by testimonials. I may, perhaps, be allowed to say a word with respect to the testimonials from colleges. So far from considering the giving of testimonials a mere matter of form, I am sorry to say that in not a few instances I have had individuals communicating with me, and inquiring whether, under all circumstances, I expected that a college testimonial should be exhibited, and stating that, for reasons given, such testimonials had been refused. In no instance did I feel at liberty to dispense with the college testimonial, and least of all when it had been refused. I mention this fact for the purpose of showing that the colleges refuse as well as give testimonials. I have myself observed the differences of form in which testimonials are drawn up. My practice has been to write to the head or tutor of the college, inquiring why a special form of testimonial has been given. This remark applies particularly to Cambridge. The simple inquiry which I have instituted will enable the Bishop to satisfy himself whether anything is meant by the form in which the testimonial is worded. I may just refer to one point which is not alluded to in the petition. The petitioners might have remembered that, besides the testimonial presented to the Bishop, the laity themselves have the opportunity of testifying as to the fitness of the candidate. In some instances they have taken up the matter, and communicated with the Bishop, and have mentioned circumstances which have prevented the ordination of unfit candidates. I should be glad if the inaccuracy of the statements of the petitioners could be pointed out to them, and I hope my right rev. brother the Bishop of Lichfield will state to his friends in Derby, that the Bishops of the Church are not so inattentive to one of their most solemn duties as they seem to conceive.

"The BISHOP OF CHICHESTER.—I wish to make one remark with regard to the employment for a short period of clergymen of whom little or nothing is known. They are in the habit of taking up their abode at various places for a short time, representing that the state of their health requires a cessation from duty. A clergyman in this position soon forms a sort of acquaintance in the place, and states that although he is not equal to the performance of regular duty, he should be happy to render occasional assistance. Having once obtained employment, he gradually finds his health improving, and that he is able to perform his duty for a month, or two or three months. The clergyman of the parish often thinks that such an employment is a matter of no great importance, and unattended with any great risk. I have suffered in more instances than one from a want of caution on the part of my clergy, and have represented to them that, however short the period of such employment may be, they ought to call my attention to the case of the gentleman who applies for temporary employment. I make this remark, because within a few months a clergyman who has been employed under these circumstances so disgraced himself that he was obliged to leave the parish.

"The BISHOP OF BATH AND WELLS.—I may mention a practice which has been adopted with success in my diocese. When an application has been forwarded to me, I have transmitted a copy of it to every Rural Dean. If he finds any person on the cautionary list, whom he knows to be an unfit person to act, he transmits the name to me. If he finds any person who is not licensed, acting in my diocese, he informs me. By that means I get the name of every curate officiating in every deanery, and am able to act accordingly.

The BISHOP OF LINCOLN.—I should be sorry to allow it

to go abroad that there is even any one registry-office from which curates may be taken without inquiry. It is scarcely possible that any secretary can make himself master of the antecedents of all those who apply to him. He has not the means of doing so. I apprehend that his letters of inquiry, if he were allowed to make them, would be privileged communications. Registry-offices may be necessary—I think they are a necessary evil—but it should be understood that any clergyman taking a curate or assistant from a registry-office, if he values the welfare of his people, is bound to make full inquiries as to the character of the clergyman engaged there, as well as from any other source.

"The PRESIDENT—It is important that it should be generally known and understood, that although the Bishops generally sanction the establishment of registry-offices, they do not by any means sanction the employment of clergymen recommended by these establishments.

"The BISHOP OF LLANDAFF—The petition takes it for granted that the testimonials of the clergy are too much a matter of form. Now, every person who presents himself as a candidate for examination for Holy Orders is desired to present a *si quis*; that is to say, notice is publicly given in the church in the place where he resides, and where his character is well known and his antecedents from his youth up, and the laity are called upon to give notice whether there is any reason why the individual should not present himself as a candidate for ordination. If any person knows an objection, he has then the opportunity of stating that objection. Again, on the day of ordination all parties are called on to state any impediment of which they are aware. Consequently the whole responsibility does not rest on the subscribing bishop or clergyman. With regard to the temporary employment of clergymen, I may remark, that a person officiated for a time in my diocese who was no clergyman at all. He afterwards went into a colonial diocese, and there obtained ordination. I have known cases of clergymen in my diocese whose testimonials were not subscribed, entering the diocese of Bath and Wells, and also of London. Now, if the clergymen employing these parties had asked the question whether their testimonials were subscribed by the bishop, they would have found that they had no such testimonials.

"The BISHOP OF ST. DAVID'S — The security against the admission of persons in cases where there is a clear and notorious impediment is by no means confined to a *si quis*, or any public notice. I do not know whether it is the particular characteristic of my part of the country, but my experience there has led me to believe that wherever any such impediment exists, it is a matter of notoriety in the neighbourhood from which the person comes; and it would be remarkable if, in that neighbourhood, there was a universal disinclination to communicate the fact to the Bishop. If there be a person who labours under a stain on his character, he must be a fortunate — or rather, I should say, an unfortunate — individual, if he has no real friend who would take some step, either privately or publicly, to make it known to the Bishop. My own experience leads me to think that perhaps in most cases there would be rather a tendency to the contrary side. But it really is almost morally impossible that any grave or notorious stain on the character of a person can exist without its being communicated to the Bishop.

"The BISHOP OF OXFORD — I believe the Bishops of London and Winchester have stated correctly the great care taken in their extensive dioceses to prevent the ordination of unfit men, and it would be but wasting time to repeat the same statements as to all our dioceses. But it is desirable that it should go forth that what they have stated as to the means taken to prevent the possibility of people coming untried, is carried out effectually in every one of our dioceses; and it may save further discussion if all my right rev. brethren would assent to that. (General cries of 'Hear, hear.') I can hardly conceive a greater crime than that a Bishop should be careless in these matters; and although there may have been a time when college testimonials were dispensed with, or character passed by, I trust such things will never happen again in the Church.

"The PRESIDENT.—Of all the matters spoken of, none is more beneficial or more calculated to prevent the intrusion of improper persons than the system of previous personal inquiry of the man himself as to his fitness and his motives. The system was first begun — I think it was first regularly organised by the late Bishop of London — more than thirty years ago. I received it from him, and by keeping very strictly indeed, as a general rule, to that practice, I have found the greatest advantage. By being acquainted with the circumstances of the candidates as well as their dispositions, I have been in many instances saved the necessity of rejecting them when they came up. From seeing them three or four times, I can generally judge of their character and motives; and, if I consider that they are not fitted for the office, it is my habit to say to them, 'You do not appear to be aware of the importance of the step you are about to take. If you persevere, such a course may be open to you hereafter, and if you come with proper testimonials you will be received, but I cannot receive you to-day.'

"The BISHOP OF SALISBURY — No person can officiate without our leave, and I allow no one to officiate in my diocese more than two Sundays without my sanction. We are really responsible, and it may be necessary to make the rule still stricter. Although I suffered some years ago from irregularities of this kind, I do not think that such things exist now.

"The BISHOP OF OXFORD — The rule is the same in my diocese, except that they may officiate three Sundays. In each case the rule leads to their calling on me before they are allowed to officiate once, and in some cases it has prevented much mischief. I allow every Rural Dean to give a title to some one whom he can specially recommend, and for whom he will become responsible. There is no difficulty, when a clergyman wishes to go away for a short time, in getting a proper substitute.

"The BISHOP OF SALISBURY — The plan has acted exceedingly well in two ways; in one case, with respect to a paid person, and, in the other, where the services were unpaid. A gentleman every way qualified at the University, acting as a tutor in a deanery, and anxious to be ordained, but unable to give up his tuition, I have allowed the Rural Dean to appoint as his curate. He is to serve for two years, and officiate at every church to which the Rural Dean sends him, the only cost being that of his transit. That regulation gives great assistance to the parochial clergy."

NOTE (58), page 119.

See representation of the Lower House, addressed to the Upper House of Convocation, February 10, 1859.

NOTE (59), page 120.

See "The Form and Manner of Making of Deacons."
"*When the day appointed by the Bishop is come, after morning prayer is ended, there shall be a sermon or exhortation, declaring the duty and office of such as come to be admitted deacons; how necessary that order is in the Church of Christ, and also how the people ought to esteem them in their office.*

"*First, the Archdeacon, or his deputy, shall present unto the Bishop* (sitting in his chair near to the holy table), *such as desire to be ordained deacons* (each of them being decently habited), *saying these words,* Father in God, I present unto you these persons present, to be admitted deacons.

"*The Bishop.*

"Take heed that the persons whom ye present unto us, be apt and meet, for their learning and godly conversation, to exercise their ministry duly, to the honour of God, and the edifying of His Church.

LECTURE V.

" The Archdeacon shall answer,

" I have inquired of them, and also examined them, and think them so to be.

" Then the Bishop shall say unto the people;

" Brethren, if there be any of you who knoweth any impediment, or notable crime, in any of these persons presented to be ordered deacons, for the which he ought not to be admitted to that office, let him come forth in the name of God, and show what the crime or impediment is.

" And if any great crime or impediment is objected, the Bishop shall surcease from ordering that person, until such time as the party accused shall be found clear of that crime.

" Then the Bishop (commending such as shall be found meet to be ordered to the prayers of the congregation) shall, with the clergy and people present, sing or say the litany, with the prayers as followeth," &c. &c.

NOTE (60), page 120.

On two occasions while I filled the office of examining chaplain in the diocese of Worcester, charges were brought against candidates *after* they had been ordained, but not till then: and on my engaging, should the charges be substantiated, that the Bishop's licence would be withdrawn, the complainants declined coming forward. On two other occasions, when charges were brought just before the examination for Holy Orders commenced, the candidates who were the subject of them, were required to withdraw. In the only other similar instance which occurred during the seven years of my holding the office of examining chaplain, the charge was not made till the person affected was presented to a living. In all these cases, testimonials certifying the moral fitness of the candidates, and the necessary certificate of public notice having been given of their intention to offer themselves as candidates for Holy Orders, had been duly forwarded to the bishop.

Note (61), page 122.

I am acquainted with one instance in which, from the omission of a mere legal formality, a Bishop was involved in an expense of 500*l*., though the charge against the incumbent could not be denied. In the recent notorious case of the Bishop of London *versus* Bonwell, though the defendant was cast in every court, his Lordship's expenses are understood to have exceeded 1200*l*.

Note (62), page 125.

The following extract from an article in the January number 1862, of the "Christian Remembrancer," on Father Felix and his Conferences at Notre Dame, is well worthy of attention.

" Most worthy of imitation, in one notable respect at least, is the system of theological and pulpit training existing in the French Church. It stands in melancholy and humiliating contrast with the course usually adopted in our own. Amongst us, theology is seldom studied as a science, frequently it is not studied at all. . . . . . . And until the whole of our present painfully inadequate, vague, and shallow system of preparation for the ministry of the word and sacraments, is remodelled and placed on a more definite and comprehensive basis; until the Church herself takes up the work, and provides and prescribes a systematic course of theological training for all candidates for Orders, we fear that she will be deprived of a most substantial element of strength and influence, and that we shall continue to labour under innumerable evils.

" In another respect does this portion of the life of Father Felix teach us a valuable lesson. When once we do possess — in spite of the shadowy and unsatisfactory system prevalent amongst us — in spite of the absence of all scientific training of candidates for the priesthood — an able and eloquent preacher, what use do we make of him? How is he too frequently treated? Is he placed in such an appropriate sphere of duty as is likely to afford full and unfettered scope to his powers for good, for teaching, reclaiming, influencing the masses, and presenting to them the momentous truths of religion, with all the adjuncts and charms of a perspicuous and forcible style, and of a ready delivery and effective address? No! It may happen that he seldom has the opportunity of preaching at all; and if he has, he may possibly be prevented from doing so by other duties of an absorbing nature. Instead of regularly, or at least at stated periods, occupying our cathedral or metropolitan pulpits, where, under God, he might be the means of influencing thousands to their eternal good — he may be vegetating, unhonoured and unknown, on some paltry curacy, in some remote village, or be relegated to the headship of a school, or the vice-principalship of a hall, with but scanty opportunities of exercising his distinguishing and peculiar talents, and even then possibly, only in a very limited and contracted sphere.

"Far differently and far better are these things managed in France and other countries, as is evidenced in the life of every continental preacher of eminence. . . . As soon as a superior or a bishop perceives that a candidate for the priesthood has the stuff of a good preacher, and exhibits oratorical power, his training for the holy office of preacher is carefully attended to; full scope is afforded him for the exercise and development of his peculiar gifts, his oratorical abilities are sedulously cultivated and his efforts encouraged, and when he has proved himself an able preacher, he is eventually placed in the particular sphere in which he is likely to effect the greatest amount of good."
—(Pp. 71, 72).

NOTE (63), page 125.

I allude especially to several able articles, which have appeared in the course of the last two or three years, on the subject of clerical deficiencies, in *The Times* newspaper. The writers show, with much force and vivacity, the want of oratorical power on the part of many of the clergy of the national Church, and the injury hence resulting to the cause of religion. But they forget that their strictures, in this respect, are as applicable to the great body of our educated laity. It is notorious that few Englishmen, under the present educational system, possess the faculty of expressing themselves with force and appropriateness in public.

NOTE (64), page 126.

It is observed in the article on Father Felix and his Conferences at Notre Dame, already alluded to, that in no respect are the deficiencies in clerical education more strikingly exemplified than in the delivery of most of our preachers. "It is well known with what ease, what naturalness, and frequently perfect gracefulness, French preachers deliver their sermons. Indeed their manner of delivery is often their greatest recommendation. We have occasionally heard French sermons which riveted our attention in their delivery, but which subsequently appeared very poor in the reading. There was a good deal of shrewdness and judgment in the answer made by Renaud to one who asked him to publish some sermons which had been very much admired. 'Most willingly, if they will print the preacher also.' . . . The delivery of our preachers is, as a rule, woefully inferior. The reason of this is obvious. The elocutionary art is as sedulously and systematically studied and cultivated in France, as it is sedulously and systematically ignored, and, to use the words of a very high authority — the Bishop of Exeter — 'disgracefully neglected amongst ourselves,' and we very much fear that even now an affirmative answer might be returned to Bishop Berkeley's celebrated query, 'Whether half the learning and study of these kingdoms is not useless, for want of a proper delivery being taught in our schools and colleges?' Mr. Daniel Moore, in his able 'Thoughts on Preaching,' has well observed, that, in a practical ignoring of all the adjuncts of effective oral address, and in the almost contemptuous denial to elocution of any right to be considered an art at all, the Church of England stands almost alone; and until this evil is remedied, and elocution occupies a prominent place in the preparation of candidates for Orders, some of our best sermons will not only not command general acceptance, but will too often become practically useless."

"The tameness, the monotony, the want of naturalness and reality, the undignified attitude, the listless and inexpressive countenance*, the soul-withering coldness, with which sermons are delivered in this country, strike foreigners particularly. If there be some exaggeration, there is at the same time much truth, in the following passage from Coquerel's recently published volume on Preaching:—

"L'Evêque ou le ministre anglican commodément accoudé sur un coussin de velours assez vaste pour recevoir son cahier, lisait avec la plus confiante placidité, sans risquer d'autre geste que le mouvement de tourner les pages, et à peine se permettait-il, de loin en loin, ce qu'on appelait *the waving of the hand,* c'est-à-dire l'effort de soulever la main pour la laisser retomber aussitôt sur le rebord de la chaire. C'était un démenti systématique et permanent donné au vieux principe que l'action est l'essence de l'art oratoire; ce principe si recommandé par Démosthènes, dont Cicéron, en l'appuyant à son tour dans les termes les plus forts, rappelle le mot fameux, que les trois premières qualités de l'orateur sont, 1ᵉ *l'action,* 2ᵉ *l'action,* 3ᵉ *l'action.*"

Bouchard, a writer most favourably disposed towards our Church and nation, as well as every French traveller who

---

* Ad summum dominatur maxime vultus; hoc supplices, hoc minaces, hoc blandi, hoc tristes, hoc hilares, hoc erecti, hoc submissi sumus. Hoc pendent homines, hunc intuentur, hunc spectant etiam antequam dicamus. Hoc quosdam amamus, hoc odimus, hoc plurima intelligimus. — Quinctilian, lib. xi. cap. 3.

has attended our services, makes very similar remarks. See also the Letter of the Bishops on the necessity of training theological students in public reading, in Mr. d'Orsay's " Lecture on the Study of the English Language." Bell and Daldy, 1861.

Mr. Gresley also aptly remarks:—" The first point to which a preacher must attend when he gets into the pulpit is, *that he may be heard;* — that the sound of his voice may be heard distinctly in every part of the church. I should not have thought it necessary to notice so obvious a truth, but for the very common neglect or forgetfulness among preachers in this most essential point. How constant a complaint is it with a congregation that they cannot hear their minister; with all their attention, they cannot catch more than half his meaning!"—*Treatise on Preaching,* p. 336.

NOTE (65), page 128.

See " *Appendix to the First Report of Her Majesty's Commissioners, appointed November 18th, 1852, to inquire into the state and condition of the Cathedral and Collegiate Churches in England and Wales.—Presented to Parliament, 1854.*"

This appendix contains the answers of the theological professors and of the heads of colleges and halls in Oxford and Cambridge to this inquiry,— " The Commissioners are desirous of ascertaining the opinion of the university and of the professors as to whether the theological lectures in the university may be considered as supplying all that is wanted for the preparation of candidates for Holy Orders, or whether it will be desirable to institute theological colleges in connection with some of the cathedral churches?" (Oxford). " The Commissioners will also be thankful for the advice of the university with respect to the preparation of candidates for Holy Orders. They are anxious to know whether it is your opinion that the lectures of the theological professors supply all that is wanted for this purpose; or whether it will be

LECTURE V. 295

desirable to institute theological colleges in connection with some of the cathedral churches?" (Cambridge).

NOTE (66), page 130.

Answer returned by Dr. Jacobson, Regius Professor of Divinity, Oxford.

NOTE (67), page 131.

The judgment of the Commissioners is given in their final Report, presented in 1855, p. xix., and is thus expressed:—
"It was stated in our First Report (pp. xxiv. xxv.), that one of the main purposes for which cathedrals were founded, was to impart Christian instruction, especially to those under training for Holy Orders in the Church.

"Referring to the evidence there given, and to the remarks there made upon the subject, we have now to declare our opinion:—

"*That it would be advantageous to religion and learning, if in each of the two Provinces a certain number of theological seminaries were formed or restored.*

"In selecting places for such institutions, we suggest that regard should be had to statutable provisions, and also to existing means and appliances in the cathedral or collegiate body: *e.g.* number of canons, theological lectureships, library, hall, and other buildings for the reception of students; sufficient population in the cathedral city, that the students might be profitably trained and exercised in parochial and pastoral work, under the direction of the clergy of the city, in visiting the sick, teaching in the schools, &c.

"We would suggest, that where a cathedral is so situate, that in connection with it a theological college could be instituted, which should be under the direction of the Bishops and Chapters of several associated dioceses, the benefit of such institutions might best be secured, and the dangers apprehended from a too great multiplication of such colleges be avoided."

Note (68), p. 133.

See answers of Dr. Wynter, President of St. John's College, Oxford; Dr. Cartmell, Master of Christ's College, Cambridge; and Dr. Jeune, Master of Pembroke College, Oxford.

Note (69), p. 137.

See "Clerical Training," a sermon preached in Cuddesdon parish church, June 9th, 1857; published at the request of the Lord Bishop of Oxford.

Note (70), p. 137.

"There can be no doubt," observe the Committee, "as to the value of a practice frequently adopted by young men previous to ordination, of placing themselves under the care of an experienced clergyman, who can at once superintend their theological studies, and gradually initiate them into the pastoral duties of their future office; and we regret that this practice cannot be universally introduced."—*Report*, p. xvii.

NOTES.

LECTURE VI.

NOTE (71), page 144.

SEE a sermon preached in the chapel of Marlborough College, on Michaelmas day 1858, being the anniversary of the Consecration of the chapel, by the Rev. F. Temple, D.D., Head Master of Rugby School.

See also a "Letter to an Employer, in an account of St. Mark's School, Windsor, embodying some suggestions on the subject of education," by the Rev. Stephen Hawtrey, M.A., Mathematical Assistant, Eton, page 10, from which the following is an extract: —

"—— now in your employ, was brought up in our school. May I ask what character he bears? Do you find him truthful, open, trustworthy, intelligent, quick to learn, and industrious, sensible, modest, obliging, and, as far as you know, moral in his habits of life? .... My inquiry is purely with a view of ascertaining what effect their early education has had on the after life and habits of the boys who have been brought up at our parochial school."

NOTE (72), page 145.

The charge referred to is one delivered to the clergy of the Archdeaconry of Middlesex, " On School Rates in England and America,"—at the visitations held at St. Paul's, Covent

Garden, on the 30th and 31st of May 1860, by the Venerable John Sinclair, M.A., Archdeacon of Middlesex, and Vicar of Kensington.

NOTE (73), page 146.

" Address " by Alexander Bache, as quoted in the above Charge, from the New York Church Journal, Dec. 11, 1856, page 28. I am glad to confirm this testimony by that of the late Dr. Arnold. In his Life, by Canon Stanley, 3rd edition, vol. i. p. 131, it is observed, " For mere cleverness, whether in boys or men, he had no regard. Mere intellectual acuteness," he used to say, in speaking (for example) of lawyers, " divested, as it is in too many cases, of all that is comprehensive, and great, and good, is to me more revolting than the most helpless imbecility, seeming to be almost like the spirit of Mephistopheles." Often when seen in union with moral depravity, he would be inclined to deny its existence altogether. The generation of his scholars, to which he looked back with the greatest pleasure, was not that which contained most instances of individual talent, but that which had altogether worked steadily and industriously. The university honours which his pupils obtained were very considerable, and at one time unrivalled by any school in England, and he was unfeignedly delighted whenever they occurred. But he never laid any stress upon them, and strongly deprecated any system which would encourage the notion of their being the chief end to be answered by school education. " If," he used to say, " there be one thing on earth which is truly admirable, it is to see God's wisdom blessing an inferiority of natural powers, where they have been honestly, truly, and zealously cultivated." In speaking of a pupil of this character, he once said, " *I would stand to that man hat in hand.*"

LECTURE VI.   299

NOTE (74), p. 148.

In a leading article in *The Times* newspaper, March 30th, 1861, it is observed, " all the informants of the Commission concur in the assertion that in the choice of week-day schools, the working population is absolutely careless of the theological differences of Protestant churches or sects . . . . the child returns as a matter of course to the faith or custom of the parents, unless the activity of religious partisans has moulded his opinions through the proselytising influence of the Sunday school." While there is no doubt that the managers of schools attach great importance to the education of children in the religious creed which they themselves profess, it appears that the parents of the children do not share in this feeling. The testimony of the Assistant Commissioners on this point is remarkable. Thus Mr. Headley says, Report, p. 147: " I have heard of no single instance in which the religious teaching in a school formed the ground for withdrawing or withholding children from the school." Again, Report, p. 164: " It is extremely rare to find a church-school which does not contain several children of dissenters. I have been constantly assured, that no objection is known to be entertained to the religious instruction given in the school. When the rule of the school requires the attendance of all the children on Sunday, there often are objections made, but even then the objections do not originate so much with the parents, as with the teachers and managers of the dissenting Sunday school." Mr. Cumin states (p. 6), "I have been asked whether the poor show a preference for one system of education over another; whether they neglect the education of their children because of religious differences; and whether, in short, there is anything in the present schools which indisposes parents to send their children to school. I made the most diligent inquiry into these matters, and found no difference of opinion. Schoolmasters, clergymen, ministers, city missionaries, all told me that the poor, in selecting a school, looked entirely to whether the school supplied good reading, writing, and arithmetic." "The truth is," he adds, "that the religious difficulty, as it is called, does not exist."

Dr. Hodson says on the subject of religious instruction: "I do not find among teachers, parents, or pupils, that any practical difficulty exists. Even those who themselves have very little religious thought of any kind, have a notion that religion is a good thing for their children." (p. 64.)

The following judicious remarks are from a leading article in *The Times* newspaper of March 30th, 1861 :—" The Commissioners justly conclude that the feelings of managers and subscribers must be regarded as scrupulously as if they were shared by the parents of the children who are to be taught ; and it is certain that religious motives have been infinitely more effective in promoting the institution of schools than any zeal which may exist for the cause of intellectual training. It is useless to argue with local philanthropists on the comparative unimportance of sectarian differences. The parish clergyman will not relinquish his connection with the National Society, nor will the zealous Dissenter submit to the Catechism and the Liturgy. Impartial devotees of secular education are few and comparatively inactive ; nor is it easy to find a latitudinarian lady visitor. Twelve hundred thousand poor children are at present taught under the superintendence, and, in an altogether unreasonable proportion, at the expense, of the clergy. Any innovation which should exclude special religious doctrine from the course of instruction would throw the whole mass of scholars on the mercy of the farmers, who habitually regard a boy as an implement for picking stones or scaring crows from a cornfield. The landed proprietors, though far less liberal in their contributions than the clergy, are almost equally resolute in their repudiation of Dissent ; and, on the other hand, the Nonconformists of the towns regard the doctrinal truths to which they are witnesses as incomparably more indispensable than the mundane accomplishments of reading and writing. The Government, when it comes to deal with Popular Education, wisely contents itself with secondary arrangements for increasing and applying the power which it finds already provided. The judicious engineer will not commence his operations by diverting the water or turning off the steam."

The following passage from the Report of the Conference of the Liberation Society, p. 110, affords an instructive insight into the educational views of political dissent.

"Nor must the society neglect the great work of popular education. Great efforts are now being made by the advocates of the Established Church to lay hold of the children of the poor, and to train them up in obedience to its claims. Every insidious art is plied, with untiring energy, to scatter abroad the most pernicious notions, with a view to reclaim the population to the bosom of the Church, and to imbue the general mind with a superstitious dread of the doctrine and practice of Dissent. Rank, wealth, and power are embarking in this crusade against freedom of thought and independency of opinion. Leisure and talent, and the blandishments of condescension are put at the service of the Church. Parishes, that a few years since were silent and inactive, are now set in motion; and in every town and village in the empire strenuous exertions are being made to arrest the progress of Dissent. It will become us to educate the children of the poor, so far as we can, in accordance with the spirit of the age. Everything should be done to aid the extension of the British and Foreign School Society. Daily instruction should be provided, wherever it is practicable, in connection with dissenting congregations. The pupils in our sabbath schools should be well informed on the meaning and constitution of a church, on the spirituality of the Redeemer's reign, on the sinfulness and mischiefs of the assumptions of religious establishments. The features by which we are distinguished as Nonconformists should be by all means more distinctly taught and more generally understood. Most strenuous and unwearied exertions should be put forth by the dissenting community to rescue the rising generation from the strange, exclusive, and bewildering instructions under which episcopal solicitude yearns to place them; and towards these exertions the Anti-State-Church Association should steadily turn its eye."

NOTE (75), page 148.

"It is proved that in rural districts landowners do not contribute to the expenses of schools so liberally as the wealthy classes in mining districts or large towns. The result is, that the burden falls principally on the parochial clergy, "who," say the Commissioners, "are very ill able to bear it." Mr. Fraser collected the financial statistics of 168 schools in his district, to which there were 1028 subscribers, of these, the following were the proportions: —

		£		£	s.	d.	
169 Clergymen contributed		1782	or	10	10	0	each
399 Landowners	,,	2127	,,	5	6	0	,,
217 Occupiers	,,	200	,,	0	18	6	,,
102 Householders	,,	181	,,	1	15	6	,,
141 other persons	,,	228					

The rental of the 399 landowners is estimated at 650,000*l.* a year.

In a somewhat similar table of the subscriptions to 18 schools in his district, Mr. Headley gives the following figures:

			£
Landowners contributed	.	.	198
Occupiers ,,	.	.	38
Clergymen ,,	.	.	471

Mr. Cumin gives similar instances. "I visited," he says, "one country parish, in which the resident owners of land subscribed 2*l.* to the school, and four non-residents 11*l.* 5*s.*, while the clergyman gave 23*l.* in one year. In this parish the rateable value of the land was 3500*l.*"

"Respecting the heaviness of the burden thus borne by the clergyman, the Commissioners remark, 'that it is but imperfectly indicated by these figures. He is frequently responsible for the finances of the school; he takes the largest interest in its affairs; he has to beg subscriptions from all sources; and at last submits, most meritoriously, and most generously, to bear not only his own proportion of the expense, but also that which ought to be borne by others. It has been repeatedly noticed by the school Inspectors; and it is our duty to state, that, as a class, the landowners, especially those who are non-resident (though there are many honourable exceptions) do not do their duty in the support of popular education, and that they allow others, who are far less able to afford it, to bear the burden of their neglect.'

" The farmers, or land-occupiers, on the other hand, are not merely indifferent, they are hostile to education. Mr. Headley says, 'that they seldom feel any interest in the school, and seldom therefore subscribe to it.' Mr. Fraser reports that 'the prejudices against education, which fifteen years ago were nearly universal, are still to be found lingering amongst this class.' But he remarks that 'they have very little notion of almsgiving of any kind, and have been entirely overlooked in the efforts that have been made to improve the condition of schools.'"— See "Popular Education in England," pp. 64—5.

NOTE (76), page 149.

This has been repeatedly urged on our Bishops, and is recognised by them as a reason for admitting candidates for confirmation from the poorer classes at an earlier age than might otherwise be deemed advisable. The hope is that the intercourse with the clergyman thus revived, may enable him to resume and retain his pastoral influence over them, before they become wholly estranged.

NOTE (77), page 150.

See sermon on "the Church's Duties and the Church's Opportunities," preached in the nave of Wells Cathedral on Thursday, October 4th, 1860, at the annual meeting of the Diocesan Societies, by Charles John Vaughan, D.D., Vicar

of Doncaster, &c., from which the following is an extract :—
" Often the brief years given to school contain the whole of a poor man's training in the things of God: and heavy is the responsibility which rests upon those to whose charge those brief years have been consigned, to see that they be made really profitable, — a seed time, indeed, of that engrafted Word which is able to save the soul."

Note (78), page 150.

In a sermon preached at the annual meeting of the Worcester Diocesan Training College, entitled " *Education not Teaching but Training,*" and published in the report of that institution for 1861, I have stated at length my view of this subject.

Note (79), page 151.

See on this subject an assize sermon by the Rev. John C. Miller, D.D., entitled " The Dying Judge's Charge," p. 26. Also, extract from a speech delivered by him at the anniversary of the Sunday School Union, May 3, 1855, and quoted by the Rev. Dr. Hessey in his Bampton Lectures, 1860, p. 501, and from which I cannot deny myself the pleasure of subjoining the following passage : " I do not believe there is a single father on this platform, or in this hall, who would attempt, if he had a grain of common sense, to deal with his own children as we have been dealing with the children of the poor. Who that knows the elasticity of a child's body and mind, and the difficulty of keeping it still, even at family prayer, would ever dream, if he thought at all upon the subject, of overtasking the physical and mental powers of children, as we have so long been doing on the Lord's day ? "

LECTURE VI.

NOTE (80), page 151.

See account of St. Mark's School, Windsor, already alluded to, from which the following is an extract: "There is no sentiment I am acquainted with, bearing on this subject, that I think more true and valuable than the following;—it occurs in Professor Stanley's work on the Epistle to the Corinthians. He is speaking of St. Paul's mode of dealing with the Churches he had planted, and says:—' *Sympathy is the secret of power. No artificial self-adaptation—no merely official or pastoral relation—has an influence equal to that which is produced by the consciousness of a human and personal affection in the mind of the teacher towards his scholars—of the general towards his soldiers — of the Apostle towards his converts.*' These words ought to be engraven on every schoolmaster's heart. . . . . . So essential do I consider it to a master's success, that he should make the boys feel that he takes an interest in them, and sympathizes with them, that if I were to put my meaning in the shape of the old apothegm, I should say that the first requisite for a master is love, the second is love, and the third is love." (pp. 26. 27.) In justice to the School of St. Mark's, Windsor, I subjoin Mr. Canon Moseley's allusion to it, see vol. i. Minutes of the Privy Council, 1848—49. " At this school, the boys breakfast with the schoolmaster, each bringing his bread and butter, and the clergyman providing the cocoa. I doubt not that this meal, eaten in common by the teacher and children, has contributed largely to the high moral tone of that remarkable school . . . The most perfect idea we can form of a school approaches to that of a well-ordered family ; and of the proper relation of the teacher and his scholars, to that of a parent and his children. It is perhaps difficult to conceive how this idea is to be realised, unless they take their meals together." My own views on this subject are stated in the sermon entitled " Education not Teaching, but Training," already alluded to.

x

Note (81), page 153.

There are some very able remarks on the moral condition of the youth of the working classes in an article on "Supplemental National Education," in Macmillan's Magazine, May 1861, by Rev. H. S. Robinson, Principal of Training College, York.

Note (82), page 153.

I give the whole of this important passage: "All of us, laity as well as clergy, individuals as well as the Church, may do much by our thoughtfulness for our weaker brethren, for the young, and the poor especially, and let it be added, (in the case of those in better circumstances) by our personal self-denial, towards making Sunday that divine yet humane institution, that blessing to the whole man, which it was doubtless intended to be. I fear that we oftentimes make mistakes in this matter. To begin with children: we find it difficult to know what to do with them on Sunday; we take them to church perhaps twice; we give them services too long even for adults. They understand but little of the prayers, and less of the sermon. But this gets over only a part of the day. What is to be done with the remainder? Perhaps we have taught them a question from what is called the broken catechism:—' Can those be thought to keep the Sabbath day holy who play on it?' to which the answer is —' By no means.' And we feel bound to carry out this sort of teaching. Accordingly, when away from church, they must not do this, they must not do that— they must sit still, or be very quiet, or read only good books, and the like. Can we wonder that they associate religion and Sunday with dulness and restraint, and that when they become their own masters, they dislike a Christianity which seemed to check all natural cheerfulness, and give them little that they could feel or understand?

" And if this is the case with our own children, it is much

more the case with the children of the poor. To the restraint of two church services is frequently added the restraint of a Sunday school. The Lord's day is made to them a day of positive work. Can we wonder, again, that so soon as they grow to an age to quit that school, they associate Sunday, and everything connected with it, with heaviness and wearisomeness? In church they got little they could understand; they were frequently seated where they could neither hear nor see: out of church they were met by lessons — well intended indeed, but ensuing upon what they had done or suffered already, too much for their jaded minds and bodies. An eminent clergyman, Dr. Miller, has said publicly, that 'we need have many searchings of heart when we see the small effect produced by our Sunday schools, and by our Sunday teaching generally; and that though there are objections to detaching children from the services in the church, even this is preferable to giving them what they cannot understand.' He says in effect, that 'the whole treatment of Sunday, in reference to the children of the poor, requires revision.' Whether such continuous tension of mind, or stagnation of bodily energy for a whole day, and that on His day who cared for little children, should exist, I leave you to judge. Whether any Sunday school should be established, which does not possess a recreation ground in which the children should be allowed such regulated amusement at intervals throughout the day, as shall suit their age and requirements; and whether, again, there should not be a graduation of the spiritual nutriment of children, as compared with men, analogous to that which is applied in bodily food, I leave to your charitable consideration. At present there is undoubtedly something wrong. Persons, directly they quit school, throw off Sunday altogether in disgust, and hence the frequent confession that their first step in evil was Sabbath-breaking. There is some truth in that confession. But to state their case more correctly, they had been taught to consider the Lord's day a burden. They could not bear it—threw off that burden, and with it, all reverence for God

and all thought of the unseen and their own hereafter."—
Dr. Hessey's *Bampton Lectures*, 1860, p. 337—8.

NOTE (83), page 154.

"Let our Sunday school children," observes Dr. Miller in his assize sermon, entitled "the Dying Judge's Charge," p. 26, — "no longer be dragged to services, in length beyond their powers of patient attention and endurance, and in character unsuited to their capacities—let them have simple, short, suitable services—and when they leave our Sunday schools they will not, as, to so fearful an extent, they do now, turn their backs upon church and clergymen alike, but continue in many cases attached worshippers. Let the quality of our Sunday schools be elevated to keep pace with the elevation of our day schools—a point which has not yet excited the attention which it demands."

It is an instructive fact that while about three-fourths of the popular education afforded by public day-schools is in connection with the Established Church, the Dissenters recruit their numbers on Sunday. For every seventy-six day-scholars, the Church has only forty-five Sunday scholars, while for every three day scholars, the Wesleyans have nineteen Sunday scholars. This may partly be accounted for by the fact that the Church educates on week-days the children of Dissenters.

"I am confident," observes the Dean of Carlisle, "that the Sunday school is just the faggot above the load in many instances. The Sunday-school teachers as a body, however pious and well-intentioned, are inferior even in Scripture knowledge to the day-school teachers, and they are generally wholly unskilled in the art of training. I have seen the children of a class laughing at the blunders of their Sunday-school teachers. I firmly believe that the subsequent irreligion of so many who have been through our schools, is to be traced to the injudicious amount and quality of the whole Sabbath-day instruction. Sunday, instead of being a day of rest and relaxation, is the heaviest and dullest day of the seven to the poor children."

Mr. Fraser, one of the Government Commissioners, observes: " I was in the habit of visiting one or more schools every Sunday, but of all I saw—more than twenty—there is not one that has not left the impression of weariness and deadness on my mind."

It is right to add that the Educational Commissioners express their opinion that " Sunday-schools, when well-conducted, are an effective means of giving religious teaching, and possess other and great advantages."

NOTE (84), p. 154.

The utility of this class of schools may be judged by the circumstance that they are frequented chiefly by those who have never received elementary instruction, or have forgotten it. " At Wells," observes Mr. Cumin, " I found Lord Auckland himself, teaching a class of navvies to read and cypher. I witnessed with admiration those brawny men come into the room with clean smock frocks, and newly washed hands and faces, having walked a distance of more than two miles from their cottages to pursue their studies. Every one had his reason for coming, and one of the most intelligent had the ambition of rising to be an engine-driver." The fact is, as Mr. Wigham, the superintendent of locomotives at Bristol, said, these men know that some of the richest contractors have risen from being mere navvies, but that such a position is impossible to reach without a knowledge of reading, writing, and arithmetic, but especially the last, in order that they may be able to measure work."

It seems to be clearly made out that mixing boys with men always leads to disappointment.

The principal hindrance, however, to the success and extension of evening schools, appears to arise from the difficulty of obtaining the services of proper masters.

It is suggested that a grouping of evening schools might be organised, in which case an organising master might spend one night of the week in each school, and train the ordinary master to his duty. The Commissioners have no doubt that evening schools, unconnected with day schools or with any other institutions, would in many cases be useful; and they quote Mr. Maurice's testimony, to the effect that, at present they are "the only means of encountering the great difficulty of modern English education," See "Popular Education in England, &c." by Herbert S. Skeats; Bradbury and Evans, 1861.

Note (85), p. 154.

There are names that will at once occur to every reader in corroboration of this remark. And it is our happiness to believe, that thousands of the daughters of our people in these days, as teachers in our national schools, as district visitors, as nurses of the sick, as helpers of the helpless, and succourers of the fallen, are doing God's work amongst us, and while ennobling their own sex, furnishing the brightest and most influential example to the other.

Note (86), p. 156.

Thus a gentleman of great experience as an Inspector of Schools, in a letter to Mr. R. A. Kinglake, one of the magistrates for that division of Somersetshire, on the subject of schools for farmers' sons, observes: "The middle classes in this, as well as other districts, are more uncared for than the poor or the independent. Their parents as yet do not feel the vast importance of the matter, and the high prices of the present moment are to them a powerful argument that with their present mental acquirements they can gain money and save money. They never think, reason, or argue on the beneficial influences of a sound education—no, nor even of its pecuniary advantages. Among a hundred farmers' sons, I cannot find one scarcely who knows the nature of the soil he cultivates, what will improve it, or what are the best materials to mingle therewith. They do as their forefathers did, and what they do, they do without a reason. This ought not to be: to say nothing of morals, nothing of that high feeling which would make them useful members of civilised society, capable of well filling the sacred trusts of home life, public life, political life. One year or two of boarding school education, after a miserable drilling by a village schoolmaster, is all that now around here for miles is granted to the middle classes. If you could influence your brother magistrates to take up this matter, and to provide a school, say in the neighbourhood of Weston-super-Mare, there to give a solid useful education,—teaching agriculture not only by chemistry, but by taking some twenty or thirty acres of ground, it would be an inestimable benefit. The arrangements should be so conducted as to average in cost from 30*l.* to 40*l.* Such a school would not only be a blessing to society, but would in a short time be self-supporting, and serve, moreover, as a stimulus for the formation of similar institutions in the county. No time is to be lost if we mean to keep the farmers in their proper place, and prevent their being overtaken and distanced by other classes."

To the same effect, are remarks recently made by Lord Chelmsford, on the occasion of his presiding at a meeting of the Chelmsford Literary Institution. His lordship observed: " The nature of the instruction now given in National schools to the lowest class of the people was of a character so much higher than that which they received in former times, that it was a subject for grave and serious consideration whether increased efforts were not necessary in the classes above them to improve their own minds, in order to keep the same relative distance in advance in their mental progress. Nothing could be more prejudicial to society, than that the labourer should be better informed, and better instructed than his employer."

Again, I find in a pamphlet recently published by one of Her Majesty's Assistant Inspectors of Schools the following remark:—" The few children taught in private schools that have come under my notice, have certainly not been favourable specimens. They have generally learned to write neatly, and do some of the more mechanical parts of their school work correctly, but their minds have not been awakened; and their ignorance on many subjects which are made the matter of much interesting oral instruction in our National schools has been surprising. See " Some Points considered in reference to Secondary Schools," by H. R. Sandford, M.A., one of H.M. Assistant Inspectors of Schools; Wright, Stafford, 1861.

NOTE (87), p. 156.

The reason why the most pretentious and the most shallow of these private schoolmasters are often the most popular and attractive, is well stated in an extract from a letter given by Mr. Acland, in his work on the "Middle Class Examinations," from one whom he calls "an experienced observer, himself in trade." His words are these: "This has always appeared to me the real gist of the educational question,— popular shabbiness of estimate, with popular inability to appreciate. Those who buy bread, or meat, or clothes for their children have some tolerable judgment of the article; but in buying instruction for them, they buy in the dark, and the most conscientious teacher has no chance against the most ignorant quack."

NOTE (88), page 157.

The following passage is extracted from the pamphlet on "Secondary Schools" already alluded to:—" As a proof of how much may be done by these public Middle Class Schools towards raising in tone and intelligence the class of children they are designed to benefit, I need only refer to such institutions as the Middle Class College at Hurstpier-Point—an institution which appears to be conducted in a noble spirit, and to retain a great hold on the affections of its scholars in after life. Nothing, again, can be more promising than the aspect of the Middle Class School lately established at Trowbridge, which has been most liberally endowed by a neighbouring clergyman. One of the most important movements that have been made in regard to middle class education, is the formation in the county of Devon of a company entitled the Devon County School Association, which has already in connection with it an excellent Middle Class School, founded by the Rev. Canon Brereton, and now established on the proprietary basis, at West Buckland, and will probably soon have another. The Lord Lieutenant of the county, and other leading gentry, are liberal supporters of the movement. It is somewhat strange that all these efforts to improve the education of the middle class should be made in the rural county of Devon, while other counties, far beyond it in manufacturing wealth, and both in the extent and in the intelligence of the population, have hardly taken a step in the matter, have done little or nothing in a united way towards providing a better class of schools for their farming and trading class. Any one wishing for information as to the above movement in Devonshire, may obtain it from the Rev. C. S. Bere, Uploman Rectory, Tiverton, who has been instrumental in establishing another school on the same plan as that of West Buckland, in the neighbourhood of Tiverton." Mr. Sandford adds, " It was my acquaintance with such schools, the seeing how much could be done in them for boys of the middle class, and how intelligent, tractable, gentlemanly, under a good system, boys of that class could become, that in a great measure caused me to take an interest in the subject."

NOTE (89), page 158.

See "Educational Charities" in the abstract of the Report of the Royal Commissioners on Education, already alluded to, pp. 100—9.

NOTE (90), page 159.

On June 18, 1857, a statute was passed by convocation, having for its object the examination of candidates not being members of the University. Examinations are held once annually. The examiners, time and place of the examination, and other particulars are arranged by a Delegacy appointed under the authority of the statute. The examinations are held in Oxford and in such other places as the delegates appoint. The candidates are divided into two classes. 1. Seniors under the age of eighteen. 2. Juniors under the age of fifteen. Every successful candidate receives a certificate, specifying the subjects on which he has satisfied the examiners.

The examination of the junior candidates is in the following subjects. 1. Preliminaries, &c. &c. 2. The Rudiments of Faith and Religion. 3. Optional Subjects, &c. &c.

The examination of senior candidates is in 1. Preliminary subjects, &c. &c. 2. The Rudiments of Faith and Religion. 3. Optional subjects &c.

Local committees wishing to have examinations held in their several districts, may at once obtain all necessary information from the Rev. J. Griffiths, 63, St. Giles, Oxford, Secretary to the Delegacy. Their actual request for an examination must be made before the 1st of February.

NOTE (91), page 161.

See "And ye shall know the truth, and the truth shall make you free:"—a sermon preached in the chapel of Marlborough College, on Michaelmas day, 1858, being the anniversary of the Consecration of the chapel, by the

LECTURE VI.

Rev. F. Temple, D.D., Master of Rugby School. See also a sermon preached by the same author in Wellington College Chapel, on Sunday, Jan. 23, 1859, on the text "For as we have many members in one body, and all members have not the same office; so we, being many, are one body in Christ, and every one members one of another," Romans xii. 4. 5, from which the following passage is an extract:— "Now the lesson which St. Paul wants to teach us when he calls the Church a Body, is this; that we are bound up together in such a way that every one of us has a concern in the life of every one else. We are very apt to think that each man has himself to look after, and has nothing to do with any one else, and no one else has anything to do with him. We are very apt to say, 'What is it to any one else how I live? If I do no crime, if I pay my just debts, if I do all my duties which my place requires of me, what more can be wanted? It can make no difference to any one else what are my thoughts, what are my feelings, what is my manner. If I do my duty, no one can complain; however sulky and discontented I may be, no one has a right to interfere. If my words are not bad, no one is hurt by my thoughts. If I never say my prayers, if I never read my Bible in private, if I never think about God, if I never listen to what is going on in God's house, that may be very wrong; but it is no one's concern but my own.' We are apt to take fancies of this sort into our heads; and if we do, here is St. Paul's answer:—'We are members one of another;' we are one body; we cannot live apart from the rest, however much we may wish it. Just see how the members of the body are bound together. Is it nothing to the heart, if the foot be bitten by a poisonous serpent? Is it nothing to the foot, if the mouth drink in the infection of some dangerous disease? Is it nothing to the head, if you cut an artery in the arm and let all the blood flow out? You cannot have any part of the body hurt without the other parts suffering, and sometimes suffering very much. Just so it is with the Body of Christ. If one of us sin, even though the sin be quite secret, and no

one know anything about it but God, until all secrets be
revealed at the day of judgment, yet for all that the sin is a
secret poison, and will most certainly do harm in many secret
ways to those who live much with the sinner. I tell you
that even sins of thought have their secret issues in damaging
the Body, and how much more sins of act and word! And
on the other hand just as the body carries poison from one
member to another (if any poison be brought in), so too does
the body carry from one member to another the grace of
God. God can give His grace in many ways. He can if
He chooses put good thoughts and good wishes into our souls
all at once, and without using any instruments. But the
common way in which He does this is by making one good
man stir up another, and then making him stir up another,
and then him another, until the power of His Holy Spirit
has breathed successively upon many hearts, and has breathed
into them the breath of the life of our Master Christ."
See also a sermon preached by the Rev. E. W. Benson,
M.A., Head Master of Wellington College, on the same
occasion.

Note (92), page 162.

I speak of Dr. Arnold, as I knew him, and the work which
he effected, and the men he trained. On some points, both
political and religious, my views differed from his. But I
was his near neighbour for the last few years of his life,
while I was incumbent of Dunchurch,—and as such
had frequent intercourse with him. I had four sons at
Rugby,—and also three assistants in my parochial charge,
ordained to my cure, who received their education there,—two
of them favourite pupils of Dr. Arnold's, recommended and
introduced by him. Of the former, it does not become me, as
a father, to speak: but I may record my deep and affectionate
sense of services received at the hands of De Bunsen of
Lillieshall, Hoskyns of Tyrrold Aston, and Bere of Uploman,
who laboured with me as sons in the Gospel, and whose

subsequent course has more than fulfilled the promise of their youth.

NOTE (93), page 164.

See "Public School Education:" a lecture delivered at the Athenæum, Tiverton, by the Right Honourable J. T. Coleridge, second edition; London, John Murray, Albemarle street, 1860.

NOTE (94), page 164.

See " Sermons on The Beatitudes" with others, mostly preached before the University of Oxford, Sermon x. p. 176; by George Moberly, D.C.L., Head Master of Winchester College.

NOTE (95), page 166.

It is unquestionable that for the culture of the mind there is no discipline so good as the enlightened study of the masters of Greek and Roman Literature. The preference manifested by the great captain of our age for men to officer his troops who had been educated at our Universities, is well known. Even for commercial pursuits our Universities furnish a good preparation,—while for the senate or the bar it cannot be denied that the studies pursued there supply the best possible training; and the recent efforts to popularize the system and enlarge the course of studies, as well as to free it from antiquated restrictions and abuses, ought to go far to recommend it to practical minds.

I quote with pleasure on this point the mature judgement of Dr. Arnold, " That classical studies should be the basis of intellectual teaching," he maintained from the first. " The study of language," he said, " seems to me as if it was given for the very purpose of forming the human mind in youth; and the Greek and Latin languages, in themselves so perfect, and at the same time freed from the insuperable difficulty which must attend any attempt to teach boys philology through the medium of their own spoken language, seem the very instruments by which this is to be effected." But a comparison of his earlier and later letters will show how much this opinion was strengthened in later years, and how, in some respects, he returned to parts of the old system, which on his first arrival at Rugby he had altered or discarded. To the use of Latin verse, which he had been accustomed to regard as "one of the most contemptible prettinesses of the understanding," "I am becoming" he said, "in my old age more and more a convert." Greek and Latin grammars in English, which he introduced soon after he came, he found were attended with a disadvantage, because the rules which in Latin fixed themselves in the boys' memories, when learned in English, were forgotten. The changes in his views resulted on the whole from his increasing conviction, that "it was not knowledge, but the means of gaining knowledge, which he had to teach;" as well as by his increasing sense of the value of the ancient authors, as belonging really to a period of modern civilization like our own: the feeling that in them, "with a perfect abstraction from those particular names and associations, which are for ever biassing our judgement in modern and domestic instances, the great principles of all political questions, whether civil or ecclesiastical, are perfectly discussed and illustrated with entire freedom, with most attractive eloquence, and with profoundest wisdom."—(Sermons, vol. iii. pref. p. xiii.)

"From time to time, therefore, as in the Journal of Education (vol. vii. p. 240), where his reasons are stated at length, he raised his voice against the popular outcry, by which classical instruction was at that time assailed. And it was, perhaps, not without a share in producing the subsequent reaction in its favour, that the one head-master, who, from his political connections and opinions, would have been supposed most likely to yield to the clamour, was the one who made the most deliberate and decided protest against it."
—*Life of Dr. Arnold*, vol. i. third edition, pp. 134-5-6.

NOTE (96), page 166.

The examination system was altered in 1855. In addition to the classical and mathematical schools, two new schools were established, viz., a school of natural science and a school of law and modern history. The staff of professors who lecture on these subjects has been very largely increased.

At Christchurch, studentships, and at Magdalen College, emyships are awarded for proficiency in physical science: nd at All Souls, the fellowships are awarded with special ;ference to proficiency in the subjects of examination in the iw and modern history schools.

Thus, though the University considers the *literæ humaniores* to be the studies best suited for the general training f all her students, other lines of study are open to those rho have special tastes and aptitudes for them.

NOTE (97), page 167.

"The Labourers in the Vineyard," a sermon preached efore the University of Oxford, on Septuagesima Sunday, February 5th, 1860, by Arthur Penrhyn Stanley, D.D. legius Professor of Ecclesiastical History, and Canon of Christchurch, from which the following grand passage is an xtract:—"It may be that this question, as put in these rords from this place, is fired into the air. It may be that nose whom it most concerns are far away, standing and oitering in a still deeper idleness on this day—I cannot say f '*rest*,' for 'rest' has no meaning for those who know not that it is to *work*. But if in the minds of any who hear me he words find an echo, the answer will perhaps come back lmost in the words of the parable, — 'no man has hired us;' the life of this place is against us; its studies do not suit s; we have worked elsewhere; we have worked at school; ut we cannot work here.' No; not so. There is no fatal harm of indolence and apathy in college life. To labour here is indeed your special call. As the preacher stands Sunday after Sunday in this place, and doubts what is the special duty which he shall lay before you, there is one of which he can feel no doubt whatever; and that is, to work. In after life you may be in doubt what your calling is, but here it cannot be mistaken. Here, in the natural studies of this place, it lies straight before you. Now is the golden time which will never come back to you. The field of study may be narrower than you would wish; narrower, perhaps, than with advantage it might be. But it is wider by many degrees than once it was; it is wide enough for almost every one to find his sphere. At any rate, *do something;* if not within the prescribed limits of study, then do something outside of them; do something to justify your existence here; do something which will enable you in after years to say, 'this at least I then learned so as to remember still.' 'This idea, this book, this character then first broke upon my mind.' 'This habit, this principle got hold of me in such a year, in such a term; and by God's grace it has stood me in good stead until now.'"—Pp. 34-5-6.

NOTES.

LECTURE VII.

NOTE (98), page 173.

IN his noble charge, "The better Prospects of the Church," the Archdeacon denounces the miserable and niggardly spirit, which, as he says, during the last three centuries generally characterised whatever was done in England for the worship of God. "When," says he, "our ancestors were poor and few in number, they built churches capable of containing a far larger population than was then to be found in the land; and they decorated them with all the skill of art, and with everything that was most beautiful and most costly. But since we have become the richest nation upon earth, it has everywhere been seen, for generation after generation, how loth Mammon is to part with any portion of his wealth for the service of God. Therefore the gifts which we had ceased to use passed away from us. The skill in architecture, which had prevailed above four centuries among men whom we have the presumption to look down on with insolent contempt, passed away from us. We became more and more dexterous in all that is merely mechanical, in everything that is designed to pamper and charm the senses, but almost barbarians in the higher regions of art."—Pp. 14, 15.

NOTE (99), page 175.

The churches of St. Pancras and Marylebone in the metropolis, St. Thomas's and St. George's, Birmingham, and not a few similar structures throughout England, on which vast sums were expended, may be cited as examples. Most of these churches are of dimensions much too large for the compass of an ordinary voice, and in the case of many of them to which populous districts were attached, large sums were expended on the fabric, but no adequate provision was made for the minister. The cost of each of them would erect in these days two or three churches far better suited for the purposes of worship, and at the same time provide a parsonage and endowment.

Note (100), page 177.

"Report of Lords' Committee on Spiritual Destitution," p. xix.

The Committee had previously observed (p. xvii.), "Their attention has been given to what is commonly called the pew system, including within the meaning of that expression, seats of a form and size inconveniently large, obstructing sight and sound, and also involving in many cases a continued retention of, or claims to, seats, by persons who may have ceased to reside in the parish, or to frequent the church. By the operation of this system it frequently happens that the poorer classes of the parishioners are, to a great extent, practically excluded from the parish church."

Note (101), page 177.

In "Fuller v. Lane" (2 Add. Eccl. Rep. 425), Sir John Nicholl observes: "All the pews in a parish church are *the common property of the parish:* they are for the use *in common* of the parishioners, who are all entitled to be seated orderly and conveniently, so as best to provide for the accommodation of all."

Mr. Toulmin Smith, of Lincoln's Inn, Barrister at Law, in his work, "The Parish," has the following passage: — "It is well known that pews are a modern innovation, and one of the growths of Puritanism. The result has certainly been different from what the Puritans intended; for pews have been one of the main causes of setting up distinctions, offensive to all good taste and Christian simplicity, even in the house of God. In a remarkable old case (Year Books, 8 Henry VII. fo. 12), though the seats then found in churches were, as is now the case in continental churches, but a few loose and moveable ones, it is declared that even such a seat is '*a nuisance*,' as interfering with the right of 'ease and standing,' that belongs to the people: 'for the Church,' it says, 'is in common to every one; and there is no reason why one should have a seat, and that two should stand: for *no place in the Church belongs more to one than to another;*' while the parishioners 'are not able to have their standing room on account of these seats.' How much more, then, is this true with the modern pew system! It is of great importance to remember, that the sale or letting of pews in a parish church, whether by churchwardens or by any holder of a seat by prescription, is altogether illegal. Nothing can legalise this:—unless indeed, it be an Act of Parliament; and any such Act of Parliament would be an absolutely revolutionary measure. Neither can a parishioner, to whom a seat has been assigned by the churchwardens, let it. The latter are bound indeed to take care that no such practice grows up. It is one of the marks of the disregard of principle, which in so many respects characterises the modern Church Building Acts, that they admit of the letting of seats in the churches built under them. Thereby they do but further prove, that the 'ecclesiastical districts,' and 'new parishes' which they establish, are merely sectarian arrangements. Propositions have been made for legalising the letting of seats in parish churches. The moment this shall be done, the Church will lose every character of an institution standing in any relation to the parish as the *Church of the People*, and claiming, in that character, reverence, affection, and support from sincere men of all creeds and opinions."

To the same effect, Mr. Coke Fowler, on "The Law of Pews" (p. 69). "Can it be wondered at that such practices have done much to alienate the affections of the poor from the Church? By these means they are almost literally shut out. The law tells them that the floor of the church is common ground; but this, like many other things, is in reality only a *pleasant legal fiction!* Yet they are not so dull as not to know that the English clergy are appointed for the cure of all souls, with equal diligence, within the limits of their charge; that one soul is as precious as another in the sight of God; and that the accidents of wealth and rank can attach no spiritual value to one above the other. Can it be a matter of surprise, then, that when, knowing all this, they find the churches of England furnished and arranged on a system diametrically opposite to these truths, they turn their backs on her? It is vain to call the Church of England 'the Poor Man's Church,' whilst, upon her present system, she is emphatically the Church of the Rich."

It is difficult to see on what principle of equity, a rate can be levied on an entire community, for what is practically for the benefit of only a few. The opposition to church-rates in many instances originated, and finds its strongest pleas, in the wrong inflicted on parishioners by the appropriation of seats. Nor should it be forgotten, that the area, which, if free and unappropriated, might, in most instances, afford ample accommodation for all who attend, will be quite insufficient when seats are reserved.

NOTE (102), page 178.

In a Charge delivered to the clergy and churchwardens of the archdeaconry of Coventry, and published at their request, in 1858, I expressed my convictions on this subject in the following terms:— "The parish church is for public worship, and common prayer: its area is free and open ground; its services are for the use of all classes; every parishioner has

LECTURE VII.

a right to a place within its walls. Such is at once the theory of the Church and the law of the land.

"But what is the actual state of our parish churches? Are they common property? Is their area free? Can all the parishioners meet together on their floors, without impediment and without distinction? Can any inhabitant walk into his parish church, and claim his right to worship there, without any one attempting to question this? Wherever else he is put aside, can he say, 'Well, at least the house of God is free. I am at liberty and at home *there:* there the distinctions of the world cease; there the rich and poor meet together; the Lord is the Maker of them all?'

"Must we not, my brethren, admit, with shame, that the reverse of all this is true,— that in no place here in England are human distinctions, and the jealousies and feuds these foster, more rife and rampant than in our parish churches? And that in His House before whom all are equal, there men most assert their place and their precedence? Are not our churches claimed by the few, to the exclusion of the many? Is not the area parcelled out in portions, to which men arrogate separate and exclusive property? Do we not hear of their rights by faculty, and rights by prescription? Do they not even put locks and plates engraven with their names on these cushioned and curtained enclosures, and make merchandize of them, selling and letting them for hire?

"Now, what is this but an act of flagrant spoliation? What can be more discreditable and injurious to us as a Church? Has it not generated, not merely opposition to church-rates, but wide-spread alienation from the Church itself? Does it not in great measure account for the neglect and contempt of religion so prevalent amongst the working classes? What wonder if men rise in opposition to a system which tolerates such an abuse! It places the Church in a most unfavourable and invidious light. It neutralizes its power of doing its appointed work. It stultifies its claims as the Church of the Poor. It almost invalidates its credentials as an institution of Christ. For it is in direct contravention of the principles and precepts of the Gospel. It ignores at once the admonition of the Apostle, and the example of our Lord. The one warns us to have no respect of persons, to give no precedence in our religious assemblies to the man with the gold ring and the goodly apparel over the poor man in vile raiment — not to despise the poor. The other enjoins us to go out into the streets and the lanes, and the highways and the hedges, and to compel them to come in, that God's house may be full. The one tells us that if we have respect unto persons, we commit sin. The other enunciates as the badge of Christ's religion, that the poor have the Gospel preached unto them.

"And what pastor of Christ's Church—at least in our cities and populous places—cannot testify to the obstruction in his work which the abuse of which I speak occasions? how it practically refutes the theory of the parochial system; how it shuts his mouth when he would urge persons to frequent the buildings from which they are thus virtually excluded!

"Its results have been to raise a rampart betwixt the Church and the people, and make the clergy, in too many instances, less the pastors of the nation than the chaplains of a class. It will not admit of argument; it cannot stand inquiry; it would crumble before opposition. And if men were only half as jealous of their rights in matters of religion as they are in matters of this world, they would at once combine to put it down."

Such are my own opinions:—but the subject is of such importance, that I am thankful to avail myself of the recorded sentiments of others.

I begin with extracts from some of the leading journals of the day.

"Nine-tenths of the cry about 'spiritual destitution,' and of the demand for 'church extension,' and the rest, arise, not from the difficulty of meeting the one or effecting the other, but from the fact that interested persons want something more than 'church extension,' and relief from 'spiritual destitution.' They are jealous of new churches, new clergy, new people, and want improvement without alteration; above all, not to abate one jot of their own dignity. *No man's dignity, however, should be allowed to stand a day in the way of public good."—The Times* newspaper, Feb. 14, 1856.

" An attempt has been made, and is still making, to draw to Exeter Hall, on Sunday evenings, some of those thousands of working men who assuredly exist in the metropolis, but who are not found in either the churches or the chapels. The large hall has been opened on the Sunday evenings of the last three weeks, able preachers have been provided, and care has been taken to announce that '*all the seats are free.*'

" We cannot notice these and similar attempts, without recurring to that which is always present to our mind, as one of the foremost causes of the present alienation of the working classes from public worship. We mean the vicious arrangement of nearly all our churches and chapels.

" It is important, when we speak of this, to bear in mind the real date and origin of the evil of which we complain. The pew system, or rather the whole internal arrangement of the churches and chapels of the metropolis is not ancient; it is not Roman Catholic; nor is it Protestant. It took its rise nearly two centuries after the Reformation, in one of the darkest and most deplorable periods of the whole British history .... The first half of the last century, within which most of the present churches and chapels were built, was a period in which religion, morals, science, and literature were at the lowest ebb. Unblushing corruption in the Government, and vulgar selfishness among the people, characterised the age..... Throughout the whole, one principle of action is everywhere discernible; *the upper and middle classes built the churches for themselves."—The Record* newspaper, January 6th, 1856.

" Few people would believe how great a practical hindrance the pew system is to the advance of the Church amongst the masses in our towns. The testimony on this subject of the most practical and sagacious men is singularly uniform, and is strong in proportion to their knowledge of the poor, and the earnestness which they bring to bear upon the difficulties of their situation. In great towns, at least, it is said by those best qualified to speak, that one of the chief hindrances to their work, is the impossibility of getting the poor to feel at home in church, and regard it and its services as something real and living, the centre of their devotions, the comfort of their lives. They look on the Church for the most part as a stiff, cold, and dreary place, which they do not like to enter, and with which they feel they have little to do. They cannot walk freely into it, and kneel down where they choose — it is no home for them; it does not invite them; perhaps it will not receive them when they come. Even with the high-principled there is a reluctance felt, which their principles enable them to overcome; but with the vast majority, that are not so, the state of our churches acts as a barrier against their use, and as an argument which the clergyman finds it difficult to encounter.... The pews are costing the Church of England the hearts of thousands of the English poor ... It is the appropriation of God's house, which has cost us so dear in the alienation of the people of our towns. It is the perfect freedom of God's houses which is needed, as one great practical means towards the recovery of their hearts, and their restoration to the number of the Church's faithful children."—*The Guardian*, September 8th, 1852.

"We look upon the whole pew system, not only as one of the greatest hindrances to the successful working of Christianity, but one of the greatest curses that has fallen on the Church in modern times. And we do not believe that it could ever have been grafted on the Church, except in such an age as that of Cromwell, when worldly-mindedness and individual selfishness had darkened, and almost hid all spiritual religion; and that if the claim had been made for the first time in our day, not only common sense, but every

feeling of religion and equity, would be roused against it. Nothing but the iron rule of prevalent custom, and the prejudice of English traditions, could hide from the eyes of men the injustice of the plan. And hence we would do all that lies in our power to tear it root and branch from the Church. . . . We have ourselves seen pews in English churches twelve feet or more square, duly enclosed by curtains and tapestry, furnished with drawing-room chairs, centre table, hat-stand, and stove with fender and fire-irons."
— *North American Church Review*, October, 1855.

" It is undeniable that the pew system erects an artificial inequality, where all should be equal. Herein it violates a clear and express divine command, anticipating as it were, and made strikingly applicable to the state of things now existing in our own churches. The apostle forbids any advantage whatever to be given in churches to one class over another, as regards situation, or the union of families, or personal comfort. His condemnation specially applies to the invidious division of churches between 'pews' and 'free seats.' To all who are instrumental in maintaining such distinctions, he seems to address the emphatic language,— 'Ye have despised the poor.' 'If ye have respect unto persons ye commit sin ; 'and as if by way of special warning to those who, however unimpeachable they may deem themselves in their faith or works, yet are guilty in this point, he adds, 'but whosoever shall keep the whole law and yet offend in one point, he is guilty of all!' "— *Manchester Weekly Advertiser*, January 26th, 1856.

" The law of England undoubtedly contemplates that every seat in every church shall be free and unappropriated. All the claims of the Church on the purse of the people proceed on this hypothesis. Church-rates, *e. g.* are wholly indefensible — in point of equity — on any other. They proceed upon the assumption that the accommodation of the church is free to all parishioners; which it is not, and never can be, where pews prevail and exclude the poor. Every interference with the relation established between the benefits afforded and the demands made, tends to alienate the people from the Church, and should be avoided as furnishing a plausible charge of inconsistency against her.

"Pews are an evil, even to their occupants. The distinction made between those who have pews and those who have none, destroys the equality of all in the presence of their God; a priority of right in the house of prayer clashes with the very notion of '*common* supplications.' The present system is the prolific parent of ill-will and anger, which arise out of the disputed possession of pews. What miserable parish squabbles, what alienation from the truth, what hostile dissent have not been generated by contested rights to exclusive possession of favourite seats in church! Again, the pew system nurtures selfishness as well as pride. It separates man from his neighbour, and lowers the tone of devotion. But great as are the injuries which pews inflict upon their occupants, they are nothing to those which are inflicted upon the excluded. At present, three-fourths of the whole population of England and Wales who might attend church, have no pews! This state of things repels those who love the Church, and desire to attend her services; but how much more does it hinder those who are wholly indifferent or alien to her, who have to be won to religion of any kind, and who throw it in the face of those who try to evangelise them, that 'even if they go to church they have nowhere to sit!'

"It is no answer to this to say that in many churches where free seats are provided the poor do not use them. There are comparatively few churches in which the free seats are as good as the pews, uniform with them in pattern and construction, and equal to them in comfort and accommodation; where, however, that is the case, and the parish is properly worked, there will be found very few unoccupied free sittings. What the poor cannot endure, is to be seated in benches marked off from the rest of the church, and whose very design and position denote that they are for an inferior class of worshippers. Look at those odious benches that

LECTURE VII. 331

crowd the middle aisles of London churches: is it likely that the poor will be enticed to go and occupy them? They are filled for the most part, but it is by the domestic servants of the pew-holders. The poor are practically driven away. The effect of the pew system on the young, on assistants in shops, and the large floating, unsettled portion of the population, who are separated from their family and home, is very grievous. These having no certainty of a seat if they go to church, easily acquire a habit of not going, and, as years pass on, become confirmed in habits of irreligion or dissent. The mortification of being compelled to stand in a crowd during a great portion of the prayers, while many sittings are unoccupied, because the owner (?) of the pew objects to the admission of strangers to his circle, keeps many from church. Yet this is going on in London and the large towns every Sunday, and driving numbers to the excursion train or to the meeting-house.

"But the pew system is a wrong to the clergy. It is a great obstacle to their success. In dealing with the poor their lips are often silenced by the fact, which they cannot deny, that the poor are not provided for in the parish church. Till this reproach is taken out of the poor man's mouth, it is vain to hope for his return to the feelings and duties of a loving churchman. The obstacles which pews offer to mission work amongst the poor, have driven away many to irregular and unchurchlike substitutes for worship. . . . The destruction of pews and the multiplication of services are amongst the first and simplest methods of church extension, and is the obvious way of making one church do the work of three.

"We have here glanced at the evils of the system. We are aware of all the objections, financial and others, that may be urged against a change, but they have no stand-point in the presence of the grievous evil entailed by things as they are. While the present system lasts the Church can never reclaim the poor. Let her in faith destroy that system, and God will help her to the means of pursuing the more excellent way."—"*Article on The Pew System, and the Injuries which it Inflicts on the Church of England, in the Literary Churchman.*" (London: Bell and Daldy, 72 pp.)

"Pews keep the poor from the house of God, and are fruitful causes of dissent and irreligion. It matters not that in most of the pewed churches sittings are reserved for the poor. The feelings of a poor man are hurt when, on entering the sacred portal, he is directed to the free seats by some rude verger.

"In the sanctuary, the presence-chamber, as it were, of their common Maker, we want men to forget, as far as possible, the distinctions of the outer world, and to remember only that they are brethren, members of one family. They do not look like a congregation of brethren, when some are in warm, panelled, cushioned, and curtained pews; others on open benches. For ourselves, we could scarcely presume to expect the Divine blessing on temples and services kept up by outraging the lowliness of the poor and flattering the pride of the rich. We denounce the system as repugnant to true Christian principles and to the common dictates of Christian charity."— *Church Review*, June 18th, 1861.

"The fearfully unchristian effects of the pew system have at all times stood in such bold contrasts to the Gospel blessings on the poor, that advocates have never been wanting to maintain the true principles; and now that the Church is striving to be active in her work, it is marvellous to witness how abuses, which had hitherto been so long established as to form legal precedents, seem to crumble into dust before the obvious and clear light of justice and Christian truth."—*Christian Remembrancer*, July 18th, 1852.

"To make a special provision for the comfort of the well-educated and better disposed, whilst those who are disinclined to religion are knowingly subjected to all the discouragement of uncomfortable places, or practically — it must often happen — of finding no places at all, in the house of God, is a custom as unhappily universal as it is plainly inconsistent with Christian charity and common sense. It is impossible to overrate the amount of hindrance to the Church's work, in large towns and in country parishes, produced by the present grievous misappropriation of her religious edifices." — *Church of the People.*

See "Letter addressed to the Lord Bishop of Ely, on the equal rights of all classes of parishioners to the use of the parish Church, and the unchristian results of the appropriation of seats," by Rev. John W. H. Molyneux, B.A., incumbent of St. Peter's and St. Gregory, Sudbury, Suffolk. "The Pew System, and the injuries inflicted thereby on all degrees of men in the Church," by a layman. "Preaching the Gospel to the Working Classes impossible under the Pew System," by Rev. John W. H. Molyneux.

To the authorities quoted above I subjoin the following testimonies from individuals.

DR. STANLEY, the late BISHOP OF NORWICH, thus expresses himself in a letter dated Palace, Norwich, December 16th, 1842 : " Agreeing with you, as I entirely do, upon the injustice and evil tendency of pews, by which the benefits of our Church Services are, comparatively speaking, confined to the higher and wealthier classes, to the exclusion of the poor,—I sincerely hope your appeal to the inhabitants of Ipswich may be successful, and that they may be amongst the first to express, as a collective body, their disapprobation of a system so adverse, in my opinion, to the true interests of our national church, which professes to have so much at heart the spiritual welfare of the poorer and humbler classes of our population. I am persuaded, indeed, that one of the prominent cases of dissent, as well as utter disregard and indifference to religion, manifested by too many of these classes, is attributable in a great degree to that exclusive system of pews which has for so many years prevailed."

EARL SHAFTESBURY (House of Lords): — " I consider it a great defect in our churches — a defect which has not grown up of late years,—on the contrary, we are now learning to avoid it, — that the working classes when they attend the services of the Establishment, generally find themselves pewed up to their very eyes, shut out from the places where they can hear and be well accommodated, and not placed on a footing of equality with the rest of the congregation. You find many nooks and corners reserved for the working classes; you have free seats set apart for them; but they will not occupy those places; they think they are despised, and treated as beings of a secondary order. Unless, therefore, you show them proper respect, and in the house of God admit that there at least there is equality, depend upon it the vast proportion of the labouring population in London will *never* be brought to attend the worship of the Establishment. What the people of England want is not patronage, but sympathy,—the bringing of heart to heart,—the acknowledgment on the part of persons of all conditions, of all degrees of wealth, that they are made of like passions with themselves, with the same hopes, the same aspirations, the same sympathies, the same fears."

The EARL OF DERBY, on laying the foundation-stone of a church in the parish of St. James's, London, July, 1860:—
" It was the greatest misfortune of our day that in this great city, and indeed in all the great towns of the country, there was little room for fair play for the development of the parochial system of the Church — that system than which nothing could be so admirably adapted to its high and holy ends — that system which contemplated not merely the aggregation of men and women in the neighbourhood, but which did contemplate, in the strictest sense of the term, a community of Christian men and women, with common interests, with common feelings, with common sympathies, and with one faith in common. That Church was open to all, rich and poor without distinction, and was one which authorized the minister to be the adviser and friend of all, he knowing all who were confided to his charge, and being prepared, with a due sense of his responsibility to his Heavenly Father, to dispense the Sacraments to all alike. In large towns it would be too much to say that the benefits of the parochial system were equally well carried out; but,

thank God, in many rural districts they nearly approached to the practical working of the system. The duties of property, as well as its rights, were not only not ignored, but they were respected, and for the most part were faithfully performed. Common occupations facilitated good feeling, bringing together rich and poor in kindly sympathy. They were not severed, but were connected together by the bonds of human friendship, and by Christian fellowship. The churches for the most part were able to admit those who came to them for the purpose of Divine worship, and in a majority of the parish churches it must be the fault of the minister, if he were not known to his parishioners, and did not find out the means of working upon their affections; but, unhappily in this great metropolis there was no room for this work of Christian fellowship. The very size of many parishes made it absurd for the minister to attempt to become acquainted with more than a very small portion of his parishioners, even with the assistance of the laity, who could have personal access to a part only of the population. Again, in the churches, large as they were, they had not, in many cases, one-tenth of those who ought to be habitual attendants on Divine worship; and this because it was necessary to resort to pew rents, by which a portion of the parishioners, and others, were excluded, though they might desire to attend these holy places. It was impossible to enter many large churches without being painfully struck with the comparatively small number of free seats, and the still smaller number of the working classes by whom those free seats were occupied. In London the claims of property were but feebly felt; the owner of the soil, through special agreements, building, and underletting, held but a small portion of it, thus dividing and distributing the interests of the people, doing away with the responsibility attaching to the property in respect to those who were settled upon it. The more wealthy had, perhaps, no other property; and the result of all this was, that a vast number of the population were growing up in a state of heathenism, and did not attend the services of the Church. The poor again, to whom emphatically the principles of Christian truth should be preached, were excluded from all the ministrations of the Gospel, and access to their spiritual pastors and advisers. True indeed it was that the labours of the ministry were lightened and assisted by a body of devoted Christians, engaged in the offices of Sunday-school teachers, Scripture readers, &c., who laboured either for a very small remuneration, or gratuitously. But because this assistance was required, was it right that those whom Divine Providence had blessed with wealth should withdraw their aid, and withhold their pecuniary assistance towards facilitating the efforts of those Christian people who were thus labouring in this wide field of Christian benevolence? It was unfortunately the case that there was too little desire on the part of the wealthy to put to themselves the fearful question, for such it was, 'Who is my neighbour?' But were they to make no effort in the name of Him who had declared that none should be lost? These were some of the reflections which had crowded upon his mind as, year after year, he had marked the constant and hopeless efforts of the parochial clergy to maintain the parochial system."

The DEAN OF CARLISLE: — "Who are they that should cast a pebble of hindrance in our way? Is it those who are preaching on soft cushions to pampered hearers, in churches the very antitype of that referred to by the Apostle: 'Stand thou there, or sit here at my footstool?' Is there not very great guilt on the Church of England, that she has for so many years allowed, to say no more, the rich to accommodate themselves and to care so little for her poorer members? No wonder she has gone so far astray! My friends, the answer to this is, we ask you to come here, because many desire and cannot go to church; many desire, and cannot find a place to go in, without being insulted by distinctions in the presence of God, which are hateful to the God we worship."

The late PROFESSOR BLUNT: — "Everybody must see

that the Church of England has had its basis greatly narrowed by our pew system, till it was ceasing to be the Church of the People, with everything in it to fix itself in their affections; the while that 'the man in the goodly apparel and with the gold ring' was pretty well securing to himself the whole area of the building."

The Rev. Dr. Taylor, of St. John's, Liverpool: — "There is an invidious distinction between the rich and the poor, as well in the appearance of the pews as in their position. Those of the former are well supplied with comfortable cushions, carpets, and hassocks, while doors serve to keep out intruders; they are also fixed in the best position in the church, not only for the purpose of hearing, but also of seeing and being seen. Those of the poor, on the contrary, are plain open benches, erected in the worst part of the building; six or eight near the door, exposed too to draughts; a few of the more aged are, perhaps,—a mark of favour,—brought up and ranged round the pulpit on forms, or seated on the steps of the Communion Table; whilst if more space be wanting to accommodate them — a very unlikely thing, as may well be thought under such circumstances,— forms are placed for them along the aisles, where they are compelled to squeeze themselves into the smallest possible compass, whilst the aristocratic occupants of the cushioned, scarlet-lined pews, rustle past in their silks and satins.

"Now, I ask, is it any wonder that the free seats in too many of our churches, thus involving the badge of poverty and disgrace, should be deserted by the poor? And yet our ministers and the wealthy turn round and express their astonishment that the poor do not come to church.

" Let churches be placed on a proper footing. Sweep away all closed pews; let there be no distinction between class and class in the house of God. The soul of one is as valuable as the soul of another. Why should not the poor have as good an opportunity of hearing the word, 'by which faith cometh,' as the rich? That is a profound oracle in Exodus xxx. 12—15:—'The rich shall not give more, the poor shall not give less, when they give every man a ransom for his soul.' Wherefore? Because the souls of all are equally valuable in God's sight.

"The poor have feelings of independence and self-respect, all the more acute, perhaps, from the poverty of their circumstances—at least the more alive to what they cannot but regard as a designed insult — the invidious classification of rich and poor in God's house. Whilst this state of things continues, let us hear no more of the excess of free sittings above applicants for their use."

The DEAN OF MANCHESTER: — "The effect of it in numerous instances is to shut out the poor from our church services, and thus hinder them from partaking of the benefits we are continually complaining they so seldom seek. In our old parish churches there were no such things as rented sittings, and in country places generally, in the present day, the whole are free.* It is only in large towns and in populous districts, wherein new churches have been built, that this rule is seen; and it is to be feared that in all instances wherein it is established there are grounds of apprehension as to the Church's security."

The late WILLIAM COBBETT: — "When our churches were first built, people had not thought yet of cramming them with pews as a stable is filled with stalls. When they had reared a fine and noble building, they did not dream of disfiguring the inside of it by filling its floor with large and deep boxes made of deal boards. In short, the floor was the place for the worshippers to stand and to kneel, and there was no *distinction*, no high place, and no low place—all were upon a level before *God* at any rate. Some were not stuck into pews lined with green or red cloth, while others were crammed into corners to stand erect or sit on the floor. Those who built these churches made their calculations as to the people to be contained in them, not making any allowance for the deal boards."

* The worthy Dean is much mistaken on this point. I wish it were in practice as he states.—J. S.

Rev. JOHN W. H. MOLYNEUX:—" Men who are ill-informed sometimes speak as though a church entirely free and unappropriated, that is, *not cut up into small private properties*, was a new and unheard-of thing. So far is this from being true, that when our fine old churches were built, pews and appropriated seats were utterly unknown. This was the case for above 1600 years of the Church's history. Such inventions were left for a covetous and worldly age, when the selfish ease and convenience of rich men is thought more of than the interest of the Gospel and the good of the poor; and when all just idea of common public worship is well nigh lost.

" The very essence of the mischief of the pew system is, that it has produced indifference and dislike, to even a greater extent than inability, to attend church. It is this special evil effect of the system which constitutes the chief, it may almost be said the only, difficulty in the way of its revival; for were the people generally sensible of the value of that of which they have been robbed, did they prize it as they would do worldly advantages and political privileges, there would be such an agitation and demand, as would soon rescue the churches from appropriation. Private seats in the parish churches of London would then be as much out of the question as private paths in its thoroughfares.

" As it is, however, those who have been most injured, care least; and we have to plead for those who plead not for themselves, and to contend for those, who, for the most part, neither sympathise with, nor understand, the efforts that are made in their behalf. They have been of no account with the Church, and the Church is now of no account with them. If we wait till the people cry out for the use of the church, we may wait for ever. We might as well wait for the heathen to cry out for the Gospel before we send missionaries to them. We must anticipate the demand, and by supply create it. The Church must open her doors, and throw wide her gates, and in so doing, show that her arms and her heart are open to embrace with tenderest love, all her lost and wandering children. She must act like her Master, who said, 'ye have not chosen me, but I have chosen you.'

"If the whole is unappropriated, not a single seat need ever be lost or left vacant on the chance of its 'owner' coming. No one need ever feel uncomfortable at the thought that he is using another person's 'property.' Every family and individual at each service they attend, will place themselves just where they please, where they find such vacant places as they require. Families, including children and servants, may all sit together if they please, without the least hindrance or difficulty; and they will all feel happy and at ease, with the consciousness that they are in their Father's house, and therefore in their own home, where they have the best possible right to be.

"I know it is God's will that the church shall be for the people, and that the Gospel shall be preached to the poor: I have therefore no fear and no anxiety as to the result."— *Letter to his Parishioners.* Second Edition.

NOTE (103), page 178.

The abuse to which I here draw attention, is notorious, and of frequent occurrence; and one which, as archdeacon, I have on several occasions been called on to redress. Were the parochial clergy appealed to, they would furnish numerous instances, as within their own knowledge, of such misappropriation of *free sittings* on the part of the middle class.

NOTE (104), page 178.

This is no doubt the case in some instances; and is easily accounted for, by the fact that under the present system, the possession of a private sitting is regarded as a personal dignity. The feeling of the operative classes in this respect is thus explained in an able pamphlet on the pew system, already alluded to: —

"Of all the qualities of character belonging to the inhabitants of these islands, none stands out in bolder relief than that of sturdy independence. To be under an obligation to, or dependent upon another, is alien to our nationality.

"The classes of workmen, artisans, and small shop-keepers, demonstrate this spirit even stronger than their superiors. If there be one subject on which sensitiveness is displayed more than another, it is the imputation of poverty. On these points, a wound is inflicted by the adoption and arrangement of free seats in churches. A mechanic declines to be classed as a pauper. He enters the market for labour, and honestly earns his own livelihood. He asks, Why am I cold-shouldered in church, why thrust into the most distant parts of the building,—this too in the House of God?"—*The Pew System*, &c.

"Examine what provision is made for *the largest class of all*— the working men and their families. A few benches up the middle aisle, or at the back of the galleries, constitute nearly the whole of the accommodation set apart for those whose numbers, in the immediate vicinity, must be told by thousands. What wonder is it, then, if the mechanic, entering such a church, and feeling himself regarded almost as an intruder, resolves to go there no more? Is not the resolution, on the part of a man not yet religious, a very natural one?

"The truth is, we have gone in the very teeth of St. James's injunctions, and are now 'reaping that which we have sown.' The simple remedy is repentance, and immediate restitution." — *The Record* newspaper, January 6th, 1856.

NOTE (105), page 180.

To wit, the Incorporated Church Building Society, which has a special fund for temporary school churches and mission houses, the objects of which are, as stated in its reports—

"1.— By promoting the erection of school-churches and mission-houses, to supply temporarily (till funds for building a permanent church can be raised), the spiritual wants of densely populated districts in large parishes.—2. To aid in building permanent mission-houses in large towns, under special and peculiar circumstances.—3. To assist in erecting mission-houses, of a more or less permanent character, in the scattered hamlets and outlying districts of wide-spread parishes. Donations or subscriptions to this fund, will also be gratefully received by the Local Hon. Secretary."

The archdiaconal church extension societies of Worcester and Coventry also give grants for the erection of temporary places of worship, and of schoolrooms which may be used for the same purpose.

The following recommendation occurs in the Report of the Committee of the Lower House of Convocation on Home and Foreign Missions:—" To meet the spiritual wants of the shifting masses of population in some parts, and the growing settlements in other parts of our mining and manufacturing districts, temporary or mission-chapels are greatly needed." To which the following note is appended:—" It has been suggested, that church building societies might promote the objects here recommended, by loans as well as liberal gifts. The former might bear interest, and be secured by a mortgage on the property. The latter also might be made conditionally, so that if from any cause within twenty years the buildings should no longer be wanted for their original purpose, a certain fixed proportion of the grants should be recoverable by the society. It is obvious, that the chapels could only be *licensed*, and we would suggest the desirableness of a relaxation of that rule of most of our church building societies, by which they are precluded from giving aid to unconsecrated buildings."

NOTE (106), page 180.

The building to which I allude was erected during my incumbency, at Thurlaston, an outlying hamlet in the parish of Dunchurch, Warwickshire, from a design furnished by W. Butterfield, Esq., and has been greatly admired. It accommodates about 130 persons, and I have the happiness of knowing that the services, commenced by myself some years ago, are still continued and well attended.

NOTE (107), page 181.

Information as to the structures here alluded to may be obtained from G. Robinson, Esq. Leamington, architect of the Coventry Archdiaconal Church Extension Society, who has given much attention to the subject, and to whom the credit of originating the particular mode of construction is due.

NOTE (108), page 181.

Dr. Arnold also shortly stated his views on this point at a meeting of the Coventry Archdiaconal Church Building Society, a year or two before his death. And in his " Life and Correspondence," 3rd edition, p. 179, he thus expresses himself, in a letter written in answer to a request for a subscription towards the erection of a church: " I shall be glad to subscribe 2l. towards the endowment of the Church, and not towards the building. My reason for this distinction is, that I think in all cases the right plan to pursue is to raise funds in the first instance for a clergyman, and to procure for him a definitely marked district as his cure. The real Church being thus founded, if money can also be procured for the material church, so much the better. If not, I would prefer to see any building in the district licensed for the temporary performance of divine service, feeling perfectly sure that the zeal and munificence of the congregation would, in the course of years, raise a far more ornamental building than can ever be raised by a public subscription ; and that, in the meantime, there might be raised by subscription an adequate fund for the maintenance of a clergyman: whereas, on the present system, it seems perfectly hopeless, by any subscriptions, in one generation, to provide both clergymen and churches in numbers equal to the wants of the country."

Note (109), page 181.

I refer the reader to an article in the *Quarterly Review*, April 1861, on "Spiritual Destitution," already quoted, p. 239, in which the desirableness of such temporary buildings is strongly urged.

To the same effect are some pertinent remarks in a leading article in *The Times* newspaper of April 16, 1860, from which the following is an extract:—

"All experience shows that a population of this sort, and in this condition, cannot be dealt with as the simple folk within sight or sound of a village church, or even the small knot of gentry and tradespeople in a country town. In those vast metropolitan parishes — three exceeding 35,000, says the Bishop; four more exceeding 30,000; five more exceeding 25,000; six more exceeding 20,000, and so on — altogether sixty-six parishes exceeding 10,000, we have a chaos of social elements, a dead level of conditions, a mere undeveloped mine of moral qualities. This is not the case for individual agencies, marvellous and even miraculous as they have proved in some emergencies. Ordinary men cannot breast such waves, and even extraordinary men may fail. The Bishop hails missionary enterprise, but hopes more from any scheme for subdividing parishes into manageable districts. The latter is the work to be promoted by the Diocesan Church Building Society. Of course, there must be both churches and clergymen, and we hope eventually to see them adjusted one to the other. But, as there are not churches,— or the churches that are, so we are told, are but ill-attended; as clergy engaged in this hard service require mutual help and countenance; as the spiritual war is, in fact, the invasion of an enemy's territory, we cannot help thinking the Bishop would get more sympathy, more money, and more men for a well-devised missionary work, framed to the scale of the whole metropolis, than for more 'churches,' in the vulgar sense of the word. The handsome church, on a costly site, with its actual or threatened tower, its permanent endowment, and its staff of petty officers, is the Church's three-decker, on which we spend so much, and so often find to be useless. What we really want is the flotilla of gun-boats, to push into lanes and alleys. We want something more locomotive than church and steeple; more winning even than reredoses and copes; sweeter than church bells; and more penetrating than either the feet or the eloquence of dignified rectors. If the Church does not adapt her means to the end, and make it a 'day of little things,' Dissenters, and even Roman Catholics, will. In fact, this is what they are doing; and this it is that enables them to make up for their immense disadvantages in social rank and position."

NOTE (110), page 182.

We find these places of worship frequently alluded to in Scripture;—as, Matthew iv. 23; vi. 5; xii. 9; xiii. 18. Mark i. 29, 39; xiv. 1; xv. 21. Luke iv. 16, 44; vii. 5; xiii. 10; xvii. 17; xviii. 4, 7, 26. John vi. 59; xviii. 20; Acts i. 13; vi. 9; x. 9; xvi. 20.

To one of them — an oratory, or place of religious retirement — our Blessed Lord is supposed to have resorted — Luke vi. 12; and the words τῇ προσευχῇ (in our translation, "in prayer"), may be more properly rendered "the place of prayer."

NOTE (111), page 184.

"When a nuisance of long standing is to be abated," writes Archdeacon Hare, "it is requisite that many persons should join in lifting up their voices against it." I will therefore further refer to a passage in Mr. Perceval's delightful "Christian Peace Offering" (p. 139), where, after speaking of the churches which he has seen in the Romanist countries, " of the largest dimensions, crowded from one end to the other, without distinction of age, or sex, or rank — without regard to personal accommodation — all, like one body, on their knees, and all with one voice joining in the responses"— he contrasts them with our churches, "into which the pride of the world, instead of being at least left at the threshold, enters openly, and where the ease and comfort of the rich and great is sought to the inconvenience of their poorer brethren, and not to their inconvenience only, but oftentimes to the hindrance of their sight and hearing; nay, where litigious squabbles and miserable jealousies are often carried into the house of God, and maintained with personal violence, about the possession of this or that pew." — *The Better Prospects of the Church. A Charge to the Clergy of the Archdeaconry of Lewes, by Julius Charles Hare. M.A.* Notes, pp. 48, 49.

To the same purpose a writer in the *North American Review* observes :— " We acknowledge that we have never entered a Romish church on the Continent, and seen how the whole space is left open every day as a place of retirement and prayer for *all* classes, and watched the little children as they came in, in pairs or singly, go down on their knees and hold up their little hands in prayer before the altar—or seen the steps of the churches at early morn covered with the tools of the labourers who, on their way to their daily task, had stopped to ask God's blessing on the day — or, as twilight drew its curtain round the rich and poor side by side on the same stone floor—without breathing the prayer that we might yet behold something of this in our own land, in temples of a purer faith."

NOTE (112), page 187.

These words occur in the speech of Lord Ebury, in the [Ho]use of Lords, May 8, 1860, and indicate his views on the [R]evision of the Liturgy. That his object is to benefit the [C]hurch, as well as to conciliate Separatists, will be dis[pu]ted by no one who is acquainted with his Lordship's per[so]nal character and active services in the cause of religion. [B]ut as, unhappily, some of his remarks have given offence, [an]d the object of his motion has been both misunderstood [an]d misrepresented, it is only fair to state his design in the [w]ords employed by himself:—

"As I have been so often asked the question what my [o]wn views are, I am perfectly willing, as far as I can, to [an]swer it; though, of course, it can only be in general [te]rms.

"The Commission would, I presume, be composed of [ec]clesiastics, with the admixture of a few laymen; at all [ev]ents, of some civilians, to assist in the review of our [Ca]nons and constitutions. It would be animated, doubtless, [b]y the spirit which is so well set forth in the letter of the [A]merican Episcopal Convention to the Anglican Bishops [(1]786), namely, 'not to depart from any doctrine of our [C]hurch, but carefully to consider the alteration of such [th]ings as are calculated to remove objections, which it would [ap]pear to be more conducive to union and general content obviate than to dispute.'

"As to the Canons, in regard to the validity and operation [of] which the greatest variety of opinion prevails — and [w]hich, if allowed to remain as they now are, it is possible [m]ay become the source of even more vexatious litigation [th]an they ever have been previously — I presume those that [ar]e deemed obsolete will be expunged, while any that it is [co]nsidered useful to retain will be couched in comprehen[sib]le language, and placed in harmony with existing use. [A]lthough, in old phraseology, in their entirety they are called the Book of Canons, yet there is, in fact, no Book. They are of two sorts — the old black-letter Canons, framed before the Reformation, and sanctioned by Act of Parliament, 25th Henry VIII., so far as they be not contrary to custom, statute, or royal prerogative; the others, of 1603, which were never confirmed by Parliament, and which are supposed to be binding on the clergy alone, though doubts have been frequently expressed whether, in fact, they are binding on any one; and, in truth, they are almost universally disregarded. The historian of the early Puritans says of them:—

'The disgrace of these barbarous canons belongs to the Convocation in which they passed; but prejudice, fomented from time to time by some of her assailants, still lays it to the Church of England; and it must be allowed that some degree of censure fairly belongs to her for permitting the canons to remain so long without revision, for the canons in their present state are discreditable to the Church, unsuited to the age, and urgently wanting revision.'

" With regard to the Prayer Book, the changes most generally desired seem to be these:— First and foremost, and that without which other alterations would scarcely be considered a boon, stands the abolition of the terms of Subscription, enforced by the Act of the 14th of Charles II. They were not considered essential in the Church of Jewel and Hooker, during the stormiest periods of our Church-history. They are a disgrace to our statute-book in the year 1860. Then the abbreviation of the Morning Service and Daily Service, the objections to which may be summed up in the language of Archdeacon Berens:—

'Our Morning Services last too long, both in a moral and physical point of view — too long for keeping up a proper degree of attention and devoted feeling — too long physically, inasmuch as to the very old and very young, and to those who labour under a want of health, it often occasions a painful weariness.'

LECTURE VII. 349

On a former occasion I gave a detailed specification of repetitions and anomalies contained in the Morning ice. I presume it is not necessary that I should at them now; I will therefore merely remark, in passing, the repetitions are generally considered even greater rances to devotion than the length.

Then, as an attempt at rigid uniformity is as useless as it expedient, the officiating minister should be at liberty ade selections for services within certain limits, when onsidered them better adapted to the circumstances of ongregation than those prescribed.

Next, the remodelling of the Calendars and Rubrics; a t almost universally admitted; specially substituting the ired word of God for the apocryphal lessons.

I think it is also desired that the Psalms should be nged for three services, with optional selections, as in American Book of Prayers.

As to the Athanasian Creed, it has been proposed either the damnatory clauses should be expunged, or that the ic should be so far altered as not to make the reading of ompulsory; in fact, in most churches it is very seldom l, and in some not at all. Both in this case, the saying)aily Prayer, and the Services for the Saints' Days — the of Uniformity and Terms of Subscription are perpetually ated; and it were much to be wished that the ordering hese should be so altered as not to make their use ab- tely imperative.

The occasional services — for Burial, Visitation of the k, Baptism, Marriage, Catechism, and Ordination — should come under review, in order, as I mentioned in my vious address to this House, to see whether certain ressions contained in them might not be so modified as give a more unequivocal latitude to difference of opinion n they do at present; and, where unity is indispensable, e clearly to define our Church's teaching, in matters ch have within the last few years, and which are still, ing rise to the most lamentable and violent contests before courts of law.

"The Burial Service, as it is now required to be performed, has been declared to be a scandal by four thousand clergymen of various shades of opinion.

"It is in the knowledge of your Lordships that the Marriage Service is habitually mutilated.

"Lastly, I see no reason why we should continue to pray in bad grammar, false concords, and obsolete terms; and it is, therefore, much wished that more suitable terms should be substituted for them, especially such as would not easily be misunderstood by the poorer classes."—*Speech of Lord Ebury, in the House of Lords, May 8th,* 1860, *on the Revision of the Liturgy,* pp. 22, 23, 24, 25.

NOTE (113), page 187.

"What," asks Dr. Cardwell, in his account of the Revision of the Liturgy in the reign of James I., "must the Puritans have thought of the complete and almost contemptuous refusal that was given to them respecting the vestments, the ring in marriage, and the cross in baptism? observances which, when treated as mere rites, were held to be unobjectionable, but when considered on the principle of obedience to church authority, were pronounced to be indispensable. 'I charge you,' said the king, 'never speak more to that point, how far you are to obey the orders of the Church.'"

Again, in his narrative of the changes effected in the reign of Charles II., after recording Dr. Tennison's computation of 600 minor alterations authorised in the Book of Common Prayer by the Convocation of 1662, and finally ratified by the Act of Uniformity, he remarks, "It will be observed, that in this long enumeration there is no mention of any of those characteristic points which had been the subjects of strife and division in the Church, from the earliest days of Puritanism. That the use of the Apocrypha; the expressions complained of in the Litany, and in the services for Baptism, Marriage, and Burial; the Rubric with regard to vestments,

kneeling at the communion, the cross in baptism, the
 in marriage, the declaration as to infants dying imme-
ly after baptism, the absolution of the sick, though some
ιem slightly modified, continued in principle the same.
 hese and several others had been conceded by the Com-
ιe of 1641; they had also been virtually withdrawn by
 Royal Declaration of October 1660; and some of them
 been abandoned by the bishops in the Savoy Conference.
 they were all of them retained by the Act of Uniformity,
 he plea that the Nonconformists had lost whatever
 ι they might once have had for consideration and for-
ance, and that the other party saw nothing in such
ations but inconvenience and error. And this feeling
 so strong, both in Convocation and in Parliament, that
ral changes of an opposite character were approved,
ch could not fail to be galling to the Presbyterians."
listory of Conferences, &c., by E. Cardwell, D.D.,
 144, 386-7.
'hus also Bishop Short, in his remarks on the Act of
 formity and its consequences:— " Had a contrary line of
 cy been pursued; had some further alterations been
 le in the Common Prayer Book; had the old law been
 wed to stand with regard to conformity; and particularly
 a wish existed and been expressed by the upper orders
 ιng the clergy, that union might be cultivated in the
 ιrch as much as possible; many of the more moderate Non-
formists would probably have joined the Establishment.
: the very declaration contained in the Act was obviously
 oduced to prevent the possibility of such an event." . . .
,'hen Lord Manchester," states Dr. Calamy, "told the
 ιg, while the Act of Uniformity was under debate, that
 was afraid the terms of it were so rigid that many of the
 ιisters would not comply with it, Sheldon replied, ' I am
 ιid they will.' Nay, 'tis credibly reported he should say,
 ιw we know their minds, we'll make them knaves if they
 form.'
'Doubtless Sheldon might deem this line of policy, of

ejecting all the Nonconformists, to be the wisest for the Church; but the events which have since occurred must convince every man who can judge of such questions, that intolerance is but another name for selfishness, and will generally defeat its own ends."—*Bp. Short's History of the Church of England.* Pp. 510-11.

Note (114), page 189.

In his recent work on the Revision of the Liturgy, Dr. Vaughan has argued with great force in favour of retaining the words in the Office as they now stand. But the fact remains, that in 1850, 4000 of the clergy, in addressing the Primate on the subject, represented that the phraseology complained of " imposed a heavy burden on their consciences, and was an occasion of scandal to Christian people."

Note (115), page 191.

"Lights and Shadows; or Church Life in Australia," by T. Binney. Pp. 55-6-7.

Note (116), page 192.

"The Liturgy and the Dissenters," by Rev. Isaac Taylor, M.A. Third edition. P. 33.

Note (117), page 193.

"There is no fear," says Mr. Binney, "of the beautiful Liturgy of the Church of England being tampered with by her true and loving children—a Service which, for myself, I have once and again acknowledged that I seldom hear devoutly and appropriately conducted without tears."—*Lights and Shadows*, p. 135.

Some of my readers may recall a similar testimony borne

. Cumming, of the National Church of Scotland, when bing the impression produced upon himself the first he joined in the Litany. The only objection urged other member of the Scotch Establishment against our gy was, that it was too spiritual. It was doubtless the ned devotion of the Service which in this instance was ained of.
ught to add the terms in which Mr. Binney qualifies the age quoted above :—" But that the ' Offices ' shall be red, and thus brought into harmony with the mind of the and personal church — the men and women who really tute the congregation of the faithful, who have scriptural in their purified reason, and the life of God in their ouls — that this should be done, is only what is panted rayed for now by a majority of the members of the opal Communion, who are alive to its interests, disished by intelligence, or piety, or both."—P. 135.

NOTE (118), page 193.

Appendix I. to an able sermon, entitled " The Dying ," in which Dr. Miller, of St. Martin's, Birmingham, ls the result of a scheme attempted by himself, and has since, in part, been successfully adopted by other men.
also " Chronicle of Convocation " for Session Feb. 10, in which the present Bishop of London is reported e used the following language :—
think that it is of great importance that your Lordships l consider very fully the degree of elasticity of which resent Services are capable. Your Lordships drew up irculated a paper, some years ago, on the subject of the the Litany ; but I believe it will be found that it is y sufficiently understood by the clergy in the more c parts of the country, and certainly is not generally n to the laity, that the use of the Litany by itself is ily lawful, but is actually encouraged by the assent of

a majority of your Lordships. This seems to me a very important point. I have conversed with many persons who have thought deeply on this subject, who consider it of great importance that your Lordships should let it be understood, after mature consideration, in what points you believe there is elasticity in our services. I believe that there is great elasticity in those services. I believe that the use of the Litany itself is almost sufficient to meet the demand for a more elastic service. If it be found, also — and I believe it may — that the Communion Service may be used as a second service, that will be a great means of making our services suitable for occasions when you do not wish to have the whole service. If it be true that you can preach without using the whole of these services, it would give a degree of elasticity which I think would satisfy every reasonable man. And I believe it will be found, when the matter is thoroughly investigated, that there is no need of revision, even with a view of making our services more elastic."—P. 14.

See, further, in a speech delivered by the same prelate, as reported, Feb. 11, 1859, the following passage:—" It has been said that the Bishops wish to sit still and do nothing. Now there are no persons more alive to the necessity of our services being made more elastic, or who have taken a more active part in rendering them so, than the Bishops. Who but they have been the chief movers in our several Special Services? They have, moreover, taken the opinion of three eminent counsel on the subject — Sir F. Kelly, Mr. Roundell Palmer, and Dr. Phillimore — who are of opinion, notwithstanding what has usually been supposed to be the interpretation of the Act of Uniformity, that the section which requires the service of the Book of Common Prayer to be read in the church, chapel, or place of worship where a sermon or lecture is to be preached, before such sermon or lecture be preached, applies to lecturers only, and that 'it is not necessary that the Common Prayer and Service should be read in presence of the preacher of the sermon or

re, or upon every occasion on which a sermon or lecture
be preached, if the preacher be a rector or other parish
t.' That, of course, opens a very wide door, for it im-
that a sermon may be preached without the regular
rs of the Church having been read. I would call your
ships' attention to the great elasticity which has been
ι by the adoption of that opinion by this House, and to
ower of acting throughout the length and breadth of
and upon the declaration made by your Lordships some
ago with reference to the use of the Litany."—*Chronicle
invocation,* p. 27.

NOTES.

LECTURE VIII.

NOTE (119), page 204.

THE words are quoted from a Sermon by Rev. F. Robertson; but as these Notes are being prepared in a foreign country, where I have no ready access to books, I am unable to verify the quotation.

NOTE (120), page 210.

The efforts of Mr. Henry Hoare in the promotion of a plan for the organisation of such conferences between the clergy and the laity throughout the country are now well known to every churchman, and have already borne abundant fruit.

For the testimony of many of our most distinguished prelates in favour of this plan, see Reports of Proceedings in the Upper House of Convocation, Feb. 11th, 1858, Feb. 11th, 1859, and Feb. 11th, 1862.

I make the following extracts from the said Reports:

"CO-OPERATION OF THE CLERGY AND LAITY.

(*February* 12*th*, 1858.)

" The BISHOP OF LONDON — I have been requested to present a petition from a number of the clergy and laity of the Church of England, whose object is to induce this House to take some steps to bring the clergy and laity into more intimate co-operation with each other for the general benefit of the Church: —

" ' To the Most Rev. the Archbishop, the Right Rev. the Bishops, and the Rev. the Clergy of the Province of Canterbury, in Convocation assembled,

" ' The humble petition of the undersigned clergy and laity of the Church of England,

" ' Sheweth — That your petitioners observe with thankfulness the progress which continues to be made towards the restoration of synodal action in the Church of England.

" ' That your petitioners have seen with satisfaction the appointment of a committee of the Lower House in May, 1857, to consider the best means of securing the united counsel and co-operation of the clergy and laity of the Church.

" ' That your petitioners appreciate highly the benefits derivable from ruridecanal synods and chapters.

" ' That your petitioners believe that ruridecanal divisions of dioceses would likewise afford convenient facilities for lay co-operation, if laymen resident within the deanery were invited by the rural dean, as occasion might require, to confer with the clergy on subjects affecting the welfare and usefulness of the Church.

" ' Your petitioners, therefore, humbly pray that your venerable House will be pleased to take into consideration the possibility and desirableness of making some provision for the more thorough revival of ruridecanal synods or chapters throughout the province.

" ' Your petitioners further pray that you will take steps for the promotion of such a measure of co-operation of the clergy and laity in ruridecanal divisions or dioceses, as in your wisdom you may deem right and expedient.

" ' And, sincerely trusting that the blessing and guidance of the Holy Spirit may be vouchsafed to your deliberations, your petitioners, as in duty bound, will ever pray.'

" Without expressing any opinion as to the particular mode in which this object is sought to be obtained, I can have no doubt, and I am sure your lordships are of the same opinion as myself, that anything which brought the laity into co-operation with the clergy in the great work of the Church, would be most valuable. The petition is very numerously signed.

" The BISHOP OF OXFORD —I understand the special prayer of that petition to be, that the bishops would, and that this House of Convocation would, as far as it is capable of so doing, express its conviction that it would be for the advantage of the Church if, generally throughout the country, there were, as there are in many dioceses, for instance in your grace's diocese and my own, meetings of the clergy in rural chapters under the direction and countenance of the Bishop; and if, once a year at least, certain laymen, invited by the clergy, would meet them to consult with them in free conference on the common affairs of the Church; and, in that way, by increasing the authority of our Church consultations, and by degrees bringing laymen in the same way to consult with the clergy under the direction and superintendence of the Bishop, that most laudable desire expressed by so many, of bringing the laity more formally into the consultations of the Church, might be obtained. Clearly it is the only way open to us, because it is impossible for us by any means to bring the laity into the Convocation of the province. That would alter entirely the fundamental constitution of Convocation, which consists of Bishops and clergy, and of them exclusively. We all desire, as my right rev. brother (the Bishop of London) says, to bring the laity and the clergy into consultation with each other. We have none of us any idea of dictating to the laity, of lording it over them, or being rulers in any way of their faith. But we earnestly wish to see them working with us

LECTURE VIII. 359

in consultation upon the common matters of the Church, and giving us the great benefit of their advice and co-operation. I heartily concur and sympathise in the prayer of the petition.

"The PRESIDENT—Perhaps it may serve the purpose, which is a good one, of the petitioners, if I state that this Synodal meeting, if it may be so called, has taken place more than once in a most important part of Kent—in the principal deanery of that county—and that it has been considered very successful. The persons who have met have consisted chiefly of churchwardens of parishes, but they have been intermixed with others who were not churchwardens. It so happens that in Kent a great number of the gentry and clergy are churchwardens of their respective parishes. The clergy themselves, through the Archdeacon, have selected certain of the clergy to form the clerical part of that Synod. They have already met twice. They have considered two or three subjects which are very important to the Church, and their meetings have been not only exceedingly harmonious and cordial, but promise to be very useful. Certainly the machinery is not very difficult where there are a sufficient number of persons to afford a selection; and with the assistance of Archdeacon and the Rural Dean I do not think your Lordships would find any difficulty in organising such Synods.

"The BISHOP OF ST. ASAPH — Perhaps your Grace may be able to state where they meet and how often, and how long they continue together?

"The PRESIDENT—I think they meet at Maidstone and sit for a day, but at no stated periods, and only to consider matters of which previous notice has been given by the presiding authority.

"The BISHOP OF ST. ASAPH—I think the details of such meetings would be most valuable and interesting.

"The PRESIDENT—Mr. Hoare's book contains every information on the subject."

Again, in Session, Friday, February 11th, 1859, we have the following discussion in the Upper House on the same subject.

"LAY CO-OPERATION.

"The BISHOP OF OXFORD — I have to present to your lordships the following petition from Henry Hoare, Esq. :—

"'To the Most Reverend the Archbishops, the Right Reverend the Bishops, the Very Reverend the Deans, the Venerable the Archdeacons, and the Reverend the Rural Deans and other Clergy of the Church and Realm of England,

"'The humble memorial of the undersigned,

"'Through Divine favour, and in a spirit and temper which have elicited very general approval, the Convocation of the province of Canterbury has of late years exercised the right, not to say the duty, essentially appertaining to it, of deliberating upon matters touching the welfare of the Church established in this realm.

"'Petitions have been prepared for presentation in both provinces. In the province of Canterbury they have been received and duly considered, and various questions have been raised, among which none, perhaps, exceeds in importance that of providing the clergy and the laity of the Church of England with some better opportunities than at present exist for joint counsel and co-operation. That subject has been considered, not only in both Houses of the Convocation of Canterbury, but also by several of the Bishops and other clergy of the province of York, although in meetings of a less strictly Synodical character than is to be desired, and has long been hoped for.

"'That the general result is, a deep conviction that the time is come for definite action; and your memorialist solicits permission respectfully to state that an important body of the lay members of the Church appear at length to be agreed upon the following conclusions, which may be taken as expressive of wishes and opinions very generally entertained by those laymen who have considered the subject: in addition to which there is reason to believe that experiments in the direction indicated would be viewed with favour by Convocation.

"'I. That the Clergy of this realm should be permitted to meet in their respective Convocations, as by law established.

"'II. That the judicial character of Episcopal and other Visitations, as by law established, should be maintained.

"'III. That where meetings of the clergy in rural deaneries are now held, they should continue to be held; and that where they are not now held, they should be set on foot, subject to the approval of the Ordinary; uniformity of practice, in every respect, being desirable in all the dioceses of England and Wales.

"'IV. That in the same divisions of dioceses, or in such others as may be more convenient to the Archdeacons and Rural Deans, the clergy of the locality should occasionally form themselves into consulting committees, at whose meetings certain of the laity from neighbouring parishes should be requested to give their attendance, for the purpose of common advice and mutual consultation on matters which, from time to time, the clergy may deem of sufficient importance to require the joint cognisance and consideration of the whole Church.

"'V. That associations should be formed, as far as may be practicable and convenient, in the several parishes, for the promotion of objects calculated to create an extended interest and sympathy in behalf of the Church; such associations being invariably under the superintendence or control of the parochial clergy, and the subjects selected for consideration being sanctioned by them.

"'Your memorialist therefore desires humbly to submit the above statements to your serious consideration, in the hope that arrangements may without delay be entered upon for carrying them out into action in the several archdeaconries of both provinces.

"' By order and in the name of the Society for the Revival of Convocation.

"' HENRY HOARE, Chairman.'

In asking your Grace's permission to move that this petition be received and laid upon the table, I am anxious to say a few words as to the effect which has followed, in my own diocese and under my own eye, the adoption of the plans to which the petitioner prays us to give our sanction and encouragement. I have only this day received communications from the Archdeacons of the counties of Berkshire and Buckinghamshire, with respect to the results of carrying out these plans, which have been carried out, to a considerable extent, in their archdeaconries. They report most strongly as to the good effect which to their own knowledge has resulted from the adoption of these plans; and especially the interest which the laity, who have been invited to join the clergy in the rural deaneries, have taken in the subjects brought under discussion. This has been very great. The laity who have taken part in these proceedings include persons in the highest positions in society, as well as the more humble members of the Church. They have joined with the clergy in worship and prayer as well as in consultation; they have taken an active part in these deliberations, have advanced their own opinions, and have discussed them along with the clergy with great freedom, and have given and received most valuable information on various matters which have been considered. With regard to church-rates, for instance, the consultations which have taken place have been the means of diffusing in these districts a great amount of information which perhaps could not have reached them in any other way. The opinion of the Archdeacons is that this is a most valuable movement; that it is entirely free from the danger which any election of laymen to serve in Church councils must necessarily involve; and indeed from evils of every kind. The laymen having merely been invited to attend at consultative meetings, the evils of elections have been avoided, and the good has been very great, and, as far as anything human can be, nearly unmixed. In presenting this petition, I feel bound to give it my warmest support, and beg to move that it be received and laid on the table. I am not aware that Convocation can take any direct steps to forward the matter, but one indirect step of great importance would be for your Grace and any of my right rev. brethren who have witnessed the working of the plan to express their opinions concerning it, so that such expression may go forth to the Church at large through the ordinary channels, and thus assist those good men who are anxious to bring about that greatest of all blessings to an earthly Church, after the direct spiritual blessing of its Great Head — the uniting together in feeling and in harmonious action the great body of her clergy and her laity.

"The BISHOP OF LICHFIELD — I quite agree with what the Bishop of Oxford has said as to the advantages likely to accrue from the joint consultation of the clergy and laity on Church matters, which Mr. Hoare is so earnestly promoting. The subject has been already considered in one of the archdeaconries of my diocese, and I hope it will soon be taken up in the others, arrangements being in progress to effect that object.

"The BISHOP OF ST. ASAPH — Mr. Hoare was kind enough to visit one or two deaneries in my diocese, and with my full sanction and assistance, the clergy have invited the laity in their neighbouring localities to attend their meetings, and have not found the slightest objection to that course of proceeding.

"The BISHOP OF SALISBURY — I have not the advantage possessed by my right rev. friend the Bishop of Oxford, of being able to state to your Grace and my right rev. brethren any experience of the working of the plan of Mr. Hoare; but I have seen that gentleman on the subject, and he has so satisfied me of its utility, that I fully intend to introduce it into my diocese. My present position is this: — Mr. Hoare has kindly promised to attend the meeting of the Deans and

Rural Deans which is annually held at Salisbury, for the purpose of laying before them a statement of the success which has attended the working of his plan; and I trust, if it should please God to allow us to assemble in this place next year, to be able to communicate to your Grace that the plan has worked as successfully in my diocese as it has done in that of Oxford. I entirely concur in the object which Mr. Hoare has in view, and hope that his plan will result in closely uniting together the laity and the clergy in the great work of strengthening the Church.

"The BISHOP OF EXETER—I wish, in a very few words, to express my entire concurrence in the views which have been expressed by my right rev. brethren. I fell in, at an early period, with the plans of Mr. Hoare, and expressed a wish that they might succeed. At the same time I saw some difficulties in the way, and thought it my duty to express them. One great difficulty which exists is this. That there should not be an election, is quite clear; but after the experience of what has occurred in the diocese of Oxford, I trust the difficulty of selection will not be so great as I imagined would be the case. It appears that the Rural Deans select those laymen whom they wish to consult. I am of opinion that that is a very desirable course, but I cannot be blind, and we ought not to be blind, to the possible danger of producing a collision, which it will require great prudence on the part of the Deans to prevent. I think, upon the whole advisableness of the plan, that it is strikingly just, and I should be sorry to say a word to discourage it, but I considered it desirable to point out the difficulty. I do not offer these observations in the way of objection to the plan, but rather as a caution in the way of carrying it into effect.

"The BISHOP OF LLANDAFF—During the nine years and a half which I have been connected with the diocese of Llandaff, I have received a great deal of assistance from laymen of high rank in that diocese, and I think that the feeling of co-operation which has been evinced during that time is increasing. But it certainly has struck me very strongly that what we require is, some plan for exciting the sympathy, not so much of the higher ranks of the laity, as of the middle classes, on behalf of the Church. I believe there is a great deal of sound good feeling in the middle classes in favour of the Church, and that they only want some centre around which they can meet. I think it probable that the kind of organisation recommended by Mr. Hoare might serve that purpose, and prove particularly beneficial to the interests of the Church. I cannot speak of this particular plan in the same manner as some of my right rev. brethren, not having had the benefit of their experience in the matter; but although the plan has not been adopted in my diocese, it has not been overlooked. Our present position is this:— There are nineteen rural dignitaries in my diocese, who meet annually, at my residence, to consult respecting the general interest of the Church in that diocese and elsewhere. At the last meeting, the general subject of lay co-operation was brought forward, and I requested the several Rural Deans during the year to take the opinion of the clergy as to the best way in which lay co-operation could be stimulated in the diocese; and at our next meeting I hope we shall hear of these deliberations throughout the diocese. I mentioned the subject to Mr. Hoare the other day, and invited him to attend, in the hope that he will do so, and give us the benefit of his advice and experience on the subject, and I shall be heartily glad to find the matter set on a proper footing. There are two things which I should like to know with respect to these meetings, so far as they have been carried out. In the first place, I wish to be informed by whom the invitations to the laity have been given; and in the second place, I should like to know whether different subjects have merely been discussed, or whether any vote has been taken upon them.

" The BISHOP OF OXFORD — In my diocese the invitation has, in every instance, been given by the Rural Dean of the district, in his own name and that of the clergy. Hitherto,

I may safely say that every danger pointed out by my right rev. brother, the Bishop of Exeter, has been avoided, and I do not think that the least feeling of jealousy has been excited by the course which has been adopted. The laity, who are marked out by character and position, in different ranks of life, have been invited, and in almost every instance they have attended, and we are not aware of any jealousy on the part of those who have not been invited. It was necessary, of course, to pass over some, who, however, will be asked to take part in the proceedings in another year. This shows that we are not acting in any exclusive spirit. In some parts of my diocese, votes have been taken when it was thought desirable to ascertain the sentiments of the majority. In one instance two or three plans were propounded respecting the church-rate question, and after some discussion, each plan was put to the vote, for the purpose of ascertaining the opinions of the assembly. This was done without the slightest tinge of hostility, and merely from a desire to ascertain which plan commended itself to the largest number of those present.

"The PRESIDENT—The diocese in which I reside had the benefit of the first trial of this scheme, and the manner in which the selection of the laity was made, in the deanery to which I am referring, was by the clergy of the different parishes meeting together, and suggesting the name of some person connected with each parish. With respect to the quality of the persons selected, they have been generally such as would be selected to fill the office of churchwarden. In a large parish like Maidstone, two persons might be selected. I am happy to say that, so far as our experience has gone, I can give the same satisfactory testimony as that which has been given by my right reverend brethren. The plan is, in fact, not a new one. In my former diocese I derived great advantage from the clergy and laity meeting together to discuss important subjects. The question of education was the subject of discussion in a large meeting of the clergy and laity of Lancashire and Cheshire. The clergy and laity also met together to consider the best method of promoting church-building, to meet the wants of the diocese. I can speak with great confidence as to the advantages of such a system, which has been attended with no disadvantages, and I believe that the more general it becomes, the better will it be for the interests of the Church.

" The BISHOP OF WINCHESTER — I cannot allow the discussion to close without making a few remarks on the subject, although I have not had the advantage of meetings of this particular kind in my own diocese. I have, however, had some communication with Mr. Hoare respecting his plan, and at his invitation, have written an expression of my acquiescence in that plan, and of the satisfaction I shall feel, if, through the Archdeacons, it can be carried into effect in my diocese. I am not sure that either of the Archdeacons has as yet taken any steps in the matter, but I am satisfied that one of them will co-operate in the movement. The other, unfortunately, is at present unable to do so. For myself, I can say that I shall most readily assist in any movement which may be made with that prudence and caution which its importance requires. In my own diocese, meetings of a similar character have been held, which have been attended with singularly good results. About eighteen months ago conferences took place between the clergy and laity of sixty or seventy parishes in Hampshire with reference to Sunday-schools; but although they met on that subject, it was not at all unnatural that others should be introduced, and many important matters relative to the religious and social condition of the several parishes were entered upon. I attended many of these conferences, and in some instances from sixty to eighty persons were present. Invitations were sent to the churchwardens, the schoolmasters, the pupil-teachers, and all those who, from their position, were likely to be interested in the proceedings. The conferences which I personally witnessed were of the most gratifying character. The attendance was not confined to one sex, for both schoolmasters and schoolmistresses were present. The meetings lasted from two to three hours, according to circumstances, and the result has been that in all those parishes a mutual feeling of sympathy between the clergy and laity has been created and extended. In large parishes, where the clergyman has a great difficulty in communicating with the whole of his parishioners, these meetings have been attended with the greatest advantage. The friendly intercourse thus commenced has been continued, and all parties have expressed personally to myself the gratification which they have experienced from the movement, and I hope these conferences will continue in future years. I thought it desirable to state these facts, inasmuch as they have a bearing on the subject, although the proceedings are not exactly those contemplated by Mr. Hoare.

"The BISHOP OF LINCOLN — I wish just to mention, in addition to the evidence that has already been given, that in two deaneries in my diocese, these meetings of the clergy and laity have taken place with the greatest success. There was not the least mixture of evil in them, and on separating they not only felt that the bonds of the clergy and the laity had been more closely knit together, but that much valuable information had been obtained; and I would recommend that in other deaneries the same plan should be adopted. What passed on my last Visitation has tended in no small degree to remove the objections of many of the clergy, who feared that some difficulties might arise from the clergy and laity meeting together for the purpose of consultation. We, for the first time, invited the Churchwardens to dine with us at the Visitation, and, after dinner, some little discussion took place relative to charities and matters of that kind, and the universal opinion was, that these meetings were good both for the clergy and the laity. In my diocese, which is, comparatively speaking, thinly populated, the difficulty which has been alluded to exists only in a mitigated form; because, where there are few persons, the selection can scarcely be called a selection. I hope, in the course of a short time, the system will be extended throughout my diocese."

Similar approval was expressed in the Upper House, Feb. 11th, 1862, on the presentation of a petition from Mr. Hoare, in the following terms:—

"The BISHOP OF LONDON—I have to express regret that owing to my leaving town for a few days, I had not an opportunity of receiving this petition in time to undertake its presentation to your Lordships' House. But I would seize the present occasion for the purpose of acknowledging the value of the services which have been performed by the gentleman whose name is the last appended to that petition. His exertions have been indefatigable, and I am sure that anything which emanates from him will not fail to receive the most serious attention of this House. I shall be glad to have that petition laid upon the table, and its prayer acceded to by your Lordships.

"The BISHOP OF OXFORD—I entirely agree with the Bishop of London, that a great debt of gratitude is due to the gentleman whose name appears last on the petition— Mr. Henry Hoare. No man could have devoted his time, his money, and his great abilities more assiduously and more self-denyingly to any cause than Mr. Hoare has done for the purpose of aiding the Church of England—first, in bringing the clergy to understand and consult one another, and then in bringing the laity to assist them by mutual counsel, advice, and co-operation. I am sure every one of my right rev. brethren will acknowledge that we owe an unspeakably large debt of gratitude to Mr. Hoare for the course which he has for so many years pursued.

"The BISHOP OF WINCHESTER—Concurring in all that has been said with respect to the obligations we are under to Mr. Hoare, there is one point in his character to which I would call especial attention—and that is, the extremely judicious manner in which he has carried on his movements. He had to enter upon a new course, which in many quarters was not very popular; and so far as my own observation has gone, I must say that he has exhibited a degree of forbearance and patience beyond all praise, and has succeeded in subduing opposition, and to a great extent in conciliating those who, in the first instance, entered into a consideration of his views with feelings of dislike and distrust.

"The ARCHBISHOP—I believe the exertions of Mr. Hoare were first begun in my diocese, in which he resides; and I should be wrong if I allowed the opportunity to pass without stating my high estimation of the earnestness with which he has devoted himself to the object which he has undertaken. His disinterested and unremitting efforts for the benefit of the Church cannot be too highly prized.

"The BISHOP OF SALISBURY— Mr. Hoare has visited my diocese once or twice, and has created amongst both the clergy and the laity a most affectionate feeling towards him for the honest sincerity with which he has propounded his opinions; and his thorough good humour has rendered him one of the most popular men in my diocese."

The Report of the Lower House alluded to will be found in the Chronicle of Convocation, February 11th, 1859, pp. 113, 114, 115, and is as follows:—

"The Committee of the Lower House of Convocation of the province of Canterbury, appointed to consider 'the best means of obtaining the counsel and co-operation of the laity of the Church in annual visitations or diocesan synods, or in any other modes that may be deemed expedient,' have to report as follows:—

"They are unanimously of opinion, that the well-being of the Church greatly depends, under Almighty God, on the mutual good-will and cordial co-operation of its members, clergy and laity; and it is their earnest desire that the end proposed may be attained.

"At the same time, they thankfully acknowledge, that a spirit of harmonious action between the clergy and laity has long shown itself with excellent results, in the administration of the affairs of many religious and charitable societies in this country.

"The special duty, however, of the present Committee is to suggest means for eliciting, strengthening, and consolidating such co-operation, by regular diocesan organisation, particularly of a synodical character.

"The Committee are of opinion, that the means employed for obtaining such co-operation, should be regarded, in the first instance, as of a tentative and provisional kind.

"It may also be anticipated, that no uniform plan can be devised, which would be equally applicable at once to all dioceses.

"*Parish Vestries.*

"I. The primary elements of lay co-operation may be found in Parochial Vestries, in which the clergyman and his parishioners meet together for consultation on matters ecclesiastical as well as temporal.

"*Ruridecanal Chapters or Meetings.*

"II. The Committee would next advert to the ruridecanal chapters or meetings, which are of very ancient date.

"They appreciate highly the benefits derived from them, and hope that such chapters or meetings may be generally revived.

"The Committee suggest for consideration whether the ruridecanal divisions of dioceses might not afford facilities for lay co-operation, if churchwardens and sidesmen of parishes of the deanery, and perhaps other laymen of the Church, were, as occasion might require, invited by the Rural Dean to confer with the clergy on subjects previously proposed.

"Such meetings, it is supposed, would be preceded by common prayer in the Church, and it is to be wished that an opportunity might also be offered for partaking of the Holy Communion.

"*Archidiaconal Visitations.*

"III. The next advance towards a fuller development of lay co-operation may be seen in the Visitations held by the several archdeacons; fifty-five in number, in this province.

"The Committee are not unmindful that such visitations were originally of a disciplinarian and judicial character.

"In course of time, however, and under the influence of various circumstances, these Archidiaconal Visitations took the place of the two yearly synods, anciently held by the bishops of the several dioceses. (Bishop Gibson, Codex, p. 958.)

"They are, in fact, the only constitutional assemblies of the clergy and laity of the archdeaconry, as such, which are at present known to the law.

"The Committee do not enter on the question, whether the present organisation of these assemblies is the best that could be devised; but they are of opinion that it is capable of improvement in its application.

"They do not recommend that any attempts should be made at present to create new agency for lay co-operation in the archdeaconries; but that, in the first instance at least, resort should be had for that purpose to the constitutional organisation already existing from time immemorial.

"They feel persuaded, that these visitations afford valuable opportunities for obtaining the co-operation of the clergy and laity, and for promoting the practical efficiency of the Church.

"The churchwardens are legally the lay representatives of the several parishes of the archdeaconry, and are cited as such to the visitations. They are the guardians of the fabrics and goods of the parish-churches; and are the trustees and dispensers of a large annual revenue, amounting to not less than 300,000*l.*, for the maintenance of the parish churches, and of their religious services.

"The sidesmen (or synodsmen) also are by the 90th Canon recognised officers of the Church, whose duty it is to assist the churchwardens in the execution of their office, and are as such to be cited to the visitations.

"Everything therefore ought to be done to increase the efficiency of these officers, and to strengthen the bonds of union which connect the clergy with them.

"It may be hoped, that if the importance of these offices were more generally understood, and if the holders of them were duly recognised as persons charged from ancient times with solemn duties, and if, as occasion might require, they were called into consultation with the clergy at these visitations, they would be stimulated in their efforts to do their duty; and the office of churchwarden would be raised in public esteem, and would be sought by earnest and zealous laymen, to the benefit of religion, and to the promotion of charity and unity.

"The Committee take for granted, that the conferences at these synodical visitations would be limited to questions concerning the practical efficiency of the Church, especially within the archdeaconry; and that no question of a purely doctrinal character would be submitted for discussion at them; and that the archdeacon, as president, would give previous notice to those who would be summoned, what the subject would be, on which he would request the opinions of those convened, and that sufficient time would be allowed for deliberation.

"For the more intimate and hearty union of those who are convened to these visitations, and for the blessing of Almighty God on their joint deliberations, it is to be wished, that an opportunity should be offered to all who are summoned to them, of joining together in the participation of the Holy Communion.

"*Episcopal Visitations.*

"IV. The Committee next proceed to consider the case of the visitations held by the bishops of the several dioceses, of which there are twenty-one in this province.

"The average number of the clergy in each of these dioceses is not less than 650, and the churchwardens probably amount to more than 900, on an average, in each diocese.

"In most dioceses, the bishop's visitation takes place only once in three years; the archidiaconal visitation being held in the two intermediate years.

"The bishop of a diocese has no regular opportunities of meeting his clergy in any one place; or of collecting the general opinion of the clergy and laity of his diocese; or of communicating his own judgment to them in any one diocesan assembly.

"Formerly, as has been already observed, diocesan synods were held by each bishop of the province twice in every year.

"The English reformers recommended in the Reformatio Legum (de Synodis, p. 109, ed. Cardwell) that a diocesan synod should be held by each bishop annually, to which all the clergy of the diocese should be convened, by means of the rural deans; and that such synods should be opened with the Litany and the Holy Communion, and an address from the bishop or archdeacon; and that the synod should consist of the clergy and such of the laity as the bishop might request to remain; and that its deliberations should, if requisite, be continued for several successive days.

"Your Committee gratefully recognise the benefits at present arising from the meetings of the churchwardens, together with the clergy, at the visitations of the bishops; and they see in those visitations the basis of arrangements which might, if strengthened and amplified, be made available for the consultation and co-operation of the laity with the clergy of the diocese, under the presidency of the bishop, according to the principles and arrangements already stated in the case of archidiaconal visitations.

"But they would further express their earnest desire, that, by a subdivision of dioceses, the clergy and laity of every diocese might be enabled to meet under the presidency of their bishop, and be associated with one another, under his paternal authority, in the Cathedral Church of the diocese, for mutual counsel and edification, and for Christian fellowship in the offices of religion.

"Your Committee are aware, that many persons, whose motives they respect, are desirous of a more rapid and larger development of lay co-operation than has been recommended in this report.

"They do not profess to determine, whether such an expansion may not hereafter be necessary. Time and experience will show. If any organic changes are requisite in the present system of lay-representation, they are of opinion that suggestions for such changes should come from the laity rather than from the clergy. But they earnestly hope, that a fair trial may be made of our existing organisation.

"They respectfully commend the present subject to the consideration of the archdeacons and rural deans of the province of Canterbury; and they would invite reports stating to the House the results of experiments made by them for the purpose of obtaining lay co-operation of a synodical character.

"Your Committee would also recommend that a dutiful representation should be made upon this subject by the Lower House to his Grace the President, and their lordships in the Upper House.

"In conclusion, they unite in fervent prayer to ALMIGHTY GOD, 'by whose Spirit the whole body of the Church is governed and sanctified, that every member of the same, in his vocation and ministry, may truly and godly serve Him, through our LORD and SAVIOUR, JESUS CHRIST.'

The association of the laity with the clergy in archidiaconal and ruridecanal conferences, has been tried in my own archdeaconry with the best results.

NOTE (121), page 213.

The Times newspaper.

NOTE (122), page 214.

It might have been thought that nothing could add lustre to the example here alluded to, or to the loyalty and love with which it is repaid.

But when it could be said of our royal mistress, that " in the very presence of death, and in the first moment of her agony, she rose beneath the overwhelming weight of her crushing sorrow, resolving, under God's blessing, to do her duty to the country,"— when in her own words " her own misery only makes her feel more for the widows of her people," what limits can be fixed to the national devotion!

I desire to adorn these pages with the letter written by Her Majesty's desire, on a recent calamitous occasion, to Mr. Carr, the head viewer of Hartley Colliery, and which was read by the Incumbent of Earsdon at a large religious meeting held on the pit-heap:—

" Osborne, Jan. 23rd, 1862.

" Sir,— The Queen, in the midst of her own overwhelming grief, has taken the deepest interest in the mournful accident at Hartley, and up to the last had hoped that at least a considerable number of the poor people might have been recovered alive. The appalling news since received has afflicted the Queen very much. Her Majesty commands me to say that her tenderest sympathy is with the poor widows and mothers, and that her own misery only makes her feel the more for them. Her Majesty hopes that everything will be done as far as possible to alleviate their distress, and Her Majesty will have a sad satisfaction in assisting in such a measure. Pray let me know what is doing.— I have the honour to be, your obedient servant,

"C. B. PHIPPS."

LECTURE VIII.

NOTE (123), page 215.

These words were spoken some months before that illustrious Prince was taken from us, of whom it has been said, that to do justice to his memory sounds like adulation, and to speak the simple truth is to pronounce a panegyric.

History will record his virtues: monuments will be erected to his memory. But what tribute can compare with that rendered in the following letter by her who knew him best?

"Osborne, Feb. 19th, 1862.

"My Lord,— The Queen wishes me to add a few words to the answer to your letter, which you will receive with this, expressive in a more special manner of Her Majesty's personal wishes.

" She is aware that she could not with any propriety contribute, as a wife, to a monument to her husband; but she is also the Sovereign of this great Empire, and as such, she cannot but think she may be allowed to join with the nation in the expression of a nation's gratitude to one to whom it owes so much.

" Who has a dearer interest than the Queen in the wellbeing and the happiness of the people? And if it has pleased God to make her reign, so far, happy and prosperous, to whom, under Divine Providence, is this so much owing as to her beloved husband — in all matters of doubt or difficulty her wise counsellor, her unfailing guide and support?

" No one can know, as the Queen knows, how his every thought was devoted to the country — how his only aim was to improve the condition of the people, and to promote their best interests. Indeed, his untiring exertions in furtherance of these objects tended, in all probability, to shorten his precious life.

" Surely, then, it will not be out of place that, following the movement of the people, the Queen should be allowed to consider how she may best take part with them in doing honour to her beloved Prince, so that the proposed monument may be recorded to future ages as reared by the queen and people of a grateful country to the memory of its benefactor.

"I have the honour to be, your lordship's most obedient and faithful servant,

"C. GREY.

"The Right Honourable the Lord Mayor, &c."

NOTE (124), page 217.

See a speech entitled "Woman's Work," delivered in the Lower House of Convocation, on Tuesday, July 9th, 1861, by Richard Seymour, M.A., Rector of Kinwarton, Proctor for the clergy of the diocese of Worcester, on moving the following resolution:—

"That this House do agree to present to His Grace the Archbishop, and to the Upper House, praying their Lordships to deliberate and agree on certain rules by which women, whose hearts God has moved to devote themselves to works of piety and charity, may be associated together on terms and conditions distinctly known as those which the Church of England has sanctioned and prescribed":—in which the whole of this subject is treated with singular pathos and ability.

See also a leading article in the *Guardian* Newspaper, March 6th, 1862, on Convocation on Sisterhoods, with some admirable remarks on the subject itself and the debate thereon in the Lower House of Convocation.

The subject was discussed in the Upper House, on Friday, the 7th, when the following representation from the Lower House was read:

"'*To the Archbishop and Bishops in Convocation assembled.*

"'The Lower House beg to represent,—That their attention has been called to the manner in which Christian women have of late years devoted themselves within the Church of

England definitively to the aid of Christ's ministers, in alleviating the sorrows of the sick and suffering, and in other pious and charitable works. That they desire to express to their Lordships their conviction that such ministrations on the part of women are to be regarded with great thankfulness, both as a revival of the Scriptural and primitive practice of the Church of Christ, and as eminently conducive both to the temporal and spiritual good of all connected with them. Believing, therefore, that such efforts deserve all the encouragement and guidance which the Church can give, they pray your Lordships to take into your consideration the modes and limitations under which such encouragement and guidance may be given. And in order that this desire may take effect, they respectfully request his Grace the President and their Lordships to direct the appointment of a joint committee to consider this subject, and to report thereon to the Convocation of this province.'

"The BISHOP OF LONDON — I should be glad to see a committee appointed on this very important subject. It is probably known that in the diocese of London various efforts have been made in this direction, and that these efforts are increasing. In times past they were viewed with a good deal of jealousy, and were supposed to be confined to persons entertaining one set of opinions; but now they are pretty generally recognised throughout the various sections of the Church. As nothing but good can arise from these individuals devoting themselves for Christ's sake, if their labours are judicious, so it is desirable that we should consider what advice can be given and what checks can be put upon any tendency towards a want of that judiciousness which is necessary in such matters. I may mention that in the large parish of St. Pancras, under the superintendence of the parochial clergyman, and with the full sanction of Canon Champneys, certain ladies are allowed to labour amongst the destitute poor of the district. The effort is only just beginning, and it is difficult to say with what degree of success it may be attended; but it is an effort which will be watched with great interest by all those who are anxious for the spiritual good of the district and the general good of the Church. Similar efforts were made long ago in the diocese of London, and although they were naturally viewed with some jealousy, I have great reason to be thankful for the amount of self-denial and goodness of every kind which has been evinced by those who have devoted themselves to the work; and I must say that I think we ought not to be too critical in judging of the way in which they perform a work for which we ought to be very thankful.

"The BISHOP OF OXFORD — As I have had some experience on this subject, I can echo every word which the Bishop of London has said as to the self-denial of these ladies, to their readiness at the suggestion of those placed over them to give up everything that might raise a suspicion, and the noble devotedness of their character in regard to this work. I have seen the effect of this in many places. Some suspicions were at first naturally entertained; but their noble conduct in this town, and in my own diocese, in ministering to the poor when every one else had fled from the dreadful scene of pestilence, won the hearts of those who at first suspected them; and it is impossible to feel too thankful to Almighty God for the rise of such a work amongst us. I think, after what has fallen from the Bishop of London, that it would scarcely be wise to act on the suggestion of the Lower House. There is a certain shrinking delicacy in such movements, and I think it would be better to leave those in London under his care, and those in other dioceses under the care of their spiritual guides, than to establish any formal rules, or to take any formal steps in Convocation. It is possible the time may come when it will be wise to do so; but at present I think it more advisable to leave the bud to unfold itself in a quiet way, rather than to take any formal steps in the matter.

"The ARCHBISHOP — From what I hear of these ladies and the way in which they are acting, I think it would injure the cause we desire to promote if we were to interfere with the exercise of their free judgment and discretion. We must believe their inclinations to be most excellent when they devote themselves in this manner to so great and self-denying a work; and we have no reason to suppose that that self-denial will not be accompanied with so much judgment as will enable them to carry on their work without any interference on the part of others; and any premature step might have the effect of checking the rising flame instead of promoting its progress.

"The BISHOP OF LANDAFF — It would give me great satisfaction to see this work extended in the Church of England provided it can be conducted, as I believe it may be, with a due regard to the sound religious feeling of the country. There are many cases of distress which no persons are better qualified to mitigate than well-educated Christian ladies; and I know there are a great number of unmarried ladies, of widow ladies, and others whose peculiar circumstances enable them to devote themselves almost exclusively to works of charity, who would be glad to have the opportunity of so doing. If we give them that opportunity, we shall provide for a want under which the Church of England has long suffered. At the same time I cannot help feeling very strongly that their assistance should be accepted in such a way as to commend it to the sound feeling of the country. For the reasons which have been given it may be inexpedient to appoint a committee on the subject, but I hope that what has been stated will induce those ladies, and especially the managers of the institutions with which they are connected, to avoid anything calculated to give offence; because it is unquestionable that the real hindrance to the spread of this means of usefulness has been the institutions themselves. Your Lordships may have seen a little work which has been recently published, entitled 'The Experiences of an English Sister of Mercy in the Crimea,' by Margaret Goodman; and I think it quite impossible for any one to read that work without feeling thankful that this lady and some others plunged into the miserable haunts of Devonport in order to visit persons afflicted with the cholera.

Their service in the Crimea and at Scutari must be viewed with equal admiration. But I think the work itself suggests the need of caution which has occurred to my own mind, and I have the less hesitation in saying this, because it is the impression of the lady herself, who, referring to some of the regulations of the institutions, after pointing out their great value, says that when she returned from the Crimea she found the regulations such that she could not continue her assistance. I shall be heartily glad if the work can be carried on effectively, with a due consideration for the sound religious feelings of the country.

"The BISHOP OF ST. ASAPH—The question before us is not whether the work may be carried on, but whether we, as a body, ought to interfere in the matter. I think more good will be done by the general expression of our earnest desire that it may be carried on, than by our interfering with the manner of so doing. I know not what the ladies may require beyond the sanction of the clergymen of their own parishes, but if they wish for any further authority, I am sure the Bishop of the diocese will render them every assistance. If we were to lay down any rules, perhaps some of the Bishops might not altogether agree with them, and an obstacle might be thrown in the way of that work, on the prosecution of which the reformation of the great mass of the lower classes of our population is dependent.

"The BISHOP OF LLANDAFF—The difficulty is not so much with regard to the rules under which the ladies should work, as to the rules which ought to guide the institutions in which the ladies are trained for their special work. That is the point to which my observations specially referred. If there are to be such institutions, they ought to be conducted on principles of which we can all approve.

"The BISHOP OF ST. DAVID'S—The petition, as I understand it, refers to the agency of ladies of England. If they are to engage only in charitable ministrations separately and individually, I do not think it would be necessary to make any regulations respecting the mode of administration. But

LECTURE VIII. 383

I apprehend that in most cases they form a body living together, and that the object of the petition is that an inquiry may be instituted as to the rules by which such institutions may be best administered. If these societies were placed under proper management, all the difficulties which have been suggested by the Bishop of Llandaff would be removed, because it is only in the interior of such houses that any misdirection of charitable efforts could take place. I wish all such establishments could be placed under proper control without at all interfering with the voluntary agency of the members. I know not how far they are at present under the control and authority of the Bishop. If they are, I do not see the necessity of placing them under any other restraint, and I think the matter may be safely left in the hands of the Bishop, who ought to have the power to make such regulations as he may think fit.

"The BISHOP OF LONDON—The efforts made in London vary very much in character. Some of them are directly under my superintendence, the ladies having made it a condition, on forming themselves into a society, that they shall have access to the Bishop and be able to consult him, and look upon him as the Visitor of the institution; and wherever they carried on the work in a manner of which I approved, I consented to give them my counsel and assistance. Of course there are other institutions with which ladies are connected, for visiting the poor and the sick, which have not sought to place themselves in connection with us—some of them from a love of independence, and others from knowing that my sentiments are not exactly in accordance with their regulations. Although it has been taken for granted that this is more or less a new work, we must not forget that there is one institution in this diocese which dates back considerably into the Episcopate of my revered predecessor. I allude to St. John's House of Mercy, the existence of which ought never to be forgotten. That institution was formed for the training of nurses, and the lady at the head of that institution is acting as matron at the Hospital at King's

College, simply from a love of the bodies and souls of those who are brought there. I believe the connection between King's College Hospital and that institution has been of the greatest use to the hospital, and I trust it is likely to introduce into the hospitals of the metropolis generally an element which has hitherto been wanting. Recently, through the kind care of Miss Nightingale, an addition has been made to the sort of training carried on in King's College Hospital in connection with St. John's House of Mercy. It would be almost presumption in any one to think of praising Miss Nightingale in relation to this subject, but I think it right to mention that she has devoted part of her energies to the improvement to which I have alluded. It has been taken for granted that this representation refers altogether to institutions of persons living in community. But, whether that be the case or not, I think this is a proper occasion to remark that the women thus employed are under a regular superintendence. A great effort was made in the parish of St. Giles, by persons who hung rather more loosely to the Church than was desirable, to reclaim persons who were leading a vicious life, and to visit the poor in their own homes; and the incumbent of that parish has found nothing but good resulting from the efforts of those Bible-women. In the parish of St. Clement Danes there is a movement most strictly connected with the Church of England, and a considerable number of mission-women have been sent amongst the poor; and from that parish the work has extended in a variety of directions. Ladies well known to many of your lordships have undertaken the superintendence of these women, and the sphere of their operations is gradually increasing. They are sent into various parts of the metropolis, each lady considering herself responsible for the work of her paid agent, and all of them being desirous of placing themselves under my direction, and in every instance taking care to do nothing which is not sanctioned by the incumbent of the parish.

" The BISHOP OF LLANDAFF—The Bishop of London

has called your Lordships' attention to the usefulness of the ladies in connection with King's College Hospital; and that circumstance recalls to my mind a fact relating to a charity at the University of Cambridge for the relief of sick students. It was suggested by Dr. Haviland that a portion of the income should be devoted to the training of nurses; and I remember the doctor saying that Mr. Valentine Blomfield had lost his life entirely in consequence of an ignorant nurse administering to him the wrong medicine. How far the late Bishop of London may have been influenced by this calamity, which came so near home to him, in supporting St. John's House of Mercy, it is impossible for me to say.

"The BISHOP OF OXFORD — With your Grace's permission, I will now move the following resolution: —

"' That this House has read and considered the address of the Lower House as to the devotion of themselves by Christian women within the Church of England to works of piety and charity. That this House agrees with the Lower House in believing that such efforts deserve all the encouragement which the Church can give them, and such guidance as may help those who are making them to be dutiful members of the Church of England. That they deem it most expedient that this guidance should be sought directly from the parochial clergy and the Bishops of the districts in which such devoted women labour: and they commend them and their work to the prayers of the Church, that all so labouring may be upheld and directed in their life of charity and labour of love by the blessed Spirit of the God of peace and love.'

"The BISHOP OF ST. DAVID'S — Believing that these institutions may confer important benefits on society, I feel very anxious that they should be kept on a safe and sound footing. We must all be aware that there is a peculiar danger incident to institutions of this kind where a number of ladies live together — a peculiar danger of excitement, which, if they are not under proper control, may tend to dangerous consequences, both as regards the welfare of the institution itself and the effects which it produces. I think it desirable that all those who have such institutions within their sphere should watch over them with great care, and take all possible steps to induce their managers to submit their rules to the sanction of the Bishop, or some other efficient authority; and that wherever the Bishop is requested to take upon himself the office of Visitor, he should examine the rules and offer such suggestions as he may think proper previous to giving his sanction to the institution. I hope that the feeling expressed in the resolution will have a beneficial effect on the spirit which animates the supporters of these institutions, and have much pleasure in seconding the motion.

"The BISHOP OF LONDON — Looking at the word 'devoted,' etymologically, it might be supposed to have some reference to 'vows.' I believe that any clergyman administering a vow to any person subjects himself to severe penalties. Anything like a 'vow' on the part of individuals to devote themselves to this work is the last thing we would recommend. It is most desirable that this should be clearly understood.

"The BISHOP OF OXFORD — In my diocese I have uniformly made it the condition of my connection with these institutions, that their statutes shall state explicitly that they are bound only so long as they please to continue in the society.

"The BISHOP OF CHICHESTER — The word 'devoted' is evidently used in the popular sense.

"The motion was put and agreed to, and ordered to be communicated to the Lower House."

NOTE (126), page 219.

This extract is from a work entitled "Female Improvement" by the late Mrs. John Sandford, which first appeared thirty years ago.

I subjoin a few passages from the context:

"The ordinary circumstances, also, in which woman is placed, seem to point her out as the most suitable agent in many benevolent designs. She enjoys a leisure which is seldom granted to the other sex. In what way can she employ it so well as in relieving the ills of her fellow-creatures? One of the most obvious offices of benevolence is that of visiting the destitute and sick; and it is one for which women must be considered, in some respects, as peculiarly qualified. Their kindness of address, their gentleness of manner, their winning tones of voice, may find acceptance where the more decisive manners of the other sex would procure a less courteous welcome; and these recommendations often more than compensate for their want of authority and physical strength. In times of sickness a woman has natural and easy access. And as she smoothes the pillow of the suffering and the dying, she may gently, and as far as her province will allow, probe the wounds of conscience, and then pour into them the 'oil and wine' of Christian consolation.

"There are situations where this duty involves but little personal sacrifice. Amongst a rural population, where the hamlet lies in some sequestered glen, and in our way thither we drink in the pure breezes of the park or of the down;—where the cottage itself is clean, if not picturesque, and its inhabitants welcome our approach with the honest smile of simple hospitality — there, we may well say, it is a pleasure to lift the latch, and to communicate to those who at least are willing to listen, that instruction which is the most valuable for them to receive. We may meet here, it is true, with ignorance and sin; we may find sickness and sorrow; and to conflict with the one, or to seek contact with the other, involves an effort. But it is not what nature recoils from, as it does from scenes of unmitigated evil; and there are refreshments in the occupation itself, which, even at the time, compensate for the sacrifice of time and ease.

"It is not so, however, when a similar office leads us, not to the quiet village, but to the alleys of a densely populated city. Those who pass only through the spacious streets and squares of the metropolis,— who visit no abodes but those of the wealthy,— who give of their abundance through the instrumentality of others,— know by hearing only of poverty and destitution, and have little idea of the realities of want. Could they see the picture which a London court presents,— the infant swarm issuing from its garrets or its cellars, whose countenance bespeaks misery, and whose accents tell of sin, — could they see the denuded walls, where a fellow-creature pines in sickness,— the straw pallet where, perhaps, a poor woman meets her hour of anguish, and gives birth to a child of want and sorrow,— they would feel almost a compunction in the enjoyment of their own luxuries, and would sincerely desire to afford relief.

"It may, indeed, be asked, whether scenes such as these are a fitting spectacle for any woman; whether a sphere so arduous, is suited for female enterprise? Universally, it is not so. It is not one on which very young women can embark, for it requires experience, firmness, and qualifications which belong only to maturer years. The delicate in health are equally unfit; and as domestic duties have a prior claim to any foreign efforts, there are many whom these will not allow to extend their active labours beyond their own homes.

"But amongst those in whom the love of Christ is a constraining motive, and who are ready both to endure and to labour for His sake, there may be found, perhaps, not a few, whom age, health, and courage render fitting agents for one portion at least of the work of benevolence.

"Is it not then possible to bring, as a subsidiary assistance, the piety and zeal of women: to concentrate more than has yet been done, the desultory efforts of such as are already stirred up to the work, and to excite others who are ready to respond to the only constraining motive?"

Thus wrote an English wife and mother in 1832. She

fell asleep in Christ some years ago. But others have effected what she prayed and worked for.

"*And I heard a voice from heaven, saying unto me, Write, Blessed are the dead which die in the Lord from henceforth: yea, saith the Spirit, that they may rest from their labours; and their works do follow them.*" Amen and Amen!

BY THE SAME AUTHOR.

REMAINS of BISHOP SANDFORD. 2 vols. 8vo. 1830. Longmans.

FELLOWSHIP WITH GOD: a Course of Lectures delivered at Long-Acre Chapel, London, 1834.

PAROCHIALIA; or, Church, School, and Parish. 8vo. 1845. Longmans.

VOX CORDIS; or, Breathings of the Heart: a Manual of Private Devotion. Parker. 1849.

The BLAMELESSNESS of HER CLERGY a SAFEGUARD of the CHURCH: a Sermon preached at the Triennial Visitation of the Lord Bishop of Worcester in the Parish Church of Southam, 1845.

The PEACE of JERUSALEM: a Sermon preached on the Third Jubilee of the Society for the Propagation of the Gospel in Foreign Parts, preached in the Church of St. Michael, Coventry, 1851.

CLERICAL CREDENTIALS: a Sermon preached at the Lent Ordination in the Cathedral Church of Worcester, on Sunday, March 8, 1857.

CLERICAL TRAINING: a Sermon preached in Cuddesdon Parish Church, June 9, 1857.

EDUCATION NOT TEACHING, BUT TRAINING: a Sermon delivered in Saltley Church, at the Annual Meeting of the Worcester Diocesan Training College, October 25, 1860.

CHURCH EXTENSION: a Speech delivered on the Institution of the Church Extension Society for the Archdeaconry of Coventry, December 1851.

INAUGURAL ADDRESS, delivered in the Town Hall of Birmingham, at the Anniversary Meeting of the Queen's College, 1852.

SOCIAL PROGRESS: a Lecture delivered to the Members of the Leamington Athenæum, January 7, 1856.

VISITATION CHARGES delivered at Birmingham, Coventry, and Southam, at the Visitations held in 1852, 1853, 1855, 1856, 1858, 1860.

BY THE LATE MRS. JOHN SANDFORD.

WOMAN, in her Social and Domestic Character. 4th Edition. Longmans.

FEMALE IMPROVEMENT. 3rd Edition. Longmans.

www.ingramcontent.com/pod-product-compliance
Lightning Source LLC
Chambersburg PA
CBHW022119290426
44112CB00008B/729